REVELATIONS

ALSO BY MARY SHARRATT

Summit Avenue

The Real Minerva

The Vanishing Point

Bitch Lit (coeditor)

Daughters of the Witching Hill

Illuminations

The Dark Lady's Mask

Ecstasy

Mary Sharratt

REVELATIONS

Houghton Mifflin Harcourt

BOSTON · NEW YORK

2021

hmhbooks.com

Library of Congress Cataloging-in-Publication Data
Names: Sharratt, Mary, 1964– author.
Title: Revelations / Mary Sharratt.
Description: Boston : Houghton Mifflin Harcourt, 2021. |
Includes bibliographical references.
Identifiers: LCCN 2020033855 (print) | LCCN 2020033856 (ebook) |
ISBN 9781328518774 (hardcover) | ISBN 9780358450238 |
ISBN 9780358450436 | ISBN 9781328518781 (ebook)
Subjects: LCSH: Kempe, Margery, approximately 1373– | Julian, of Norwich, 1343– |
GSAFD: Biographical fiction.
Classification: LCC PS3569.H3449 R48 2021 (print) | LCC PS3569.H3449 (ebook) |
DDC 813/.54—dc23
LC record available at https://lccn.loc.gov/2020033855
LC ebook record available at https://lccn.loc.gov/2020033856

Book design by Michaela Sullivan

Printed in the United States of America
DOC 10 9 8 7 6 5 4 3 2 1

For Joske, my companion on the journey

Pilgrims are we all.

—Piers Plowman, XI 240

PROLOGUE
The Mysteries

York
Anno Domini 1417

Y STORY IS NOT a straightforward one. Women's stories never are. To burst free of our fetters, we must first have an awakening. We must be summoned by God. This was how I came to find myself preaching to the women in front of York Minster.

"Every living creature will be saved," I told them as they circled round me. "Those were Dame Julian's words." As I spoke, I heard Julian's voice. Her wisdom caressed me like a feather.

Pilgrims come to see the Corpus Christi mystery plays thronged the cathedral yard. On a decorated hay wain that served as a stage, a costumed troupe from the Mercers' Guild enacted the End of Days, the separation of the blessed and the damned. But the women seemed to have eyes and ears only for me. Burghers' wives, servant girls, pie sellers, and baker women, they leaned in to hear my every word.

"Dame Julian told me she could see no hell. No wrath. Only love. Like the sweetest mother's love for her only child." I swallowed, waiting for that to sink in.

In the awed silence that followed, cooing sounded above our heads. We looked up to see a mourning dove, her wings gleaming gold in the midsummer sun.

Lest I attract too much attention, I drew away from my audience. Ducking my head, I followed the stream of the devout into York Minster, that lofty cathedral bedecked with leafy birch boughs for the feast of Corpus Christi. One Mass had just ended. Before long, another would begin. Palmers lit candles as they recited the Lay Folks' Catechism, for which they would earn an indulgence of forty fewer days in purgatory — or so they'd been told.

Though I tried to hide in plain sight among all the others, I stood out. Clerics regarded me with reproving glances, something I had learned to endure, being such an odd creature, a perpetual wayfarer with no desire to ever return home. A lone woman wandering the wide world with no husband, son, brother, or father to stand at my side and uphold my honor.

Entering the side chapel of the Holy Cross, I knelt on the cold stone floor and began to chant the Veni Creator Spiritus. My gaze anchored on the crucifix painted so harrowingly that I saw it through Julian's eyes, as if I were privy to her first revelation those forty years ago. As she lay deathly ill, she beheld Christ's face above hers, and through this grace, she had recovered. But only yesterday the news had reached me that, at the age of seventy-four, Dame Julian of Norwich was well and truly dead.

Though I knew her to be in paradise with our Beloved, our God, I was destroyed by the thought that I would never see her again upon this earth. I was insensible in my sobbing until I felt a sharp tug on my sleeve.

The hairs on my flesh stood on end. A canon with a jeweled pectoral cross loomed over me. Other clerics gathered round, regarding me as if I were some diseased beast who had no right to set foot in this place.

"Madam, why do you weep so noisily?" There was no compassion in the canon's voice, only an aridness that filled my throat with dust.

"Sir," I said, struggling to make the obligatory reverence while he held fast to my sleeve. "You are not to be told."

At that, I attempted to wriggle free, but the clerics formed a solid wall round me.

"You, wolf, what is this clothing you wear?" The canon stared at my white gown and kirtle, my white hood and cloak. "Are you a virgin?" His voice thickened with the insinuation.

"Sir, I am a good Christian wife who has taken a vow of chastity. An honest pilgrim." I pointed to the scallop shell pinned to my cloak, a keepsake from my recent journey to Santiago de Compostela.

"A wife and yet you travel alone?" The canon shook his head. "Do you have an affidavit from your husband giving you permission to tramp across the land?"

"Sir, my husband gave me leave with his own mouth." I tried not to tremble before his chilly blue eyes. "Why are you questioning me and not the other pilgrims here who have no more affidavits than I?"

"What cloth is that?" The canon fingered my sleeve, as if hoping to prove that I'd run afoul of the sumptuary laws.

"Plain wool, sir," I said. "Even the lowliest beggar might wear it. Now if you would let me be on my way."

How I wished I hadn't left my pilgrim's staff behind at my lodgings — it would come to good use right now as I attempted to force a path between two of the skinnier clerics. But the canon laid hold of my arm.

"The law forbids women to preach, and yet I witnessed you performing that very act in the shadow of this holy minster," he said.

"Sir, I'm no preacher." I forced myself to hold his gaze. "Never have I spoken from any pulpit. But the Gospels give me leave to speak of God."

My words only angered the canon all the more. How I infuriated and confounded these men by my very existence — a free-roving woman, neither a proper wife nor a cloistered nun, who presumed to speak of divine love and redemption. A masterless woman without a father or husband to rein me in.

Another man butted in, this one not a cleric but a worldly man, dressed like a princeling in calfskin boots and a brocade doublet. Around his neck he wore the chain of the office of mayor.

"Declare your name and business, woman," he said.

"My name is Margery Kempe." A deathly cold crept up my legs. "I hail from Bishop's Lynn in Norfolk. I'm a good man's daughter. My father was the Mayor of Lynn five times and an alderman in the Guild of the Holy Trinity," I added, careful to convey the fact that I came from worthy kindred. "My husband is a burgess of that town."

"Saint Catherine was eloquent in speech, describing what kin she came from," the canon said. "But you're no saint."

"You," said the mayor, jabbing his stubby finger at me, "are a strumpet. A Lollard. A deceiver of the people. I believe you've come here to take our wives from us and lead them off with you."

"I'm no Lollard, sir." A cold wash of panic filled my belly. "I've nothing to do with Wycliffe's disciples."

Two years ago, John Wycliffe had been declared a heretic. Though the ordained priest had been dead for more than thirty years, they ordered that his corpse be dug out of his grave and burned, all because he had translated the Bible into English. William Sawtry, a vicar from my own parish church of Saint Margaret's in Lynn, had been burned for Lollardy.

"We have witnesses who heard you quoting the Scriptures," the mayor said. "How should you come to know the gospels in English unless you're a Lollard? One of Oldcastle's whores," he added, referring to Sir John Oldcastle, the renegade outlaw who had escaped the Tower of London and who threatened to bring down the King in order to establish a Lollard commonwealth.

"Good sirs, I *can't read!*" I cried in desperation—may God forgive my lie. "I learned my scriptures from listening to sermons and speaking with godly folk," I added, now telling the truth. "I swear that I uphold the teachings of the Holy Mother Church. I support neither error nor heresy—"

The mayor held up his palm to silence me. "Save that for the trial. You're under arrest, Margery Kempe."

I

Incendium Amoris

I

Anno Domini 1390

WHEN I FIRST SAW the Mysteries at York, I was seventeen and as vain as Salome.

All the way from Bishop's Lynn in Norfolk we had ridden, a seven-day journey. We were well rewarded, for the City of York was a moving pageant. Scattered through the streets and squares were the wagons, wains, and carts where the plays were performed that narrated the entire sweep of history from the Creation to the End of Days. Such a spectacle! Yet I can say without lying that as I rode past those decorated stages all eyes were on me. Even the players forgot their lines as they gaped and stared.

How could they not? I rode a dappled chestnut mare, her bridle inlaid with polished silver shining in the June sun. White roses and green ribbons were plaited in her flaxen mane. And I was showier still. As befitting the Mayor of Lynn's only daughter, I wore gold piping on my towering headdress. My long trailing sleeves were dagged with tippets and slashed to reveal the many-colored brocades beneath. Pearls and coral beads gleamed at my throat. Even my Ave beads, hanging on display from my girdle, were of Baltic amber. My father had grown rich as a trader, exporting wool and grain and importing wine, timber, and fur. His ships sailed as far as Russia. Father was not only Mayor of Bishop's Lynn, but a member of Parliament and a justice of the peace. A descendent of the de Brunhams of Brunham Manor in Norfolk, his kin had served as clerics for the Black Prince.

My lofty perch in the saddle allowed me to see over the heads of the poorer, horseless folk as I watched the Mystery of Creation. A young man in a flesh-colored tunic—intended to hint at the nakedness of Adam—lay on his side while an old man with a beard of purest white waved his hands. Then, up from behind the reclining young man, rose a girl in a flesh-colored shift, as though she had been conjured from the boy's side. We gasped as we beheld Mother Eve—a tanner's fourteen-year-old daughter with long golden hair. She stood beneath a sapling apple tree placed upon the cart. From its branches hung fruit fashioned from crimson leather and a real dead snake—the Tanners' Guild had stuffed it to make it seem as lifelike as possible. Eve put her ear to the wicked serpent's mouth before offering Adam the apple. We all crossed ourselves and held our breath as we witnessed the original sin, our fall from grace.

Yet I was lighthearted. Flanked by my parents and our servants, I gladly accepted the cup of caudled ale that the alewife pressed in my hand. Sipping the spiced brew, I reveled in the performance, the sheer pageantry of these Mysteries, so unlike anything I would have ever seen in mercantile, money-counting Lynn.

When the first Mystery ended, we wound our way up Petergate to see the next. We passed jugglers, minstrels, acrobats leaping backward to land upon their hands, and even a dancing bear. Still, I was the one who turned everyone's head. A confectioner fawned as he lifted his tray of sweetmeats for my perusal. I took my time in making my selection, intently examining his delectable morsels of honeycomb, currants, and almonds as I reveled in his admiration.

Mother rolled her eyes. "Margery, you've grown insufferable! Remember, my dear, pride comes before the fall."

Once Mother had been the great beauty of Lynn, or so Father told everyone in his jovial way, but birthing twelve babies had taken its toll. Though she was no less sumptuously attired than I, she had lost half her teeth and her face looked tired and pale. The greatest injustice my mother suffered was that only two of her children had survived—my brother, Robert, who couldn't join us in York because he had sailed across the seas to trade, and I. Even our family's wealth and position were no match for the contagions that killed infants in their cradles.

"Leave Margery be," Father told Mother. "Soon enough she'll be married and having daughters of her own."

At that remark, I only smiled, confident that Father would want me to take my time choosing a husband. After all, my dowry was the envy of Lynn. I'd no intention of settling for the first herring merchant or wool dealer to call at our big house in Briggate near the Stone Bridge, which my father owned. With my riches and youth, my green eyes and honey-brown hair, I could pick and choose a man with the same dreamy whimsy as I'd plucked the most delectable sweetmeat off the confectioner's tray.

But even then, there was more to me than that, a part of myself I'd learned to hide. Beneath my costly linens and silks, my soul was always hungry, always craving something greater than the narrow streets of Lynn and a future of dutifully bearing babies. I envied my brother, who owned a ship and sailed to the great Hanseatic ports—Bremen and Hamburg and Danzig. How my spirits feasted on the City of York, second only to London in the entire realm. All these new sights, from the castle to the Merchant Adventurers' Hall. The great minster put our parish church of Saint Margaret's to shame. Never in my seventeen years had I seen so much stained glass. With Mother and her maidservant at my heels, I traipsed through the vast nave, craning my neck to examine every window. My favorite was the scene of Saint Anne teaching her daughter, the young Virgin Mary, to read. Mother had taught me to read in English, as befitting my station as the mayor's daughter. But I hungered for more. I wished I were some high-learned soul who was truly literate—literate in Latin. I burned with curiosity to decipher the secrets hidden in the arcane tomes that the clerks hoarded in their libraries.

I made do with the one book I owned, a lavishly illuminated book of hours, which was my most treasured possession. As the minster bells rang the office of Sext, I knelt beside Mother and opened my book to the appropriate page, moving my finger beneath the beautiful black letters spelling out the words of our Latin prayers.

As ravenous as I was for books, I took the greatest pleasure in maps, which raised me to the heavens and gave me a picture of all that lay below—the jagged coastlines and serpentine rivers. The City of York was marked by its heraldic white rose, its castellated walls, spired churches, and mighty minster. I knew Lynn by its famed harbor bristling with ships. So great was my love of maps that Father nicknamed me Compass Rose.

"Compass Rose," he said to me when our week in York had reached its end and it was time to journey home. "My eyes aren't as sharp as they used to be. Read the map for me, won't you?"

We had just ridden out of Walmgate Bar, York's eastern gate. The Vale of York spread before us, green hedges glistening with dew. Taking the map from Father, I unscrolled the tableau of rolling hills, towns, and hamlets, and traced the roads and highways with my finger. I felt as though I held the world in my hands.

The journey, I confess, delighted me far more than the destination. What a thrill it was to ride across the land even when the clouds showered hail and forced us to shelter beneath thickly leafed trees. Seeing the terrain constantly change before my eyes made my heart beat faster. When we crossed the mighty Humber on a wide ferry barge, I was breathless with elation. Ah, to feel the waves beneath me while the wind whipped my skirts. I stretched out my arms like wings and thought I might take flight with the gulls reeling above our heads.

But four days later, when we boarded Father's own ferry to cross the Great Ouse to Lynn, I shriveled inside to see the familiar city walls looming across the water. Rather than give thanks for our safe travels, I lamented that my first and only journey and exodus from Lynn was already over.

Surely it was wicked to be ungrateful for my lot. Lynn was a large and important town, boasting five thousand inhabitants and a rich, bustling port filled with foreigners selling exotic wares. Mother's kitchen was fragrant with rare spices, such as cinnamon and black pepper. I heard French and Flemish spoken in the Saturday Market. German cobblers made my shoes. But I recognized every face, from lowly artisans to the richest merchants and aldermen. I knew every servant girl, every friar, every single beggar and simpleton who haunted our streets. I could have found my way from one end of Lynn to the other through obscure alleyways with my eyes sewn shut. What was worse was that everyone knew *me*, my every vanity and foible. Wherever I went, a train of gossips clucked and mardled in my wake, their whispers pitched so I could hear every word. *There goes Margery Brunham in her trailing tippets! She's so conceited. I hope a seagull soils her headdress.*

What a wonder it would be to leave this place behind and sail away in one of those tall-masted ships that jostled for space in the harbor. I wondered if I would feel any less ridiculed in foreign lands among strangers.

2

WO YEARS PASSED AND I turned nineteen, fair of face and graceful of figure. Mother insisted I pick a husband soon, but she could have spared her breath. My heart was set.

Martin hailed from a family of wine merchants and was hardly a day older than I—the handsomest youth I'd ever clapped my eyes on. But he was a youngest son, and my parents were dismissive of his prospects and insisted I could do better. If that wasn't discouragement enough, Martin's widowed mother, a wine merchant in her own right and member of the Guild of the Holy Trinity, disapproved of me, thought me foolish and frivolous. But our parents' conniving couldn't keep Martin and me apart. We danced together at every fete and contrived to sit near each other at every banquet.

Martin and his family were among the many guests who came to share our table for the Twelfth Night celebrations. While a minstrel played his pipes, I smiled at Martin over my silver-rimmed cup and lost myself in his eyes, which were as dark as the sable adorning his doublet. Bloodred claret gushed from our servants' ewers in a never-ending fountain as Father led toast after toast to his friends in the Guild of the Holy Trinity, the foremost merchants' guild in Lynn. We feasted on roasted swan and peacock.

The piping trailed off as the mummers made their grand entrance in their bearskin jerkins and garishly painted wooden masks. As they stood before our holly-bedecked hearth, their beastly forms threw eerie shadows on the wall, making me shiver. Mother looked down the table to fix me with her pointed gaze, indicating that the mummers' dance was not a spectacle for a maiden's eyes. So I was to be banished just as the proper entertainment was about to begin? Though simmering in annoyance, I kept my composure. Smiling sweetly, I bade everyone goodnight, then cast a secret glance at Martin.

All eyes were on me. The men at the table rose to bow. At Father's right hand sat his dearest friend, John Kempe the Elder, burgess and town chamberlain of Bishop's Lynn. His son, likewise named John, sat near Mother. Both men seemed improbably old to me, gray riming their beards like frost. John the Younger ogled me. Avoiding his gaze, I cast down my eyes. A virgin in my father's house, my hair was uncovered and swept past my waist. Gilded rosemary crowned my brow. My brocade skirts swept the costly Italian tiles of our parlor floor.

I did not go upstairs to my chamber but instead crept downstairs and let myself out into the moonlit garden. There, in the most private corner, behind the well and the apple tree, I waited and hugged myself for warmth. The year was 1392 and I hadn't traveled more than five miles from Lynn in the two years since my return from York. Still, I fevered with anticipation that this might soon change. Such a fire burned inside me, rendering me oblivious to the snow beneath my thin soles.

Before long, Martin appeared, having used the spectacle of the mummers' dance to slip out of the parlor unnoticed. My arms wrapped around him, and I rubbed my cheeks against the leather and sable of his doublet. When he buried his face in my loosened hair and declared his love, I felt as blissful as Eve before the fall. Beneath the moon's pearly light, I held his face in my hands and stared in adoration. By Our Lady, I could never get over his beauty.

"Ask Father," I pleaded. "Ask him *now*. You'll never find him more cheerful than on Twelfth Night. He'll say yes. I promise he will."

If Martin had one fault, it was that he was so shy and unassuming, so fearful of offending my parents. But tonight, I prayed he would be bold. The thought of Martin returning to the parlor, taking Father aside, and asking for my hand in marriage left me giddy. I imagined a spring wedding, a posy of bluebells, a brimming bridal cup filled with mead and woodruff blossom. And the delights that would follow in our bridal bed — the very thought was enough to make me swoon.

"Just *ask!*" I threw my arms around his neck. "He's most indulgent. He *wants* me to marry for love."

"Margery, your father's no fool," Martin said. "He's had far too much wine to give his consent on so serious a matter. Your mother would never stand for it. Besides, I'm bound for Gascony this fortnight. My first trading mission."

My chest ached with frustration to imagine my beloved faring forth while I stayed behind, bereft of him. His face softened as my tears began to fall. He kissed my eyelids and then my mouth until I thought I could simply melt into him like a snowflake.

"Don't give up hope, my love," he said. "On this voyage, I can finally prove myself. Prove to your father that I'm worthy of you."

His eyes never leaving mine, he unhooked the chain with the golden Saint Christopher medal from around his neck, pressed it into my palm, and closed my fingers around it. His departed father had given him the medal, his most cherished possession. That was my Martin, so generous, without a thought to himself.

"By all that is good, I can't take this," I said, attempting to give it back. "You'll need it to keep you safe on your journey. What if there's a storm?"

He silenced me with a long kiss. "Your prayers will preserve me. And my medal will keep *you* safe until I return and make you my bride."

At that, he clasped his chain round my throat. His sacrifice moved me to unhook my necklace of pearls and coral beads, and offer it to him. But he refused it.

"Your mother will notice it's missing and demand an explanation. Here, give me a lock of your hair instead. It's far more precious." From his belt he took his knife and cut a tress, then kissed it and tucked it inside his doublet while I concealed his medal beneath my gown. The golden image of Saint Christopher, patron of travelers, pressed upon my racing heart. Having exchanged our tokens, we swore our undying love. We plighted our troth. We kissed until we finally summoned the strength to wrench ourselves apart.

"Mind how you go," I said, my fingers twining in his hair.

"Fare you well, Margery, my love," he whispered, kissing me one last time.

After Martin had set sail, Robert returned from Danzig to marry Alice, his betrothed, a meek, pious girl two years my junior. Such a wedding feast there was! I blushed when Father pinched my cheek and declared to the merry crowd that the next wedding would be mine. Under Mother's watchful eyes, I danced with every eligible man in Lynn, including John Kempe the Younger, who professed that I was the prettiest young thing he'd ever seen, all the while treading on my toes, the great lummox.

"You could do worse," Father told me privately. "He owns a warehouse full of Flemish linen and German hops."

Inwardly, I seethed. To think I had believed that Father had wanted me to marry for love! Clearly, I was wrong.

Soon after my brother's wedding, John Kempe, a brewer as well as a cloth dealer, gifted Father with a barrel of beer and asked him for my hand. I refused, aghast beyond all measure that a childless widower of thirty-six years thought he could have me — and my dowry! — for the price of a barrel of beer.

"Oh, you're a haughty thing," Mother said, astounded at my rejection of so worthy a man, the town chamberlain's son. "How much longer do you intend to wait? Soon you'll be the oldest virgin in Lynn outside the cloister."

My habit of perpetually questioning every single thing, even the necessity of being respectably married off by the age of twenty, was enough to drive Mother to despair.

Later I overheard Father assuring Mother that John Kempe was patient enough to wait and ask me again in half a year's time. It was all I could do not to shriek. I held Martin's medal in my clasped hands and prayed to Christopher and all the saints to keep my beloved safe, to bring him back to me.

Each day Martin was gone, Lynn grew narrower, its gray walls closing in to crush me.

To ease the ache that never left my breast, I walked with my brother along the harborside and took solace in a rare moment alone with Robert away from Mother's and Alice's judging eyes. My arm linked with his, I listened with longing to his tales of faraway lands.

Of the broad-gabled houses of Danzig, the countless warehouses, the great markets.

"Their women are so beautiful, tall and fair like angels, but none would marry me," he confided. "The Germans believe that English folk have tails like devils." In his many years away, he'd lost his broad Norfolk accent and spoke almost like a German, and yet in a tone so mischievous that I couldn't tell if he was joking or telling the truth. "Deo gratias, Mother found my Alice for me!"

Not wanting to linger on the subject of Mother arranging marriages, I pointed to Robert's ship, called the *Saint Savior*.

"What a fine craft she is!" I said, squeezing his arm.

The dry-docked vessel was being repaired and repitched in preparation for her long return voyage across the North and Baltic seas. The shipwrights, mindful of Robert and me watching, seemed to work with added diligence. If the fair weather continued, it wouldn't be long before *Saint Savior* could sail, her hold laden with English wool.

"Alice is sure to love Danzig," my brother said, with easy confidence. "The markets are magnificent. You can buy *anything*. Narwhal tusks! Ivory from African elephants! Indian silk! Arabian perfume! When we reach home"—I caught my breath to hear Robert call Danzig his home—"Alice and I shall build a hostelry for visiting English merchants. That way she'll have an occupation to keep her busy and in good company while I'm at sea."

Not wishing to dampen my brother's spirits, I nodded along though I couldn't imagine shy, retiring Alice acting as a hostess to strange men.

"I wish I could come with you," I said. "Alice might feel lonely without another English *woman* to talk to."

Were it not for Martin, I would have insisted that Robert take me along. I, his sister, would make a far better landlady to visiting merchants. Didn't Father trust me to entertain his distinguished guests? There was never a lull in the conversation when I sat at the table. But then I imagined the happiest of all outcomes—Martin could join us in Danzig where we could marry without my parents protesting that he was a youngest son. We would live together in bliss a world away from the gossips who had known us since we were babes in swaddling clothes.

Robert shook his head. "Mother would disown me if I took you away. Besides, I'll wager you a sack of good wool that you'll be wed by summer's end. Master Kempe is certainly taken with you."

Bridling at the thought of John Kempe, I looked down the Great Ouse and imagined my Martin's ship appearing. Listening to my brother's tales, I stared out at the harbor where Hanseatic merchant ships came and went, carrying goods and artisans in a perpetual whirl of leaving and arriving. Every one of them on the move while I remained planted in Lynn like some tree.

My parents held a farewell feast for Robert and Alice. I drank the spiced claret and toasted them until I was hoarse. Then, on the first of May, I waved goodbye as *Saint Savior* lifted anchor and disappeared down the wide river.

Spring's blossoms ripened into summer's fruits, and all the while, John Kempe paid court. Despite my attempts to rebuff him, the man was indefatigable, as loyal and adoring as the family hound. Gossips muttered about how God would punish me for my arrogance. Who did I think I was?

I couldn't even speak of my love for Martin, of the promises we had exchanged. My secret smoldered inside me, consuming me from within. Day after day, I accompanied Mother to the markets and to Saint Margaret's Church, my daily round through the twisting streets, and I remained aloof to John's increasingly ardent declarations. In thrall of Martin, I believed I'd the power to make time stand still, to remain that lovely virgin walking to church in my French gown and Flemish headdress. The envy of all and beholden to no one. As fixed and unchanging as a moth trapped in Baltic amber until Martin returned and broke the spell.

3

OME September, the bells of Saint Margaret's tolled for Martin's funeral Mass. His ship went down in a gale off the Brittany coast. My beloved sank to the bottom of the sea, taking my heart with him. I didn't even have his corpse to weep over. His blessed, beautiful flesh. *Beata viscera.*

I sobbed so grievously during my beloved's funeral that Martin's mother glared over her shoulder at my mother, who, taking her hint, guided me out of the door into the churchyard where I could weep myself empty without creating a disturbance. I braced myself for Mother's anger, her lecture and scolding, but instead she held me more tenderly than she had in years.

"Sweet child," she said. "I knew you were besotted with that boy. A first love is the sharpest arrow. It pierces the heart. Once, when I was even younger than you, I suffered just the same."

In my amazement, I stopped crying to stare at Mother. Never had I been privy to such a confession.

"Let this be our secret," she said, her brow touching mine as she held my shoulders. "Once I was nearly destroyed by grief."

Mother's words plunged me into silence and wonder. I recalled Father's tales of her being the most beautiful girl in Lynn. What had become of Mother's first love?

"Of course, you must mourn your Martin," she said gently. "But you'll turn twenty next year. You must look to your future, my darling. You can still find happiness. I did. If I hadn't been brave and accepted your father, I would never have had *you*, my dear."

She hugged me tightly. But we straightened and drew apart when we heard approaching footsteps. I blinked to see John Kempe staring at me. How downcast he appeared to find me so undone for another man. Yet his eyes shone with undiminished love. Bowing, he offered me his handkerchief.

For close to a month, I could only weep. I hardly left my chamber. The very thought of food galled me, and my gown hung loose on my frame no matter how tightly the maid tried to lace me in. I left our house only to go to church.

On the Feast of Martinmas, when the children paraded through the dark November streets with their lanterns, I lit candles at the altar of Saint Martin. The saint's painted image with his black hair and liquid eyes was as beautiful as my dead love. Leaning down from his gray steed, Saint Martin cut his cape in half to clothe a beggar. *Sancte Martine, ora pro nobis.* I folded my hands in prayer and closed my eyes while imagining Martin's fur-lined cloak wrapping around me. For a fleeting moment, I felt alive again. His ghostly arms held me. His spectral lips kissed mine.

On my way out of the church, I was so transported that I nearly careened into a creature clad in a rough woolen gown and veil. Her bare feet trod the frosty burial ground. She staggered under the weight of an enormous candle that threw unsteady light on her bruised and haggard face. Her eyes were dull and empty as though she didn't see me at all. Any comfort I'd gleaned from my devotions to Saint Martin vanished. I shivered and crossed myself, thinking this creature must be a phantom.

Mother appeared at my side, took my arm, and marched me quickly away. "That's Hawisia Moone," she whispered. "The Lollard."

Shock seized me. Mistress Moone had been so beaten down by her gaoler that I'd not recognized her. She was a widow who had run a small inn by the shipyard. Once I heard her preaching in the Saturday Market, and if that was not scandalous enough, what she actually proclaimed to the folk of Lynn sealed her doom, namely, that any man or even any woman who lived a good life was as worthy a priest as any ordained clergyman or even the pope in Rome. That the divine sacraments, the Host, the act of confession, even baptism, were meaningless. That it was far more virtuous to give money to the poor than to the Church. Charity for the needy and sincere devotion to God were the marks of a true Christian, not obedience to bishops. All the trappings and pomp of the Church were mere idolatry.

So this was the penance the bishop had meted upon Mistress Moone—to walk barefoot round and round the graveyard in the November darkness bearing the heavy candle. As harsh as this seemed, the bishop had been mild to her—the ultimate punishment for heresy was death by fire.

My bones shook to recall our old vicar, William Sawtry, who had read Bible verses to us in English without the bishop's permission and told us that every Christian was worthy enough to learn and understand the scriptures. Father Sawtry was the first to ever be burned at the stake for Lollardy in all England. How I missed and mourned him. It seemed a travesty that such a good man could be condemned to burn in Smithfield as though he were a traitor to the realm. I'd never been afraid to confess my sins to him for he'd always been so kind. Unlike our new vicar, Father Spryngegold, who struck terror in my heart.

I had loved Father Sawtry's sermons. Thanks to him, there's many a Bible passage I could recite from memory. *Did that make me a heretic, too?* I wondered. *No better than Hawisia Moone?* That deadened look in her bruised, defeated face was enough to harrow my soul.

On Sunday, as Father Spryngegold mounted the spiraling steps to the pulpit, it was plain to see he had no intentions of sparing us.

Before Father Spryngegold came to our parish, I'd believed that no matter how threatening the world could be everything was the handiwork of God and watched over by angels and saints to whom I could pray for solace. But Father Spryngegold was forever reminding us that our every deed was witnessed by countless demons.

"Demons were with us from the very beginning of creation." His voice raised every hair on my skin.

I edged closer to Mother for warmth—it was so cold in that church that our breath plumed like smoke.

Even before Eve committed the original sin and condemned us all, rebel angels, cast out of heaven, rained down from the sky above the Garden of Eden, or so Father Spryngegold told us. When the fallen angels touched the earth, they became demons. Hell and all its horrors were established before Adam and Eve were driven out of paradise.

"Above all, women are beloved of demons," Father Spryngegold said, glowering down from his pulpit.

He pointed to a fresco on the wall showing a demon riding the long silken train of a woman's gown while another demon hovered close to eavesdrop on two women putting their heads together to gossip. He muttered at some length about the evils of Hawisia Moone, the Lollard. After undergoing her penance, she sold her inn and vanished from our parish. I tried to imagine what had become of her. Perhaps in some village or town far away, she could start a new life among folk who didn't shun her.

"Unlike men, women are not made in God's image," Father Spryngegold informed us. "Eve is an inferior creature, fashioned from a rib. When she seduced Adam, she made sinners of us all."

Father Spryngegold declared that men's souls strove to rise to God but were dragged down by the wicked lure of women who tempted them with their unclean bodies that oozed with unholy excretions and the pustulent sin of Eve.

I looked to Mother, trying to see what she made of this. Her face was pale and she shivered just as I did. Not a single person could ignore Father Spryngegold when he delivered his homilies, such was the awful might of his words. He'd a great reputation as a holy and ascetic man whose fasts could rival those of any hermit.

"The lustful eye of a woman," he said, "ruins a man and dries him out like hay. A woman's gaze is the devil's mirror. Woe be unto even the most pious man who looks into a woman's eyes too often. No man should trust a woman after she deceived Adam. This is why she must veil her head and forehead in shame." His voice rose like breaking thunder. "Woman's love is no love but bitterness!" His fist crashed down on the lectern, causing us all to leap and gasp. "It should rather be called a school for fools!"

His words rendered me sick. Is this what I did to Martin, stealing away his soul's salvation when I took his holy medal from him?

Would that medal have saved him, body and soul? What if my love and desire had dried him out like hay even as his corpse lay in its watery grave? The frigid stone floor beneath me lurched, and I thought I would vomit on my mother's brocade gown.

Seemingly indifferent to my distress and that of the women around me, Father Spryngegold launched into the most horrific part of his sermon, describing in starkest detail the End of Days when God would destroy his creation and allow demons to overrun the scorched earth. He pointed toward the huge fresco above the rood screen that framed the high altar. At its apex sat Christ as the Judge of Souls. On his right hand, angels escorted the souls of the blessed into heaven.

"But few are the blessed," Father Spryngegold reminded us. "Most mortals must endure purgatory even if they die in the grace of the Church."

The scene on Christ's left side revealed the destiny of those who died *without* grace. Without being shriven of their sins and receiving the final sacraments. All who died a sudden death, like Martin, might meet this fate. Demons drove the souls of the damned into the hellmouth where unending fire and torment awaited them. The fresco spared no detail of the unspeakable degradations that demons performed on men and women. They hacked their bodies to pieces, shoved burning torches into every orifice, boiled them in oil, pierced them with skewers—tortures that would not end in merciful death but go on and on for all eternity.

In the freezing and dim November church, the demons in hell seemed to come alive, writhing with menace and triumph.

On the way home from church, I saw demons lurking in every shadow. I leapt out of my skin at the sight of a black cat darting out of a ginnel. That night as I lay in bed, I writhed in dread to hear the owl's cry. When I finally slept, demons danced through my dreams. Night and its creatures, such as owls, were ruled by devils as were women and cats.

I fingered Martin's Saint Christopher medal. When I closed my eyes and strove to picture his beautiful face, I only saw his bones, picked clean by fish, knocking together in the cold tide. *Your prayers will preserve me,* he'd said. If I'd only prayed harder, would he still be alive? If I'd been better, more devout, purer in spirit, would Martin have survived? What if I was, in fact, responsible for Martin's damnation? Absolution seemed beyond me—I was too petrified, too ashamed to confess my sin to Father Spryngegold. My stricken conscience pressed down on my soul like a coffin lid.

Hard on the heels of Martinmas came the Advent fast and the squally days of December. At least now I'd an excuse to refuse all sustenance but water and dry bread. Hunger eased my pain, unhooking my soul from my wretched flesh. Mewed up in my chamber while the outside world withered and died into the rising darkness, I willed my physical form to shrink and vanish.

"Fasting doesn't mean starving," Mother admonished, bringing me a bowl of fish broth.

But I was too listless to swallow more than a few mouthfuls. Devils seemed to gather round me, blackening the air with their whirring wings. Honey-tongued, those infernal spirits seduced me with the longing for death, for the deep peace of the grave where I'd be reunited with Martin at last. If I was damned anyway, why not surrender? Many a tale I'd heard of girls struck down with the greensickness. They stopped eating and dwindled to bone while their families could do nothing but watch and mourn.

Opening my book of hours, I gazed at the brightly painted image of Saint Martin until the colors blurred together.

Almost half of Advent had passed when Father stormed into my room, seized my shoulders, and shook me until my teeth rattled.

"I've had *enough* of this lovesick nonnicking of yours!" His voice blared like the trumpet of the Apocalypse. This was no longer the indulgent man I knew. Raw, he looked, his face set in stern furrows. "I'll not stand by while you waste away of vain self-pity."

Standing silent in his shadow, Mother held a bowl of pottage.

"We've coddled you long enough," he said. "You'll finish that pottage if I have to pour it down your throat. And then you'll make up your mind. Either you marry poor John Kempe or else I'm packing you off to Carrow Priory. If you want to fast until your hair falls out, you'll do it in a nunnery. Not in my house."

Too frightened to look at him, I gazed toward my white-lipped mother who trembled as much as I did in the force of Father's wrath. His final word.

Mother fed me the broth spoonful by spoonful as though I were a little child. All the while she spoke to me in a careful, coaxing voice. Both of us suspected that Father was listening with his ear to the door.

"Carrow Priory is a fine Benedictine house," she said. "Just outside the walls of Norwich and richly endowed. They'll be sure to welcome you as a postulant."

They'll be sure to welcome my dowry, I thought, trying not to gag on the pottage.

"You so love books, my dear," Mother went on. "The Sisters will teach you to read and write in *Latin*. You shall be as high-learned as any clerk. Why, I've even heard it said that there's an anchoress, Dame Julian, who took her vows there before she was enclosed in her cell. She's *written* a book, just like Bridget of Sweden did, but here in Norfolk." Mother's voice rang with the wonder of it all.

I remained unmoved. I'd heard of Bridget of Sweden, of course, the sainted mystic who had received holy visions of the Nativity and Passion. I'd heard of Dame Julian, though I doubted that the story of her writing a book could be true. Mother, I imagined, was telling me tall tales to insure my obedience. If Mother only knew that the very thought of an anchoress raised my skin. What manner of woman chose of her own free will to be bricked inside a single room for the rest of her days—she would either have to be very holy or stark mad.

Having swallowed down the last of the broth, I willed myself to fall into a sleep from which neither parent would ever be able to rouse me. But before I could sink down into the blankets, Mother gripped my arm and looked me in the eye.

"*Or,*" she said, "you can marry the man who adores you. Look what John brought you today."

Out of her pocket Mother took a silken pouch and placed it in my hand. She hovered so close, I knew I'd have no peace until I opened it. When I upended the pouch, a silver oval tumbled into my palm. A medal of Saint Margaret. Wielding her cross like a sword, she swaggered over the dragon she'd slain. Margaret, my name saint and patron. *If only I could be so courageous as I forged my future path.*

After Mother finally left me alone, I pulled the bed curtains fast around me and reflected upon my fate. Sweet Martin lay dead at the bottom of the sea. God had taken him and I could never be his wife. Perhaps God had indeed punished me for my willful pride. Now, out of the many paths and choices I once thought were open to me, only two remained.

One, to reward gentle, patient John for his long-suffering devotion and become his bride. My parents would certainly welcome this with blessed relief. My twentieth birthday was fast approaching. If I waited much longer, perhaps even John wouldn't want me anymore.

Two, to marry Christ and take the veil. Transform the ephemeral and doomed love I had shared with Martin into an eternal love for my Savior who had died for my sins, vanities, and carnal lusts. I would travel the forty miles to Norwich, then disappear behind cloistered walls and bid farewell to the great world. Never see Danzig. Never see York again or even the Saturday Market or the ships in Lynn Harbor. The thought of being trapped forever inside a priory—an even more confining space than the gray walls of Lynn—made me want to cut my throat.

Seeing me struggle to know my own mind in the face of Father's rage, Mother tiptoed into my chamber the following morning while I lay frozen in bed. This time she brought a rolled parchment.

"Don't tell your father," she said mysteriously before laying it at my side.

Intrigued, I unscrolled the parchment. It was a map of the great pilgrimage routes across Europe. I made out the isle of Britain, shaped like a pregnant woman on her knees, then the massive lands of the Continent and far and fabled Palestine.

Perching on the edge of my bed, Mother pointed to the most sacred shrines. "Santiago de Compostela," she said with hushed reverence. "Rome."

Then we both moved our fingers to the place on the map that marked out the holiest of holies—Jerusalem—illuminated in gold leaf.

For the first time in months, joy spread through my chest. My heart exulted at the very notion of setting off on pilgrimage and leaving this sad, narrow life behind. I imagined faring forth into a brand-new existence where I would become a different person. Someone brave, bold, even blessed. Pilgrimage would cleanse me of my sins, and I could at last make my penance for what role I may have played in Martin's death.

Mother brushed my lank hair from my cheek. "John Kempe, I'll wager, will take you to see the Mysteries at York at the very least."

On the first day of Christmas, John paid us a visit. While my parents looked on, I poured his wine and served him spice cakes. Though I was still weak and thin, I was dressed in my finest. Mother had even made me bathe though the servants muttered that bathing in midwinter would be the death of me. My freshly washed hair hung loose and uncovered as it had on Twelfth Night almost a year ago when I'd sworn my eternal love to Martin.

"You're so pale from your illness," John said, his face rumpling in concern. "Drink your wine, dear girl. It will bring some color to your cheeks."

I didn't want to let the wine jumble my thoughts. Setting down my cup, I leaned toward John and rested my hand on his broad arm. I made myself speak, unflinching and clear.

"If I agree to marry you, John Kempe, do you promise to go with me to the shrine of Our Lady of Walsingham in the first year of our marriage?"

My heart swelled, thinking about the pilgrims' map. Asking him to take me to Rome or Jerusalem would have been preposterous. However, it seemed reasonable enough, in my mind, to ask him to travel with me to Walsingham right here in Norfolk. Come spring, provided the ground wasn't too muddy, we could ride there in a day. I trembled with the urge to make my first journey since my family's travels to York three years ago.

Father frowned, as if perturbed by my presumption. Mother ducked her head and smiled.

"My daughter is very devout," she told John brightly.

Father raised his eyes to the ceiling but said nothing.

John laughed as though my request delighted him as much as it surprised him. He raised his cup to me. "Sweet Margery, name the date of our wedding and I solemnly swear we'll ride to Walsingham to ask Our Lady to bless our marriage."

Mother clapped her hands in glee. Even Father finally smiled and embraced me.

Just after Candlemas, a mere thirteen months after Martin and I had shared our last kiss, I became Margery Kempe. Every burgher of Lynn crammed into Saint Margaret's for our wedding Mass. Father kept slapping John's back in congratulation. Mother could not stop kissing my cheek and assuring me all would be well.

After the wedding feast with its singing and dancing, John ceremoniously took my arm and escorted me to my new home in Fincham Street. A tall, crooked old house, it was, and attached to his warehouse and brewery.

Laughing and merry from the spiced mead we'd shared in our bridal cup, John and I stumbled over the threshold. As soon as we barred the door, John's huge hands wrapped around my waist and lifted me into the air. He gazed up at me, his hard-won prize, and beamed.

"By all the saints, I'll make you happy, Margery."

The place where my heart used to be remained numb. Still, I smiled and resolved to make the most of what was left to me.

"Husband," I said.

When my feet touched the ground once more, I closed my eyes and kissed him with full-throated longing, pretending he was Martin. His silvering beard brushing my lips was astonishingly soft. John swept me in his arms as if I weighed no more than a March lamb and sprinted up the stairs to our bedchamber. Together we tumbled into our bridal bed, which Mother had bedecked with rosemary and dried rose petals.

I held my breath, for I didn't know what to expect. Surely I would disappoint him, for he must know deep inside that I was hopelessly enamored of a dead boy. But his face was tender, as though he possessed enough love for the both of us. Enough to make up for my lack of true love for him. His kisses were so gentle, causing my limbs to unclench while my thoughts whirled in confusion. Though I'd believed I could never desire any man but Martin, something rare began to stir inside me. When John began to peel off layer after layer of my clothing, my fear and shame dropped away. What transpired next caused me to sway and arch my spine and throw back my head. Never had I suspected that such pleasures existed. *Can heaven itself be sweeter?* Such were the blasphemies dancing inside my head on my wedding night. I could only marvel that what we were doing wasn't a sin.

4

HEN JOHN AND I rode to Walsingham that May morning, the world seemed fresh and new, redolent with promise. The hedges were frothy white with hawthorn, the meadows a tapestry of cow parsley and buttercups. The woods, thick with bluebells, rang with cuckoos' cries. My husband and I cantered along, my chestnut mare shoulder to shoulder with his bay stallion.

I prayed that this pilgrimage, taken in the third month of our marriage, would cleanse me of my sins—of how I'd tortured John, my parents, and myself with my stubborn love for Martin. Of how difficult I'd been, the way I questioned and challenged every single thing that was expected of me. Let this journey transfix me in every way and transform me into a good and virtuous wife so I could adore my husband every bit as much as he appeared to adore me.

Soon enough the roads grew crowded with fellow pilgrims. As holy shrines went, Walsingham was second only to Canterbury in all England. The mood was jubilant as we greeted our companions on the journey.

Much later in the day, when the shadows grew long, we reached the Slipper Chapel, a mile and a half from the main shrine. After paying a groom, we left our horses, removed our shoes, and proceeded as barefoot penitents. For all my fine brocade and linen, I was no more exalted than the peasants and washerwomen who shared the path. My feet smarted on the stony ground, but I limped onward, resolute in my quest. I lifted my voice to join the others in their hymns.

We grew silent as we approached the narrow pilgrims' gate leading into Walsingham Priory. I waited behind the others in the queue until it was my turn to enter the small chapel. After John and I laid down our offering of two golden noble coins, we kissed the finger bone of Saint Peter. Next we processed to the well house where we slaked our thirst on the waters from the two holy wells.

Only then did we reach the culmination of our journey. One by one we filed inside the Chapel of the Virgin. More than three centuries ago, a Saxon noblewoman received three divine visions that moved her to build a replica of the Virgin Mary's house in Nazareth right here in Norfolk. Suddenly, I was no longer in England. The outer world and all sense of time dropped away as I beheld the fresco of the Annunciation. The Angel Gabriel appeared in a blaze of gold before Mary, who looked up from her prayer book in rapture. I dropped to my knees before the statue of the Virgin flanked by Saint Catherine with her book and wheel and Saint Margaret with her cross and dragon. My eyes filled with tears as I kissed the reliquary containing a vial of the Virgin's milk. For one heart-stopping moment, I felt complete. At peace. Pure and new like the Virgin's heavenly blue mantle draping her slender form.

"What a blessing on our marriage," John said that night in our lodgings.

As he reached to tug off my nightshift, I held his wrists to make him stop.

"Not *tonight*, John," I said, wanting that state of grace I'd felt in the shrine to linger on.

"Never fear, love," he said, kissing my lips. "What we're doing is holy. We'll be blessed with a fine child."

In the three months of our marriage, I'd discovered that it was impossible to hold off John even on holy days and fasting days when canon law forbade conjugal union. So I'd no other choice than to succumb once again to the force of his desire. After all, hadn't I prayed to love him more?

Two things must be said of John Kempe.

The first is that he was so jovial and good-natured because he knew that this served his purpose. He was decisive, my husband. He never wavered. He was a man who always got what he wanted in the end even if he had to wait for it. He was a patient hunter who bided his time until his aim was perfect before loosing his arrow.

The second thing I must say of him is that, in his way, he meant well enough.

In the beginning he gave me such pleasure that I bloomed for all to see. Even the market women remarked how well I looked, how wedded life suited me. It seemed impossible that I had ever been despondent enough to lock myself in my chamber and refuse to eat. I never forgot Martin, who would dwell forever inside my heart. But thanks to John, I discovered how wide my heart truly was, with more than enough room for both Martin and my husband. Folk in Lynn still mocked me for my showy headdresses, but I was deaf to their jibing. In truth, I was happier than I'd ever been. Until about a month after our return from Walsingham when I began to grow sick in the mornings.

"God be praised!" John cried, clasping his hands before his heart. "A fine son it will be. By my troth, we conceived the baby in Walsingham!"

That night, for the first time in our entire wedded life, he left me alone in bed. While he snored contentedly with his back to me, I lay with my hands on my belly and pondered my fate. In the space of a day, my husband had gone from never taking his hands off me to hardly touching me at all for fear of damaging our unborn child. I didn't know whether I was frustrated or hurt or secretly relieved to finally have some respite from his lust.

My pregnancy should have proved that I was indeed a good wife, bearing John's child. I should have been blissfully aglow like the expectant Virgin Mary and content to spend my days stitching swaddling clothes. Surely no reasonable woman in my place would have cause to complain. It soon proved that I was no reasonable woman.

Though Mother fairly spouted with advice on what I must eat and drink, and what I must avoid, I was wretchedly ill and bad-tempered. I sickened at the sight of fish and despaired at the way my once graceful body now bulged and protruded like some misshapen sea creature dredged from the deep. My ankles bloated, barrel thick. My back ached. Soon enough, just walking to the Saturday Market seemed an impossible labor. Melancholy closed in on me as thick as winter fog, for it seemed my days of dreaming over pilgrimage maps were well and truly over. No longer a happy young bride, I became a miserable shrew who scolded John for farting in bed and for the mess he made in the chamber pot that the servants refused to clean, leaving that task to me. I suffered great attacks of fever all the way up to giving birth.

In darkest February, slightly more than a year after John and I married, I went to my childbed. My labor was harrowing, and I became convinced that God was punishing me for being such an awful wife. I cursed and swore so outrageously against my poor husband, he surely must have heard it—as must have everyone who passed our house in Fincham Street.

After a full day and night of agony, I was delivered of a healthy son whose broad head nearly shattered my pelvis. John was so pleased, he forgave me for my foulness. Our baby boy was beautiful and perfect —the very sight of him brought tears to my eyes, for I knew I didn't deserve such grace. Roiling in fever, I was too weak to hold him, let alone nurse him. When John took my hand and spoke to me, I saw his lips move but couldn't hear his voice. All I heard were the sooty-winged demons who smirked at me from the rafters where they hung upside down like bats. *Come away with us, Margery. You're bound for hell. You're damned.*

I was so insensible with fever that John and Mother feared the worst. They sent for Father Spryngegold to give me the Office of the Dying.

This was my last chance to confess and receive absolution. I gazed into Father Spryngegold's fish-cold eyes. *Now or never.* Could my soul still be saved? Demons crowded the chamber. Plump and stinking, they perched on the bedposts, picked their noses, and sniggered at me. My mouth was dry, my throat tight with terror.

"*Mea culpa*," I said, struggling over each syllable. "*Mea maxima culpa.*"

My eyes filled as I tried to find the words to describe my mortal sin of taking Martin's holy medal from him. Of loving a dead boy more than my living husband. The demons only leaned closer, one of them stroking my cheek with his oily talon.

"Don't you see them?" I asked, clutching Father Spryngegold's sleeve with my last strength. "They're everywhere. Why don't they flee *you* if you're a holy man?"

Shouldn't the demons vanish at the very sight of the priest with his crucifix, holy water, and communion Host?

He sighed. "They told me you were deathly ill, not a witless lunatic. If you please, Mistress Kempe, make your confession or keep your sins to yourself. I've a dying alderman to attend to and I can't waste any more time with your wittering."

He looked at me so pitilessly that I couldn't say another word. The demons crinkled their leathery faces and roared in laughter.

By and by, I recovered in body if not in spirit. Believing myself damned, I went out of my mind for the best part of eight months. Demons followed me everywhere. They pawed at me and dragged me around the house. They shat on my distaff and danced jigs on the butter churn. Whenever I opened my mouth, streams of curses gushed forth. I railed against my husband and my parents. Against God, his blessed mother, and all the saints. Yet even then I fasted on bread and water, as if this could atone for my blasphemies and the sins I'd been unable to confess. I didn't trust myself to touch my own baby. I was thankful that Mother and the wet nurse cared for little Jack, who grew plump and rosy as I dwindled.

The demons closed in on me. Their claws raked my flesh and their voices grew shriller, commanding me to jump out of the attic window. To take the kitchen knife to my throat. The only way to silence them was to shriek and bite my own hand so savagely that I bore that scar for the rest of my days.

The servants forcibly restrained me day and night to prevent me from wreaking any further harm. Surely I was doomed beyond redemption. John despaired of me. Even Mother feared I was a lost cause.

On Martinmas morning I awakened to a perfume sweeter than roses on Midsummer's Eve. The most exquisite music filled the chamber, as though an organ, psaltery, rebec, and recorder were playing in intricate harmony. Angelic voices sang.

Is this the demons' latest trick? I lay in my bed and my warders were out of earshot, so it took me some time to work up the courage to open my eyes. The music swelled to even greater splendor, as though it had the power to melt away all my pain.

Then I saw him sitting on the edge of my bed. His gaze transfixed me.

"Martin?" I whispered.

Had my true love come back from the beyond to save me and raise me up again? His beauty stunned me — the most handsome and dazzling form that could ever be seen by human eyes. He had grown a beard, and instead of his sable-trimmed doublet, he wore robes of purple silk. Every hair on my body stood on end when I realized this wasn't Martin. Wasn't Martin at all. Golden light blazed from his body to fill the chamber.

My hands were bound together with rags, so I couldn't reach out to touch him. But he leaned in to caress my cheek. *Margery, why have you forsaken me when I never forsook you?* He looked at me with such overpowering compassion.

All the darkness inside me fled before his radiance. I knew then and there that I wasn't damned. That no demon would have power over me ever again. He was the absolution I had craved. The absolute love.

Love douses all sin, he told me, his voice brimming in tenderness.

The air around him blazed like lightning. I watched him step inside that shimmering gold nimbus. He moved not with haste but with elegant grace so I could see him clearly until the light closed around him.

Trembling, I laughed and wept at once. I felt so light and unburdened, as though I could simply float out the window. My hands were still bound, but with patience and diligence, I managed to undo the knots with my teeth. When my hands were free, I untied the rags that bound my ankles. I rose from the bed, made use of the chamber pot, and dressed myself without calling for the maid. I brushed my hair and tucked it inside a linen snood. There was still water in the basin to clean my face and hands. My chamber door was locked, but I jiggled the keyhole with a pin until it sprang open.

With calm assurance, as though I had never been ill or raving, I descended the stairs to the kitchen where Emma, the maid, was kindling the hearth fire in preparation for breakfast. At the sight of me, she squawked, leapt halfway to the ceiling, and crossed herself.

"Mistress Kempe!" she cried. "How did you get out of your chamber?"

"Give me the keys to the buttery, if you please," I said. "This morning I shall eat meat with my husband." The thought of meat left me surprisingly hungry, for I'd eaten little apart from invalid's food for the past eight months.

Emma shook her head, looking at once confounded and suspicious. "I'm not allowed to give you the keys, mistress. You're not in your right mind."

"Do as you're told," I said, every inch the Mayor of Lynn's daughter. "Or must I dismiss you for your insolence?"

I held out my hand imperiously. Sucking on her teeth, Emma surrendered her ring of iron keys into my open palm.

I was heading toward the buttery when John bounded in.

"Margery?" he asked, fixing me with an incredulous look before turning to Emma, who threw up her hands.

"*I* didn't let her out, Master Kempe," she said, her face flaming red. "I'll wager it was that dolt of a wet nurse."

"By Our Lady and all the saints, it's a miracle!" I told John before embracing him and laying my head on his chest where his heart thumped away in bafflement. "Jesus Christ appeared to me in all his glory and dispelled my darkness."

Emma shot a look at John as if to say, *Here's the proof that she's truly mad.*

Before Emma could do or say anything more, the wet nurse entered with my eight-month-old son.

"Little Jack," I said, taking him in my arms and cooing at him until he smiled at me. I kissed his downy head.

"Sweet Margery," John said. "We thought we'd lost you."

John and I shared our breakfast, laughing together as if no tragedy had ever befallen us.

"Alas that I ever did sin," I said, taking a swig of small beer and spearing a sausage with my knife. "It's so merry in heaven!"

5

 HAD THOUGHT THAT MY vision of Christ would change me forever, that I would live the rest of my earthly days enveloped in bliss. But I was still a wife of Lynn, fettered by my womanly condition. By Candlemas, I was pregnant with my second child. Neither John nor anyone in my household believed that my vision was real, though my husband was prepared to humor me in his sheer relief to have a sane wife once more. During my months of lunacy, my parents had paid the Brothers at the Carmelite friary to say Masses for me. Thus everyone in Lynn attributed my recovery to this miraculous intervention. The fact that even Mother dismissed my vision was a blade in my heart, and yet I went on believing in my revelation.

With an unclouded mind, I bore a daughter with wide green eyes and fair hair. We named her Isabella after my mother. This baby I doted on, nursing her myself, singing to her, and carrying her in my arms the whole day through, which sent little Jack into fits of jealousy. While she slept, I cuddled him in my lap and told him every story I knew about the great world. Of his uncle in Danzig and of my dreams of traveling to Jerusalem. Had it stayed like this, I could have found my happiness as a wife of Lynn, content with my lot.

Yet before I could even get used to having a slender waist and being light on my feet, I was pregnant again. Our second son we named Robert, after my brother. The baby's sable-dark eyes reminded me of Martin's. In unguarded moments I'd find myself daydreaming that this was Martin's child, the living proof of his ghostly love. Sweet Robbie died at eight weeks. I had not even begun to grasp the enormity of my loss and grief when I fell pregnant once more.

And so the years passed, taking my youth and dreams of pilgrimage with them. Many a day, in thrall of morning sickness, I could hardly rise from bed. Countless nights I never slept, having spent the dark hours tending colicky infants. Still, I strove to do my duty serving John as a good wife must. When he returned home of an evening, I sat him in the best chair before a roaring fire and knelt before him to tug off his boots and give him fresh hosen and shoes. When he was poorly, I served him a caudle of boiled beef cheek. I took great pains to keep him in fresh linen, to keep our bedsheets white and clean, and to banish fleas in the summer months. But it seemed I could never keep servants for long—Emma left after complaining that so many crying babies addled her brains. My hands were perpetually raw from scrubbing swaddling clothes and soiled clouts.

Catherine, my second daughter, was as quick and alert as a hare. Next came Anna with her formidable gray eyes. Her shrieks could make even John's hair stand on end. But Margaret was the quietest baby I ever bore, which made me fear she would not make old bones —a prophecy that proved true. We lost her before she was even a year old. Simon was as pretty as a girl with his long black lashes, earning Jack's mockery as well as his affection. More brothers followed. Edwin was bold and intrepid, constantly getting into mischief. Lucas was a sunny child from the day he was born, sweet and eager to smile.

Mother of seven, I was, and pregnant yet again. I began to wonder how many more pregnancies my body could endure—what if my poor exhausted womb fell out along with the next baby? Together with John's young brewery apprentices who slept in our attic and ate at our table, we'd more children than stools in our house. Oh, the din and mayhem. Jack dropped a toad down the back of poor Catherine's underdress, making the girl leap out of her skin. Isabella rushed to her sister's defense and beat her brother over the head with her distaff while Lucas howled in his cradle. Fierce little Anna caught the toad and hurled it out the window, where it chanced to land in the cowl of a mendicant friar whose hands flew up in horror as if a biblical plague of frogs were raining down upon him. While I struggled to pull apart the sparring siblings and comfort Catherine and the wailing baby, Edwin and Simon seized their chance and stole off to the buttery, which the clueless maid had left unlocked. I found them there later. The little boys giggled like imps, their grubby paws in the honey pot. I was tempted to hide in the cellar and hold my hands to my ears for a moment's peace.

If I was at wits' end, John was well pleased with his lot. When we went to church, he fairly sparkled with pride to have his progeny marching behind him while I, baby Lucas in my arms, swayed from the weight of my enormous belly. John loved to brag over his beer that he had married the most fertile woman in Lynn. My fecundity served as proof of his virility. Perpetually pregnant, I could only force a smile as neighbors and even Mother exclaimed what a blessing it was and how grateful I must be. Each new baby, they said, was a gift from God.

During darkest December, I nearly bled to death bearing a baby girl who perished before she could be christened. As long as I live, I shall never forget the sight of her tiny body, perfectly formed but stone-cold. Her ears like delicate pink shells. Those puckered pink lips that would never speak, never cry. To think I had birthed this soul only to lose her to both this life *and* the next. Though it had broken me in half to lose Robbie and Margaret, at least we'd been able to give them a Christian burial and I could pray that we might one day be united in heaven. But this baby girl, who I couldn't even bring myself to name, would wander forever in limbo, the cold and shadowy edge of hell. Though she had done no wrong, she'd no baptism and thus she was barred from paradise on account of the stain of original sin. She couldn't even be buried in consecrated ground. I wept in disbelief that God could banish my baby. My grief blackened everything. I cried so long and hard that neither John nor the children could sleep. The new maid ran away at first light.

After losing my baby girl, I lost all desire for John. In my distress, I just wanted him to leave me alone and keep his beastly lusts to himself. But this he could not countenance. My husband insisted on his conjugal rights no matter how much I wept or pleaded. With my last strength,

I struggled to push him away, but he pinned me down and shoved my legs apart.

"How dare you even question my right?" he asked with a long-suffering air as he forced himself on me. "I'm not a cruel man. I've never once beaten you. You'd be hard-pressed to find a milder husband in all Lynn. I've held my tongue when you drove the servants away and burned my dinner. But now you've gone too far."

Six weeks on, I was gagging with morning sickness, yet I still had no respite from John. Before he had at least left me alone when I was pregnant, but now he expected to lie with me even though I carried a child in my womb. To make it worse, he muttered endearments all the while to silence my protests, as if he thought he could strong-arm me into desiring him again.

My stomach swilled with nausea as I stood in the kitchen and prepared to make eel pie. On my cutting board lay the eel, still writhing with life. Cleaver in my fist, I pretended the long, snakelike thing was John's manhood. With a grim smile, I chopped the creature to pieces. Such wicked thoughts paraded in my head. I imagined being strong enough to strangle my husband the next time he tried to bed me. I imagined God striking him dead. The conjugal debt of matrimony had become so abominable to me that I would have rather swallowed the ooze and muck from the gutter. But after almost eleven years of marriage, I was forced to concede that my body was no longer my own. All that remained to me was my soul.

To make matters even worse, John was a fool with money. In the early years of our marriage, he was elected town chamberlain like his father before him, but he didn't hold that office for long. And dare I say that for a father of so many children John was unforgivably careless and lazy. Soon it proved his fortunes and prospects would never be as glorious as my parents had hoped. Though I tried to help him with his bookkeeping, his debts mounted and his brewery brought him no great fortune. Of my immense dowry, nothing remained.

My only reprieve were my weekly visits to Master Alan, the holy and high-learned anchorite who read to me from the books I loved and so fed my mind and spirit.

Leaving the glowering maid in charge of my brood, I fairly sprinted out the door, wobbling pregnant belly and all. A harsh January wind swept the streets. The cold cut through the thin soles of my shoes and pinched at my flesh. As I crossed the marketplace in the shadow of Saint Margaret's Church and the Guildhall of the Holy Trinity, I lowered my eyes to the littered ground. At the age of thirty, I still turned heads, but not in a way I liked. Even the beggars seemed to smirk at how shabby I had become, my headdresses now ragged and ridiculous. When an old woman thrust out her hand to me and my alms were too stingy to her taste, she spat at my tattered hem.

"Not so high and mighty are you now, eh, Margery Kempe?"

Her fellow paupers laughed along. My eyes stinging, I rushed away as swiftly as my pregnant state allowed.

Reaching the priory church, I took refuge in that consecrated silence that was such a balm to my fractured nerves. At the far end of the nave was the screened window looking into Master Alan's cell. He had left his shutters open in preparation for my audience with him.

I'll confess I approached his anchorage with trepidation, for I'd never quite been able to get over my aversion of the life Master Alan had chosen for himself — to undergo the funeral rites while still alive and then be walled into a single room where he would remain for the rest of his days. He had surrendered his liberty in the ultimate act of devotion in order to be buried with Christ and become dead to the world. Who but the holiest of madmen could make such a sacrifice?

When I seated myself upon the stool outside his window, I could not get over my revulsion at thinking that this man lived here like a prisoner or a caged animal. Yet when I peered through the screen, I saw not a prison but a sanctuary. Freshly cut rosemary and evergreen boughs adorned his private altar, their fragrance mingling with that of frankincense. His desk was stacked high with his treasured books. His cell was cleaner and more ordered than my kitchen, for he had servants to bring him food, books, candles, fresh linen, and water for washing through his service hatch and they also came to empty and scour his chamber pot. I glimpsed the curtained alcove where he slept and from whence he now emerged, running a hand through his wispy gray hair.

"Mistress Margery, welcome." The anchorite beamed with good cheer.

Despite his constrained existence, he seemed truly happy and at peace with himself more than any man or woman I'd ever met. Merely being in his presence filled me with a sense of lightness and joy, and lifted the many burdens oppressing my soul. Unlike Father Sprynge-gold, Master Alan did not dwell on demons or damnation but on the wonders and marvels of mystical union with the divine.

"What shall I read to you today?" he asked, sounding as eager as I to delve into the mysteries held in the illuminated pages of his books.

"*Incendium Amoris*," I said, not hesitating one second. The fire of divine love.

The thought of the book kindled a flame inside me. This mystical treatise was written by Richard Rolle—not a priest or monk but a layman hermit. Though Master Rolle had studied at Oxford, he wrote not about canonical literature but his own experience of divine union.

Master Alan sat in his chair and read the Latin aloud, then translated it sentence by sentence into English. I kept interrupting him with my endless questions. For once I could forget I was a wife of Lynn. Here I was a questing soul with a hungry mind.

"Master Alan, how may one *know* if a mystical experience is genuine and from God, and not from the False One, or else the figment of a deluded imagination?" I thought of my own vision of Christ. Not a single person had believed it was real. I didn't dare divulge my experience to Master Alan for fear that he, too, would dismiss me as a fanciful housewife.

"Rolle writes that the true presence of God may be felt in the body, not just in the mind." Master Alan seemed as comfortable discussing holy visions as other folk were conversing about the weather or the price of wool. "Three properties accompany such divine visitations.

They are *fervor*, physical warmth; *dulcor*, a sense of indescribable sweetness; and *canor*, the sound of heavenly music coming from within rather than without."

I turned my face away so Master Alan wouldn't see my tears of recognition and longing, for I had experienced all those things when Christ had appeared at the foot of my bed almost ten years ago. Even the memory was enough to leave me fevered, my skin tingling in sweetness, my soul lulled by divine harmonies. What would it be like to truly *live* as a mystic? Richard Rolle was a layman who had taken no vows. Perhaps even in my married state, I might be a mystic, too.

"*Fervor, dulcor*, and *canor* lead us to *raptus*," Master Alan said. "The rapture of divine union." His eyes shone as if he recalled his own encounters with ineffable bliss.

Raptus! The very word left me blindsided by the heat of my desire for my Beloved, which eclipsed my feelings for John, who had impoverished me and used me as a broodmare. How my love for God jostled with my unchristian contempt for my husband, those two sides of me constantly at war.

"If only I could read Latin," I said.

The anchorite smiled as though he were my dearest friend. "I would miss you sorely if I could no longer read for you, Mistress Margery. There's many a burgher who pays me to read pious texts, but you are the only one who asks such questions as to make me think and study them with a deeper understanding."

Master Alan was the first person to ever praise me for asking so many questions instead of scolding me for it or expecting me to meekly accept whatever I was told. His praise sent my spirits soaring high above the realm of soaking clouts and the pile of mending awaiting me at home.

"There are books in English, are there not?" I leaned forward, my hands clasped in my lap. "You said we might read from the *Revelations* of Bridget of Sweden."

Bridget, I knew, had been a wife and mother of eight children, and yet she had convinced her husband to make a vow of celibacy, the thought of which sent my heart spinning. After her husband's death, she became a nun and traveled to Rome where she started her own religious order. How I envied her freedom.

Master Alan nodded sagely. "Even so, Mistress Margery, it's better that I read for you with all this talk of Lollardy going round."

We bowed our heads in somber remembrance of William Sawtry. If our former vicar could be so accused for reading holy texts in English, what might they do to a housewife who decided to read for herself? Or think for herself? Or ask too many questions? Somberly, I reminded myself of poor Hawisia Moone.

My time with Master Alan came to an end all too soon—he had his devotions and private writing to attend to. With a reluctant heart, I bade him farewell and wound my way back through the blustery streets.

I loved my children, truly I did, yet my feet dragged with each step. My roiling resentment of John made me clench my jaw and fists. Instead of heading straight home as a good wife should, I returned to my girlhood home in Briggate. Surely it was a virtuous thing to visit my parents—even John couldn't begrudge me that.

Father was out, but Mother received me, her embrace enveloping me with the scent of the lavender and orange peel sachet she wore around her neck to ward off winter contagion.

"Margery, how good of you to stop in. Pity you didn't bring the children."

How uncanny it was to look at those tapestries, those oak-paneled walls, to tread upon painted Italian tiles, and to sit in a carved chair before the roaring fire while sipping mulled wine from a silver-rimmed cup. To think this had once been *my* home, that I had taken these luxuries for granted.

"Margery, you look so melancholy," Mother said, plying me with her clove-spiced honey cake. "What troubles you? Have you and John quarreled again?"

I read in her eyes how disappointed she was for me and what my life had become. Her pity moved me to finally spill out my pain that I had tried to hide from her for so long.

"By the blood of Christ, I wish I'd taken the veil instead of marrying John Kempe!"

"Margery, don't make such dreadful oaths." Mother took the cup from my hand and hugged me. "Yes, it's true he's not what your father and I hoped he would be. He hasn't done his duty to provide for you as he should. But, my dear, he's not a bad man. He doesn't beat you or the children."

I wept bitterly into my hands. If Mother even had an inkling of how I had come to hate him.

"Is there truly *nothing* left of your dowry?" she asked. "It should have been enough for you and John to live in comfort for the rest of your lives."

My rage bubbled up like a cauldron about to boil over. "He bought a herring ship and it sank because he was too careless to get it pitched. I told him to, but he called me a nag. Even as a brewer, he's the worst in Lynn. The beer I brew in my kitchen tastes better than his. Sometimes he takes my brew and sells it off as his own."

Even as Mother sat back in her chair as though she didn't know what to say, a new idea took shape in my mind. Many a married woman earned for herself from her housewifery. What was to stop me from doing the same?

"I should set myself up as a brewer," I said, my voice growing in conviction. "And keep the profits for myself and the children."

Like it or not, a woman's worth was judged by the quality of her clothing. My daughters would have no prospects whatsoever if they looked like ragged urchins.

"Go into competition against your husband?" Mother asked me, but I could see from the spark in her eyes that she thought my idea a clever one.

"If something doesn't change soon, I might go mad and smother John in his sleep," I said, trying to sound lighthearted. "Better a shrew than a murderess."

Mother smiled in spite of herself. "You were always so strong-willed, my dear."

The time had come to put my will to work.

After giving birth to my eleventh child, whom I named Alan after the holy anchorite, I transformed myself from a hand-wringing house-wife into an industrious alewife. Father lent me the money to set up my own brewery and what could John say or do to gainsay the Lord

Mayor? My beer, strong and smooth, was lauded as the best in Lynn. Father saw to it that the Guild of the Holy Trinity bought barrels of it for their feasts. Soon all the innkeepers were placing their orders. Merchants bought my brew for their seamen, for it kept well, being seasoned with the best hops. The following Christmas, I sent a hogshead to my brother in faraway Danzig.

Before the first year was out, I could array myself and my daughters in dagged sleeves and brocades. The day we first walked to church in our new finery, John was purple with indignation. "Why must you make such a spectacle of yourself? Everyone will laugh at me now."

He seemed particularly put out that my towering headdress made me appear taller than he was, as if I were the true head of the family.

Ignoring him, I turned to pinch Isabella's pale cheeks. "Hold your head high, my dear," I told her.

For a time, I was the foremost brewer in Lynn. My purse heavy with gold, I endowed the Carmelite priory and bought candles for Master Alan. I could spend as I pleased without leave from John. Both my parents fully approved of my industry and prudence. In my female lot, I was still resigned to pregnancy — after Alan came my twelfth child, Peter. But at least I could shroud my bulging belly in the finest silk while proving to all Lynn that I was far better at commerce than my husband.

Some folk muttered that I was a cold-hearted cow, that John should beat me to put me in my place. To his credit, he did no such thing. I did, alas, receive my comeuppance, but not from my husband. One year the crops failed. Hops froze on the vine. The price of grain rose so high that even small beer became an extravagance few could afford. Yet while my brewery failed, John's business limped along, for the burghers of Lynn had come to feel sorry for him, saddled as he was with such a disagreeable wife. Nonetheless, he remained deep in debt.

Undeterred, I borrowed money from my parents to start my second venture, a horse mill to grind grain. Surely this business was bound to succeed, or so I told myself. For a time I prospered, but then the impossible happened.

On the eve of Corpus Christi, the horses would only go backward, as though they were bewitched. I stood on and watched in horror as the two hitherto healthy gray mares refused to step forward no matter how brutally Hugh, the driver, whipped and beat them. A sweltering day, it was. The mares shimmered in sweat. Flies danced around them like a host of demons.

"Stop your whipping!" I shouted to Hugh. "It's too hot for them to work."

But the man whom I had trusted and paid good wages to only narrowed his eyes at me. "A stubborn nag needs to be beaten until she learns who her master is."

His hatred poured over me like pitch. He was deliberately beating my horses to death before my eyes to punish me for the way I'd treated John. My mouth filled with vomit as I dashed forward, but it was too late. An awfulness spread through my chest to see the poor creatures collapse to their knees while the flies feasted upon their bloody welts. The horses' eyes were so listless and dull, I knew they would never rise again.

Hating Hugh, hating myself, hating everything in this world, I collapsed beside the horses and wailed. I was pregnant with my thirteenth child. Like those poor, mistreated beasts, I foundered. I couldn't go on.

6

Y LIFE LAY IN tatters, my family ripping apart at the seams. That November was marked by sickness and fever, which took Catherine and Simon in the same week despite all the physick I gave them. If that wasn't enough, Father languished in bed, his lungs and heart grown weak, his once stalwart body scrawny and feeble. His mind was as foggy as the November sea. There were days he didn't recognize me. He growled and barked, as though I were a stranger.

But I rejoiced to see beautiful Isabella marry the man she adored, a fine young merchant devoted to her happiness. And I was grateful for the companionship of my eldest son, Jack. Of all my children, he was most like me. How he chafed against the shackles of Lynn, which he found so pitifully narrow. Often we put our heads together and spoke of our dreams of sailing far away.

John rebuked me for filling the lad's head with idle fancies. One thing was clear—Jack was my son through and through. He truly seemed to understand my pain and took my side in every dispute between me and my husband. If he heard me pleading in the night, begging John to leave me alone, he'd slam the walls to shame his father. As beautiful as a lion, he was a full head taller than John. Jack professed nothing but contempt for his father and refused to have anything to do with John's brewery, determined to make his own way in the world. Father and son's rows grew so fraught that I feared they might come to blows.

In the end, I intervened by scraping together the funds to send my son away to far Danzig where he could join my brother and work in his hostelry. Since Jack and his father were no longer on speaking terms, it was I who walked my son to his ship.

"Come away with me, Mother," Jack said, his light-brown hair waving in the brisk salt wind that rippled the sails and filled my heart with the yearning for escape. "Grandmother and Isabella will look after the little ones. Once we're in Danzig, you can send for them to join us. Who will protect you once I'm gone?"

His loyalty was such that I was nearly tempted to believe in the impossible, that all my travails would dissolve as soon as I set foot on that gangplank. But I smiled at him through my tears and rested one hand on my pregnant belly.

"I'm in no condition to travel," I said. "I'll not be a millstone around your neck. This is *your* journey, love. Your adventure. Go with my blessing."

When he embraced me, I could feel his racing pulse, like that of a horse that would finally be allowed to gallop headlong toward the far horizon. The greatest gift I could give any of my children was freedom. If one of us could escape, let it be Jack, whose young life was so full of promise, a blank sheet of parchment on which anything might still be written. I gazed at his ship until it disappeared around the bend in the Great Ouse.

With a heavy heart, I went to my childbed that January. When, after a day and night of grueling labor, the midwife finally pulled the infant out of me, it was tiny, misshapen, and stillborn. The sight of that lifeless blue girl-child laid my soul to waste. My keening spooked the crows that nested in our thatch. They took to flight in a thunder of caws. Would there be no end to this litany of death? My only solace was to imagine Jack's new life in Danzig and to witness how blissful Isabella was with her husband.

As soon as I hauled myself out of bed to resume my household duties, John insisted on having his way with me. The man would simply not suffer my womb to remain empty. I was to be his cow, forever in calf.

Never mind that out of the thirteen children I bore him, six were already dead — two of them without even being christened. Never mind that he knew full well I took no pleasure from the act. No matter how it broke me, John would make me bear him baby after baby until I perished or grew old and barren — whichever came first.

Once he had at least made a pretense of acting as though his unwanted attentions could rekindle my love for him. But when that failed, he had turned bitter and ravished me with unmasked violence, as if to punish me for being such a bad wife.

Sore and bruised, I lay there. Corpse rigid. Polluted. Many a story of the lives of martyrs I'd learned by heart. Their bodies had been broken on wheels, or else burned to ash, or dismembered, or run through with swords, spears, or flaming arrows. But the story that remained untold was the living martyrdom a downtrodden wife must endure. *Even death*, I thought, *would be kinder*.

Having reached my lowest ebb, I closed my eyes and prayed for all-encompassing blackness. For eternal silence. Instead, there sounded the music I hadn't heard in more than eighteen years. While John snored on, the notes of trumpet, harp, psaltery, rebec, viol, and flute rose in crescendo after crescendo, washing away my pain and longing for death. In a fiery burst of radiance, he appeared, filling my entire vision. How could I have forgotten how beautiful he was?

My skin tingled and glowed as the heat and sweetness swept through me. The brittleness armoring my heart melted as the flames surged within. *Incendium amoris.* I trembled, on fire with bliss. *Fervor, dulcor, canor, raptus.* A golden cloud enveloped me.

His voice spoke inside me, sweeter than the music of heaven. *All devotion comes from within. I live and burn in your heart as an eternal, inextinguishable flame. This is where you'll always find me. This is the power and solace no one will ever be able to take from you.*

A power, *his* power, inside *me?* A speechless joy bubbled up. I felt as though I were floating miles above the earth.

"How I wish I'd taken the veil," I told him fiercely. "How I wish I was *your* bride. A virgin for you."

John muttered in his sleep but slumbered on, his back to me.

My Beloved smiled as though I were the most treasured of all his creation. *Margery, you are a virgin in your soul. I wish you to wear clothes that are white and no other color. I shall give you a golden ring as proof of our troth.*

"A virgin in my soul but still beholden to John Kempe," I blurted, my eyes welling as a sense of futility gripped me. I feared the degradation would begin all over again as soon as this vision faded.

What my Beloved said next shook me to my bones. *The next time John forces you against your will, I shall slay him.*

Had he truly said such a thing or had I, in my wickedness, fabricated it all?

The following morning, I rose before dawn. Leaving John in bed, I slipped on my cloak and darted through the dark and empty streets. In the aftermath of my vision, I felt faint. The edges of the world seemed to blur. The very earth beneath my feet seemed to shift and resettle as I hurried to my parents' house in Briggate. I still possessed a key. The servants were yet asleep, but I found my way through the dim corridors and up the shadowy stairs. Candlelight gleamed from beneath the door of Father's room.

With a gentle knock, I entered to find Mother praying at his bedside. I knelt beside her while regarding his waxy face. His closed eyes were sunk deep in their sockets, and his chest rose and fell with his shallow breath. Though he had survived this winter, I suspected he could not endure another one. My stomach heaved. I found the privy pot just in time to catch my vomit.

"Are you pregnant again?" Mother asked. "So soon?"

For one awful moment I feared she would congratulate me and tell me how blessed I was. Instead, she seemed at a loss for words.

"My fourteenth child," I said, unable to hold back my tears. "I swear, Mother, this one must be the last. A fifteenth child would kill me—if this one doesn't."

My years of childbearing had taken their toll, robbing me of teeth and hair. My spine swayed and buckled. I couldn't stand or sit for any length of time without my back seizing up in pain. My private parts had dried out and burned in agony whenever John tried to meddle with me.

Not wanting to disturb Father, I quietly left his room and crept to his study where I hunted for the scrolled parchment I had not touched in many years. The pilgrims' map of Europe and the Holy Land. My fingers traced the routes crisscrossing valleys and plains, rivers and mountains. My son had embarked across the seas to seek his fortune. Did I, a woman in my middle years, dare to do the same?

When Mother entered the room and found me poring over the map, I faced her squarely and said the unspeakable. "If John can't be trusted to control himself, I must go away. After this child is delivered."

Self-reproach washed through me — how could I abandon a newborn baby? I waited for Mother to tell me how selfish I was for even thinking such a thing.

"Wisht, Margery, hush," she said. "We each have our cross to bear."

If I had a cross to bear, I swore it wasn't to be John's lust. My visions had proved that much. A new determination seized me, a force that even John could not ignore. I stood taller and took broader strides, impelled by the light surging from within. John and I had been married nearly twenty years, during which time he'd ample cause to doubt my sanity or roll his eyes at what he pronounced as my ravings. But for the first time I grew bold enough to abandon our marriage bed and sleep in the old truckle bed in Anna's room. I stopped eating meat. The only flesh to touch my lips was the Body of Christ, for I had begged Father Spryngegold's permission to receive the Eucharist every Sunday — a rare privilege, as most lay folk took communion only once a year, on Easter. Father Spryngegold had been hesitant to grant me this honor, but Master Alan had persuaded him.

My visions were unstoppable. I meditated not on my knees but while lying down, welcoming my Beloved as a bride welcomes her bridegroom. Suddenly this temple of flesh was my own again, cleansed and purified, as though I had bathed in a holy spring. I took him to myself as my wedded husband, my dearest darling. I took him in my soul's arms and kissed his sweet mouth, his head, his nail-pierced feet. And he whispered in my hair, *I ask no more of you but that your heart loves me who loves you.*

Marvels and wonders accompanied me throughout my waking

hours while I was immersed in the homeliest of tasks, such as scouring the privy or haggling over the price of eggs at the Saturday Market. With my physical eyes, I beheld many white things flying around me on all sides, as thick as motes in the sunlight. Delicate, they were, and their presence comforted me. The brighter the sun shone, the better I could see them. Yet I also saw them in darkness, which made me fear that they might be something infernal. But my Beloved spoke to me in my own mind, *Wherever God is, there are many angels. God is with you and you are in God. Angels watch over you day and night so that no devil can have power over you.*

That was not all. I heard birdsong from within my heart. My Beloved assured me that this signaled the presence of the Holy Ghost.

I confess it was enough to confound me. As much as I loved God, I feared I was losing my mind. There was so much I couldn't tell even Master Alan—how could that sainted anchorite comprehend my urgency to break free of my husband or my fear that I might not live beyond the birth of this fourteenth child?

For all my ecstasies of the spirit, my worldly woes remained. One morning John cornered me in the kitchen. I had thought that the stink of the stockfish I was preparing for our Lenten meal would be enough to repel him. Alas, it appeared that sterner stuff was called for.

"I hereby make an oath of chastity," I said before John could utter a single word. "I shall go to the bishop and ask his leave to wear white clothes."

For a moment John seemed to lose the power of speech. His mouth hung open like a haddock's.

"*You* must make an oath of chastity, too," I said. "Otherwise I shall leave you."

"And where, pray, shall you go?" He sounded as though he were torn between shock and cynicism.

"To Rome and Jerusalem," I said. My voice didn't even shake. "If God calls me to walk the pilgrim's path, who are you to stop me?"

"And how shall you pay your way? You'll not get a penny from me."

I laughed in his face. "I never did get a penny from you, John. It was always the other way around, was it not?" As hard as I strove to be holy, I could never banish my stinging tongue.

"You can't go anywhere without my permission," John said, an edge of desperation creeping into his voice. "You're a wife of Lynn, not a nun. If you're truly called by God, why then I'll wait to see a sign." At that, he stalked out of the kitchen, his hands shaking as though it took every ounce of his self-control not to throttle me.

Struggling to regain my composure, I busied myself with the stockfish. Using iron tongs, I pulled the now-softened preserved cod out of the simmering cauldron, then placed it in a dish to skin and debone. The silvery skin stuck to my hand like a glove.

His voice whispered from within, *Dear one, you cleave to me as tightly as the skin of stockfish sticks to your hand. You'll not forsake me for any shame a man might wreak on you.*

Closing my eyes, I swayed as though dancing in his radiant arms until clattering footsteps wrenched me from my reverie. I opened my eyes to see Anna, her young face pale but forthright.

"Mother, I think you *should* go away."

Dumbfounded, I stared at her. Had she been eavesdropping?

The girl, ever practical, took over the task of deboning the stockfish. "You're already away, don't you see? You've been somewhere else in your heart for years. I'm not calling you wicked. But it would be easier for me and the boys if you truly were elsewhere and we didn't have to listen to your quarrels and tears."

The fish skin still clinging to my hand, I moved to embrace my daughter, but she held me at arm's length while looking earnestly into my eyes.

"I want to leave, too," she said.

So it was not just Jack who dreamt of escape. My yearning for the great world outside Lynn had also possessed Anna.

"Then we shall go together on pilgrimage," I said in a warm rush. I imagined us riding into Jerusalem. Walking the Via Dolorosa side by side.

She shook her head. "I've no desire to tramp through foreign parts, but neither do I want to be like you." Her voice broke at this admission.

She turned red and looked away. I bit my lip to consider what she had overheard in the nights before I had moved to her room. No wonder she wanted to be gone from this sad house.

"I don't want to marry and have a mountain of babies," she said. "I want to join the Benedictine Sisters at Carrow. I'm old enough to be a postulant."

"My dear girl," I said with such fervor that she let me hug her. Oh, to know one's mind so young! To think that young Anna had the foresight to choose the life I wished too late to have chosen for myself.

On the Friday before Whitsunday, I went to Mass at Saint Margaret's. Neither John nor my boys were in attendance. As for Anna, Mother and I had already delivered her to Carrow Priory where she would begin her new life. I offered my prayers for my daughter and her vocation. Let her prioress be kind. Let her find friends there as well as the eternal companionship of Christ, our Beloved. I tried not to envy my daughter, but there was no ignoring how difficult it was to live with my visions in the full stream of worldly life. As a cloistered nun, I might have given myself wholly to my raptures and tears. Yet here I stood, neither a loving wife nor a model mother nor a Holy Sister.

My secret revelations weighed heavy in my heart, but I dared not speak of them. Who would believe me? My own mother had only shaken her head and blinked when I'd told her of how Our Lord had appeared at my bedside all those years ago when Jack was just a baby. If I breathed a word of my visions to anyone, even Master Alan, I feared that everyone in Lynn would mutter that I'd gone mad again.

I hid my face in my book of hours, and at that precise moment, part of the church ceiling came crashing down on me. On me and no other person.

A great cry arose from the congregation. I heard their voices, young and old, male and female, rising in a chorus of judgment upon my soul.

"It's a sure sign of God's wrath."

"The Lord smote her for her willful pride!"

"That will teach her. Maybe now she'll mend her ways."

"Surely she's dead!"

"Good riddance, the horrible squawking woman! Her poor husband will finally have some peace."

"She's pregnant, you fiends! At least have pity on her unborn child."

They swarmed around my prone body and managed to heave the masonry and broken beam off of me. Much to their disappointment, I was still very much of this world.

"All the saints be praised," I said, blinking up at them blithely. "I'm completely unscathed!"

Not a bruise or scratch marked my body.

"It's a miracle," a young girl said as she helped me to my feet.

A boy scooped my book of hours off the floor and handed it to me with a little bow.

Shouting sounded from the window of Master Alan's anchorage cell. He called for the masonry and timber to be weighed to ascertain the miraculous nature of the event. As clerics and townsfolk alike scurried to find a set of scales, one of the market women winked at me.

"All that heavy brocade," she murmured approvingly. "Like armor, it is. Spears would bounce off of it."

Yet even so, the weight of the stone and beam together was declared heavy enough to strike a person dead. Master Alan pronounced that my survival was indeed a miracle.

The news traveled faster than a tempest. Truly this was the most thrilling thing to transpire in Lynn since the dancing bear had run amok at last year's Saint Nicholas Fair. Mother rushed to the church and then John and the boys. Peter, my youngest, bolted to me and buried his face in my skirts while I stroked his silky fair hair.

Then I faced my husband and raised my voice so the entire congregation could hear my proclamation. "John Kempe, you said you were waiting for a sign from God to see if I was truly called to be a pilgrim. Well, here it is. I make my vow before all these witnesses that I shall fare forth to Rome and Jerusalem."

John's face went white, then red, but he could not speak a word with all those people staring. Peter gazed up with bewildered eyes. My other sons looked at their father, then at the ground. My mother regarded me tearfully as though I had already taken leave of them all.

For all my grand words, I was going nowhere. Heavy with child and weakened by fever, I took to my bed—Anna's old bed. Soon I was too weak to rise.

My pilgrimage will begin and end here. I would die and only fare forth to Jerusalem in the afterlife. I told myself I wasn't afraid, that any escape was better than none. I took refuge deep inside the cloister of my heart. Through the blur of agony, I saw myself standing at Saint Anne's bedside while she painlessly gave birth to the Virgin Mary. It was I, her nimble maidservant, who ran to find pure white swaddling for the glowing infant. Sometimes Jesus spoke to me. Sometimes Mary, or Saint Peter, or Saint Catherine.

My fever took me back in time. I was yet a virgin and free to choose whether to marry Christ or John Kempe. As I struggled to make my choice, Mother whispered to me of an anchoress named Julian who had written a book, just like Bridget of Sweden had, except right here in Norfolk. Then a woman's face appeared. Her wrinkles spoke of advanced age, yet her eyes, shining like heaven, reminded me of a young girl's. She was no one I recognized. At first I thought she must be Saint Elizabeth who bore John the Baptist when she was already old. This lady appeared to know me. Her eyes welled with tears of compassion, as though she felt my searing birth pangs as her own. *Margery Kempe,* she said, her voice ringing like the bells of Rome on Easter morning. *I saw you coming long before you arrived. Child of my visions.* Her voice was drowned out by a liquid roar. A river of blood.

7

NEARLY DIED BEARING MY fourteenth child, a girl I named Juliana after the anchoress I had never met. I was too weak to nurse her, too ill to believe I could ever rise from my childbed.

"Even if she survives," I heard Mother tell John, "there must be no more babies. Another would kill her." Her voice shook in rage.

I blinked weakly as John sat on the edge of the bed and took my hand so gingerly, as though he feared he might break it.

"If I make an oath of celibacy, will you stay with me, Margery?" He wept as though he'd lost me forever.

I looked up and truly saw him for the first time, as if a veil had been lifted from my eyes. Here was a man nearing the age of sixty. His hair had grown thin, his pate shone like a monk's, and his beard was almost white. His eyes were shadowed, haunted by his loneliness and terror that I would abandon him either by death or by pilgrimage. Leave him with four boys and a baby girl. All he had ever wanted was my love and I had refused it for so long, allowing fear and hate to clout up my heart. Yet, in his ignorance and manly pride, he had done everything to murder my love.

"Make your oath." In my weakness, I struggled to form each word. "In front of the priest."

Father Spryngegold had come to give me the last rites.

As John made his oath, my Beloved's voice sounded from within me, so loud and insistent that I was astonished no one else could hear it. *If you bring forth what is within you, what you bring forth will save you.*

If you do not bring forth what is within you, what you do not bring forth will destroy you.

I made my silent vow then and there. *I will bear no more children. Instead, I shall ride to Norwich and seek out Dame Julian.*

It was not just a child's new life I had birthed but my own.

Some weeks later, still weak from my childbed, I hobbled up Briggate to my childhood home. I'd learned that Father was departing this world. The door opened to Mother's blanched, tearstained face.

"By all the saints," she said. "I fear he'll go within the hour."

I climbed the stairs as quickly as I could into that chamber cloudy with frankincense. Father Spryngegold had just served Father his last Holy Communion. My eyes filled to regard that man shrunken into the linens, his skin like old parchment stretched over jutting cheekbones. Yet his eyes still moved, as sharp as a falcon's.

"Compass Rose," he rasped, calling me by the girlhood nickname I had nearly forgotten.

I held him tenderly, fearing he might break if I hugged him too hard. But when he spoke, it was with all the might and authority to be expected of the man who had been five times Lord Mayor of Lynn.

"Margery, hark." His eyes burned like flame. "You wish to walk the pilgrim's path."

I nodded, stroking his hand, thinking to coax some warmth and lifeblood back into his flesh.

"I've set aside money in my will. I bid you to go to Rome and Jerusalem to pray for my immortal soul."

My heart welled up, a fountain of gratitude, my dearest dream coming true at last. Yes, I would walk the Via Dolorosa, reliving the Stations of the Cross, until the path took me to the Church of the Holy Sepulcher, the holiest shrine in all Christendom.

The effort of his short speech seemed to drain Father's last strength. He gasped for air, then I saw the fear in his eyes, the terror of what lay in store for him after he quit this earthly existence where he had wielded such power. Soon he would be just a soul among souls, stripped of all rank and possessions, and waiting to face the ultimate judgment and all the horrors Father Spryngegold chastised us with in his sermons.

"I give you my word, Father," I said, kissing his brow. "I shall walk the pilgrim's path for you. But don't be afraid. As sure as God is great, he is loving." The words welled up as though my Beloved were speaking in my voice. "One day, I promise you, we shall meet again in paradise."

Never until that moment had I seen tears in my father's eyes. He smiled and squeezed my hand. Mother wept softly and embraced him while Isabella, Father Spryngegold, and I chanted the rosary, round after round, until Father was lulled beyond this world, his final breath as gentle as a whisper.

Every burgess in Lynn attended Father's funeral, and every pauper, too, to receive the funeral alms of bread and coins in exchange for praying for his immortal soul. I wept, raw and desolate, for his passing had left me unmoored. Though he could be harsh and stern, Father had been my king, my foundation, my bulwark. My station and rank in this world were all thanks to him, to being the Mayor of Lynn's only daughter. Now that he was gone, what could I call myself?

At last I had the means to truly walk away from John, but he cleaved to my side as though loathe to let me out of his sight. He seemed to fear I would just float away in the air like an autumn leaf. What's more, he began to court me more ardently than he had done twenty years ago when I was a beautiful young virgin. With all my heart and will, I was set on going to Rome and Jerusalem, but he would have me stay and love him.

"I've made an oath of celibacy, all for you," he said over our evening meal of eel pie. "Why should you leave me?"

More than anything, he seemed to fear a lonely old age.

"But I gave Father my word. Would you have me break my oath to a dying man?"

"Let us be pilgrims together," he said cheerfully, as though that solved everything. "Why should you wander the great world on your own? It's dangerous enough for a man, let alone a woman. I would never forgive myself if any harm fell your way."

But I knew that John, with his beer belly and bunions, would never set foot on a pilgrim's ship bound for foreign lands. Instead, he took me to see the Mysteries at York. Mother agreed to look after our children and the new baby in our absence. John wrapped his bunions in soft bandages and walked with me on foot so we could travel in humility and piety. Though my feelings about John were as muddled as ever, I must confess that the thought of visiting York again for the first time since I was a girl of seventeen filled me with joy. As we strode through meadows of new lambs and calves, John took extra care to prove how devoted he could be to my wishes. We took separate rooms at the simple country inns.

The Corpus Christi Mystery Plays brought back all the delight and sense of possibility I had experienced as a girl. I felt carefree, not like a mother of fourteen who had nearly died only months ago. John held my hand as we watched the white-bearded player pretending to conjure Eve from Adam's side. We shared a cup of caudled ale and laughed together as if there had never been strife between us.

Corpus Christi fell late that year, on the twenty-second of June. Thus, it was on Midsummer's Eve, the twenty-third of June, a Friday, that we left York and began our journey homeward. The weather being hot, I carried a bottle of beer, which we drank from in turn, while John carried a wrapped pie tucked inside his tunic. All was as serene as the blue heavens arching above us as we tramped across the green hills. Lulled by the sunlight and good beer, I imagined making peace with my life as it was, staying with John—in chastity, of course. Staying as a mother to my children. Perhaps I didn't need to go to Jerusalem after all. Perhaps the true Jerusalem lay deep inside the sanctuary of my heart, not at the other end of the world. Why, John and I could go to Canterbury instead and offer up our prayers for Father's soul there.

John took a swig from the bottle before passing it back to me. Then he spoke, suddenly quite earnest. "Margery, if a man came riding with a sword and threatened to cut off my head unless I made love to you right here and now, what would you do? Would you expect me to keep my vow even though I'd be slain?"

In my consternation, I dropped the beer bottle, which spilled a foamy puddle at my feet.

"But there is no man with a sword threatening to chop off your head," I pointed out. "Why even raise the matter after all these months?" How could he talk such twaddle? We had finally come into harmony — why was he allowing his infernal lust to divide us again?

His eyes moistened. "Because I want to know your heart's truth."

Sadness weighed on me, but I spoke my mind. "I would still cling to my vow of chastity even if a man did come to chop off your head."

John blinked, then his face hardened. "You are not a good wife."

"And you," I said sharply, "made a vow before Father Spryngegold."

"A vow no reasonable man — even a priest — would expect me to keep!"

Panic ripped through me. I took off running, following the road to Bridlington. John, being thick of girth, struggled to keep up. But soon a stitch in my side sent me tumbling to the grass beneath a wayside cross. I folded my hands in supplication and began to weep and pray. John, huffing and puffing, threw himself down beside me and seized my arms. I stiffened, fearing the worst, and began to wail, but he held up his hands in a gesture of peace.

"Margery," he said, his voice plaintive and resigned. "If I give you permission to travel on your own, will you first pay my debts before you leave Lynn? And will you eat meat with me again after all these years?"

Meat on a *Friday*, when we had just seen the Corpus Christi plays? No meat had passed my lips in almost a year. The very thought of animal flesh curdled my stomach. But my Beloved's voice spoke inside me. *Eat meat with your husband just this once and you shall finally be free.*

I dried my eyes. "Yes, John."

He took the wrapped pork pie from his tunic and shared it with me beneath the wayside cross.

I had finally won my freedom, yet still I feared to wander off into the world as a lone woman without some outward sign of my absolute devotion to God.

You are a virgin in your soul, my Beloved had told me. *I wish you to wear white and no other color. I shall give you a golden ring as proof of our troth.* The white gown and mantle and golden ring would serve as proof of my desire to live in chastity, marking me out as Christ's bride moving freely in the world, not confined by cloister walls.

But sumptuary laws ruled what a woman could or couldn't wear. Only the bishop could give me permission to dress all in white. To complicate matters, the bishop's see in Norfolk was vacant and I was obliged to journey to Lincoln, sixty miles away, with John in tow.

Five days John and I walked, crossing field and fen. Then, as my husband began to complain once more of his aching bunions, I looked up to see the miracle of the great triple spires appearing on the horizon. They glimmered faintly at first but soon took on mass and form the closer we drew. Lincoln Cathedral, the tallest building in all the world. When we reached Lincoln itself, the flat plain gave way to an impossibly steep escarpment. A maze of narrow streets led uphill to the castle and cathedral. By the time we reached the cathedral close, John and I were quite literally breathless. The cathedral, built of golden limestone, gleamed in the afternoon sun as though it were made entirely of light. From its open doors came the sound of a choir singing Mass.

Here my new life begins. I stepped through the great western portal into that vast nave glimmering with countless candles. After kneeling at the shrine of Saint Hugh and offering our prayers of thanksgiving for our safe arrival, John and I called in at the bishop's palace just downhill from the cathedral.

Alas, it was not so simple. Three long weeks the Bishop of Lincoln, Philip Repyngdon, made me wait before he deigned to grant me an audience and only after I kept reminding his secretary that I was the late Mayor of Lynn's daughter. Seemingly more in deference to my deceased father than me, Repyngdon invited John and me to dine with him. John gawped at the many tapestries lining the banquet hall, then his eyes fairly burst out of their sockets to behold the twenty-four different dishes being served. The table was so crowded with cathedral canons and visiting dignitaries, it was all I could do to get the bishop's attention.

"Your Reverence," I said, pitching my voice to be heard over the cacophony of different conversations going on at once. "Most humbly I beg you to witness my vow of chastity in the cathedral before I leave on my pilgrimage to Jerusalem."

Though John and I had made our private vows in front of Father Spryngegold, I wanted all the weight of a public ceremony with the bishop in attendance. This way, if I was questioned or challenged, I would have the bishop's authority behind me.

Repyngdon, a grizzled old man, glanced up from his bowl of hare soup and frowned. "What does your good husband say to that?" he asked in a strong Welsh accent.

"Oh, he agrees." I kicked John under the table, and he looked up, his mouth stuffed with capon, and nodded sheepishly.

The clergy exchanged glances as though my husband were more milksop than man.

Repyngdon remained skeptical. "Such vows and ceremonies are generally reserved for widows, Mistress Kempe. Not a woman with a husband still living."

As a married woman, I ranked below both virgins and widows, and thus it seemed hard for anyone to take my vows seriously when my very station in life seemed to preclude any claims of direct revelations from God. Nonetheless, I persisted.

"Your Reverence, I am going to Jerusalem on my late father's bequest to pray for his immortal soul. He was the Mayor of Lynn, as I'm sure you know."

The bishop sat up a bit straighter when I reminded him, yet again, of whose daughter I was. I knew that once, before he became a bishop, Repyngdon had borrowed money from my father in a time of need.

"I journey alone and would have some outward sign of my virtue. I ask your permission to wear a white gown and mantle and a golden ring as proof that I'm a vowess."

The bishop regarded me with dismay. "White is the color of virgins. Of brides and novice nuns. You, madam, are a mother of fourteen. Do you not fear being called out as a hypocrite?"

My eyes stung.

"May I add that the whole notion of a wife going on pilgrimage is preposterous," he said. "Saint Boniface himself urged bishops to forbid matrons to travel even as far as Rome. A great number of them perish on their travels, or even lose their virtue," he added darkly, as though a woman's lapse in moral purity was even more tragic than her death. "Few are the towns between Antwerp and Milan without a score of English harlots and fallen women—a disgrace to the entire Church!"

John seemed to choke on his capon. "Oh, Margery," he said. "Listen to the Reverend Bishop. Put this fancy behind you once and for all!"

I simmered in rage. So my desire for pilgrimage made me a *whore* in the bishop's eyes? His canons looked me up and down as though I were no better than the prostitutes who haunted the Lynn docks.

"This is why I wish to wear *white*," I pointed out thinly. "To preserve my virtue, Your Reverence. So that no man may mistake me for a wanton."

The bishop now took an entirely different tack. "It's scandalous for a *wife* to wear white. People might suspect you of heresy! Women, being weak," he added sternly, "are more prone to heresy."

"Lollard women have been known to wear white mantles," one of the canons said. "Those misguided followers of Oldcastle."

I sobered to hear him mention Sir John Oldcastle, once the King's bosom friend, who was imprisoned in the Tower of London for heresy. The man had a following across the country, and before his arrest, he had even invited Lollards to preach from pulpits in his wife's estates in Kent.

"I've heard it said that Lollard women don't only presume to preach," another cleric said, raising his voice to be heard from the far end of the table. "They even stand accused of serving the Eucharist, as though they were ordained priests."

A sense of inexplicable horror seemed to settle upon everyone except John who went on noisily chewing his capon and sucking the sweet marrow from the bones.

"But Your Reverence," I said, holding my ground. "Surely you don't believe in every idle murmur of suspected heresy when you yourself once stood accused."

The whites of Repyngdon's eyes shone starkly as I held his gaze.

Every man at that table stopped eating and fell silent, every man staring at the bishop then at me.

"Only because Your Reverence spoke in defense of the late John Wycliffe," I continued. "Because you knew him to be a good and godly man even though some of his followers were Lollards. You were excommunicated, were you not, before your superiors came to their senses and pardoned you, then raised you to your bishop's throne, may God be praised."

If the truth be told, he'd been forced to recant before he was pardoned, but I thought it best not to mention this.

Repyngdon froze like a cornered hare, too flummoxed to blink.

"Your Reverence, my late father came to your aid then. It is in his name and in Our Lord's that I ask your aid now."

In the uneasy silence that followed, the clerics gazed at the bishop, whose eyes were fixed on the wall behind my head. The only sound in that banquet hall was John burping discreetly into his hand.

"Margery Kempe," the bishop said, gathering his wits once more. "I give you my blessings for your holy pilgrimage. I shall even make a donation of twenty-six shillings to help pay for your journey," he added, as though bribing me in order to end our conversation as quickly as possible. "But if you wish for an official ceremony or permission to wear white clothing, I cannot grant them. In all England, only the Archbishop of Canterbury has the authority to entertain such an . . . *unusual* request."

"Canterbury," I echoed.

The bishop was washing his hands of me. He had done nothing short of accusing me of whoredom and possible heresy when his own reputation was far from untainted. He wished to distance himself from me so that no further suspicion would fall upon him.

John turned to me sorrowfully. "Alas, Margery, I shall never make it to Canterbury with these bunions of mine."

I held the bishop's gaze and told him loudly, for all to hear, that I would gratefully accept his donation of twenty-six shillings. I resolved to use Repyngdon's money to buy my white clothing whether the bishop liked it or not.

Back in Lynn, I settled John's debts before bidding farewell to my family. I took bittersweet comfort in the fact that baby Juliana seemed far more settled with Mother and the wet nurse than with me. Our parting kiss seemed to pain me far more than the baby girl. She only smiled and gurgled at me fleetingly before holding out her little arms to Mother.

"I'll look after her," Mother said, kissing my daughter so tenderly, as though this baby were her most treasured consolation in the wake of her widowhood and bereavement.

"Godspeed." Isabella kissed me and pressed her smooth young cheek to mine. When we hugged, her pregnant belly came between us. She was expecting my first grandchild.

"Goodbye, Mother." Twelve-year-old Edwin and eleven-year-old Lucas were by now too old to cry at our parting. Stiff and formal, they seemed embarrassed to kiss me.

Nine-year-old Alan looked sad and brave, as though he were trying his best to be manly like his older brothers. Only seven-year-old Peter cried and clung to me.

"Wisht," John said to our youngest son. "Your mother's been gone before—to York and Lincoln—and she's always come back. This is just another journey, only a longer one. She'll return with presents and stories to tell you."

As I struggled to comfort my crying son, I felt John's gaze on me, as though he were willing his words to come true. Willing me to return from the Holy Land a changed woman, cleansed of my irritating peculiarities. A woman who would quietly and uncomplainingly resume my duties as an obedient wife and a good mother, all rebellion and dissent finally driven out of me by the grace of God.

My heart tore to say goodbye to the little ones, yet deep inside I felt the same restless excitement I'd witnessed in Jack when he had embarked for Danzig. This was my adventure, unfolding at last.

8

N THE FIRST OF September, I left Lynn with outcries of scandal and judgment ringing in my ears. What kind of woman uses God as her excuse to abandon her ten-month-old baby? My stepping out of the town gates without John proved to all Lynn that I had trespassed the bounds of civilized behavior. Before their gawping eyes, I made myself an outcast. Never mind that I had John's and the bishop's permissions, as well as Master Alan's blessing, and that I traveled with a maid for propriety's sake.

The maid was Nell, the nineteen-year-old daughter of my former servant Emma who had quit my employ after my too numerous progeny had nearly driven her mad. But Emma was eager enough for her daughter to enter my service — the girl was down on her luck and I, it seemed, was her last hope. Nell's former master, the nastiest miser in Lynn, had most inconveniently perished and left her without work and without so much as a ha'penny or a crust of bread. Nevertheless, it was with a glum countenance that the girl hauled her scrawny body aboard the wool merchant's wagon bound for Norwich. It seemed to weigh heavy on her heart that she was bound to travel to the ends of the earth with the most eccentric wife of Lynn.

But Nell's reluctance could not dampen my spirits. As I leapt aboard the wool wagon, my heart raced, giddy with a sense of freedom and escape. I was headed for Carrow Priory to say goodbye to Anna, hoping that she at least would understand why I was making this journey. I hoped to see her truly happy and settled in her new home before I set off on my adventure. But my other intention, to seek out Dame Julian the anchoress, blazed inside me. *What would it be like*, I wondered, *to receive spiritual counsel from another woman?* Would she have greater compassion than the likes of Philip Repyngdon? What would she make of my visions and my quest? I worried that perhaps even she would think me a lunatic—or worse. What if she judged me as harshly as the gossips of Lynn? I had not yet dared to buy my white clothes. Repyngdon's words taunted me. *Do you not fear being called out as a hypocrite?*

Three days it took us to reach Norwich. Three days of having my bones shaken apart with each rut in the road as the oxen trundled along.

Dusty and rattled from the road, I rejoiced to arrive at Carrow Priory, just south of Norwich. When the portress let us in, I delighted to see the fountains, grapevines, rose trellises, and fruit trees inside these cloistered walls. How beautiful Anna's new home was! Truly, I could rest my heart that she was in the best possible place.

Despite her vows of poverty, Anna lived in greater luxury here, I reflected, than she had back home, for now she dwelt with daughters of the highest nobility whose dowries had so enriched this venerable house that had been founded by the Normans. My daughter was learning to read and write in Latin. She was well on her way to becoming a high-learned woman. *And I might have chosen this life, too.*

When Anna came to greet me in her white novice's habit, I could not keep myself from exclaiming how well she looked. Her cheeks were plump and rosy, as if all her sharp edges had softened. I threw my arms around her and wept in joy, but my daughter stiffened.

"Welcome, Mother," she said tepidly, then she disentangled herself from my embrace. "Please don't weep so noisily. The Holy Sisters are at prayer."

She threw a nervous look at the prioress who pursed her lips at me as though it demanded all her Christian virtue to be hospitable to a visitor as irksome as I. *What*, I wondered sickly, *had my daughter been telling her about me?*

How it hurt to see Anna recoil from me as if I were an unwelcome reminder of the chaos and misery she had left behind as a daughter of the biggest laughingstock in Lynn.

The prioress said she wanted a word with me in private.

"Anna tells me that you claim to have visions of Our Lord, that he speaks to you." The prioress seemed to regard me with a mixture of skepticism and pity. "I counsel you to speak of such things only to your confessor, Mistress Kempe, for how can you know if such apparitions are truly divine or merely a trick of the devil beguiling you into thinking you're something special."

Her scrutiny raised every hair on my head. Before I could think what to reply, the prioress briskly excused herself and left me there, her judgment hanging over me like a sword. The sense of betrayal foundered me. I had never told Anna—or anyone—about the visions and yet she knew. My own daughter had been telling tales about me to her prioress, exposing the most private part of me to this woman's condemnation. Even as I had escaped the walls of Lynn, so Anna had erected cloister walls around her heart to keep me out.

Though still numb from Anna's lukewarm reception, I set off the next morning in search of Dame Julian. The portress summoned a local boy to show me the way. I followed him while Nell trudged in my wake and muttered about her sore feet.

We entered the walls of Norwich through Ber Street Gate. A prosperous city, Norwich was the fifth biggest in the land, its cathedral even more magnificent than York Minster. Norwich boasted fifty parish churches and four large friaries. Its castle keep shone like a mighty cliff face in the morning sun. The market stalls glittered with silver cups and cloth of gold. Wealthy merchants' houses faced the broad streets and squares while behind them lay warehouses and workshops full of weavers at their looms manufacturing the worsted wool that had made Norwich so rich.

We passed through a cobbled square with a great elm tree and a parish well. Through the open windows of one timber-framed house, I saw many women working together. Some were spinning at their distaffs while others dyed yarn in vats. There was not a man nor any children in sight. Not a single cradle. But what made me stop in my tracks was that one woman stood at a lectern and read aloud for them all. In English, not Latin. The beauty of her words left me spellbound.

> Of all that God has shown me
> I can speak just the smallest word,
> Not more than a honeybee takes on her foot
> From an overspilling jar.

Over the house's front door, I saw the painted image of Saint Martha, almost as though this was a religious order, yet none of the women wore nuns' habits. This house with its wide-open windows was certainly not cloistered.

"Who are these women?" I asked my young guide.

"Beguines," the boy said.

I'd never before heard that word. But I'd no chance to question the boy further, for it was all I could do to keep up with him as he led me deep into a warren of alleys and passageways.

The prioress had informed me that Saint Julian's Church was in a humble district near the River Wensum, where workers and artisans lived. The anchoress was so self-effacing, she had taken the church's name as her own. I found myself wondering what name Julian had been christened with and what her life had been like before she had chosen to be bricked into a single cell as a living sacrifice to God. I only knew that she had taken her vows at Carrow Priory, that she could have stayed on and served as a Benedictine nun there with every physical comfort.

We must have been approaching the river, for my nose prickled at the stink of tanneries. The streets grew ever poorer. Nell shrieked at the sight of a large brown rat gnawing the rotted corpse of a pigeon. I began to fear that the boy had led us into this slum in order to rob us.

Nell gasped and pointed at the women whose yellow hoods marked them out as prostitutes. "Surely no holy woman lives in this district. Take us back to the priory," she tried to order the boy, but he just darted onward and it was either follow him or find ourselves hopelessly lost.

A pale sickly girl in a yellow hood cut in front of us. Her eyes glittered with tears and a fresh bruise bloomed on her cheek. My throat tightened to see that she looked no older than Anna. I thought she had come to beg for alms, but the stick-thin girl bolted up the narrow ginnel, her dirty bare feet flying beneath her threadbare skirts of undyed wool.

The ginnel opened up into a square. I scarcely believed it when I saw the northern wall of a small church built of gray stone. Cobbled onto the church was a cottagelike structure with a single barred window. As the girl rushed forward, two black-sleeved arms appeared between the bars and reached out to her, taking both her hands.

"That's her," the boy said, pointing at the black-robed figure behind the barred window. "Dame Julian."

I froze and squinted to make out the woman in her black Benedictine habit, this far-famed holy anchoress who had no qualms about touching a prostitute. From where I stood, I heard Dame Julian's grandmotherly voice as she comforted the sobbing girl. It was as though this poor creature was as dear to the anchoress as all the saints in heaven.

After much whispered counsel, the anchoress began to speak in a voice that carried, as though she wanted me and my companions to hear.

"Dear sister, don't tremble before God as though he were a wrathful father. For as surely as God is Father, God is also our Mother. Think of the most tender mother's love for her only child. Even greater than this is God's love for you."

Hearing those words, a sense of overpowering love and mercy that could right all wrongs blindsided me. Tears welled up in my eyes. I blinked and saw the anchoress bless the girl and give her a loaf of bread before the girl scurried on her way.

My legs shook beneath me as I approached the barred window and saw a woman of around seventy. The same aversion I'd once felt upon seeing Master Alan caged in his cell reared inside me. Except Dame Julian had it far worse, being walled in like an eternal prisoner in Norwich's most wretched slum. How had she lived to such a venerable age in this unhealthy place with the stench of urine from the tanneries hanging in the air?

When her clear blue eyes lit on mine, her smile was so radiant, it made her look younger than her years. But what robbed me of my breath was how she reached out to me with both hands and embraced me through the bars, as though she had been expecting me.

"Welcome, my sister," Dame Julian said. "At last you've come. I've been waiting for you so long."

I shook my head in confusion. "Do you know me, Reverend Lady?" I stared into her clear blue gaze. "My name is Margery Kempe. My late father—"

She cut me off. "I saw you coming long before you arrived. Child of my visions."

Her words left me thunderstruck. Everything about this woman stunned me. Never before had I stared into the face of such love in human form. If it weren't for her warm hands clasping mine, I would have thought this was a vision. Surely she must be a saint, the greatest soul I would ever encounter on earth.

"But how?" I asked. "How can you know me?"

"Tell me the day and year of your birth. Was it not the eighth of May in the year of Our Lord 1373?"

My tongue went dry. I could only nod.

"The day and year I received my showings," she told me. "My sixteen revelations of our Beloved."

To give us greater privacy, Dame Julian invited me to enter the church and sit beside her other window, the one facing the high altar. Not wanting Nell to eavesdrop, I sent her back to the priory with instructions to come fetch me an hour before sunset.

Here, with a roof over my head and protection from the bitter wind and the thieves who haunted this quarter, I laid my secrets at Dame Julian's feet. My every vision, sin, misgiving, stupidity. All the things I'd never dared tell any confessor. If Dame Julian could call a prostitute her sister, then I trusted she would also show me sympathy, wretched and flawed though I was. Weeping into my hands, I poured out my entire soul to this stranger who seemed to know me better than I knew my own self.

"The world would call me wicked. I've left my husband and children to go on pilgrimage. But the truth is that I long for my freedom as much as I long to see Jerusalem." My voice quaked at this admission. Julian's clear gaze emboldened me to spill out everything I'd been too ashamed to admit even to myself. "I'm a terrible mother. I left behind an infant not even a year old. I never wanted this life of having babies —I must be unnatural. The prioress at Carrow says I can't trust my visions. She thinks I'm deceived by Satan. Then these tears I can't control —does it mean I'm a madwoman, Mother Julian? Do the tears come from Satan, too?"

What if I had been deluding myself all these twenty years?

Dame Julian sat in silence, her eyes lowered. I began to fear my sins were enough to confound even her. She would send me home and that would be the end of my pilgrimage.

"This beautiful word *mother* is so sweet and kind, it cannot be given to anyone but God," she said at last, taking me by storm, for I could not possibly have expected such a response. "Only she who is our true Mother and source of all life may rightfully be called by that name. So, no, Margery, do not call yourself a terrible mother because you cannot match such grace in your human condition. I presume you left your infant and other young children in the proper care?"

"With my own mother," I said, drying my eyes.

"You say you've borne fourteen children." She smiled as though she understood my every travail. "Once I was married and had seven children—only half as many as you. I, too, worried that I had failed as a mother, for sometimes my temper and impatience got the better of me. Then they were taken from me. My grief was enough to drive me mad—I feared their death was God's way of punishing me for not loving them enough." Her face went ashen at the memory. "The plague visited Norwich three times before I turned thirty. The first time it took my father. The second time, my beloved sister. The third time, my dear husband and all our children."

Her pain and loss hung in the air between us, matching my own unhealed grief for my lost babies.

"All I had left was my mother," Julian continued. "In my despair and longing for comfort, I begged God to bring me to the brink of death so I could look beyond that veil into the next world. God answered my prayer. I was at death's threshold when I received the showings. They were so real, Margery. I *saw* Our Lord's passion. I felt his hot blood dripping on my face. And then he opened up his heart and showed me what lay inside. I saw such love—endless love. It was so vivid, it ravished my heart. I lost myself in him."

Her words left me swaying.

"What's more," she said. "In all he revealed to me, I saw neither sin nor blame nor wrath nor even hell. I could only conclude that sin has no substance. It cannot be discerned at all save for the pain it causes—for a time. In this sense, you could even say our failings and mistakes are necessary, for they serve to purify us and make us know ourselves and ask for mercy. Think of this, dear Margery—all our trials and anguish are tastes of Christ's passion. But behind the reality of our deepest suffering lies the mystery of God's love. Know that all is well."

Her words lifted me to such a high place that I could gaze down upon the world as though it were a map. I was lifted higher and higher until I could behold this precious tender world and all the starry heavens nestling like a hazelnut in God's palm.

"After that," she said, "I couldn't go on living a worldly life, so I chose this life as an anchoress. It had to be this way, you understand. I couldn't bear to stay on as a Sister at Carrow and have my prioress and her priest cross-examine me about my visions at every turn. I needed privacy and solitude to make sense of it all. I've devoted the past forty years to contemplating all I've seen. But I never for a moment doubted what our Beloved revealed to me. And neither, dear Margery, should you doubt what he has shown to you."

Dame Julian, the holy and high-learned anchoress, spoke to me as though I were her peer. A mystic, like her. This made me weep all the more—in gratitude and wonder.

"When Our Lord visits us with the gift of tears," she said, taking my hand, "it serves as proof that the Holy Ghost dwells inside us. No evil spirit can grant the gift of tears. Saint Jerome wrote that our tears torment devils more than all the agonies of hell."

She leaned forward as if intent that I commit her every word to memory.

"The seat of God is in your soul. Dear sister, how can you believe in God if you don't believe in yourself? Until you have faith in your calling and all the grace he has revealed to you?"

The room seemed to shift around me as her words nestled in my heart. Even the air I breathed seemed redolent with blessing.

"Set all your trust in God and don't worry about what the world says of you." She cracked a smile. "If some people dislike you, perhaps that means you're doing something right."

I laughed for the first time in days. All my life I had been seeking someone like her. A wise friend. A spiritual authority. A confidante who understood my womanly condition and to whom I could tell everything, holding nothing back. Dame Julian gave me the greatest gift any human being could give—permission to trust myself.

"So my quest to leave my family and go on pilgrimage isn't selfish?" My heartbeat quickened.

She squeezed my hand. "As surely as I needed to enclose myself in a solitary cell to make sense of what I saw, it seems that you need to go out into the great world as a pilgrim to make sense of what our Beloved has shown to you."

I finally worked up the courage to ask what riddled me most. "How did you know my birthday? Or that I would come?"

The anchoress and I had lived our separate lives in towns more than forty miles apart. We had never met before and were not even the most distant of kin.

"Our Beloved revealed your face and your quest," she said. "I would know you anywhere."

As she spoke, a sleek ginger cat emerged from a dark corner and leapt into her lap.

"Such an infernal creature is allowed inside your anchorage?" I asked in alarm. From earliest childhood I'd been taught that cats were creatures of the night, in league with demons.

Dame Julian laughed. "How can any of God's creatures be infernal? Of course, I keep a cat. I live by the river. If it wasn't for dear Rufus, this place would be swarming with rats."

Rufus blinked his green eyes at me as though he were every bit as wise as his mistress.

As I laughed with Julian, a sense of buoyancy seized me, as if the two of us could fly away like swift-darting swallows, utterly unburdened.

"Dame Julian, is it true that you wrote a book?"

"Indeed I have." A shadow fell across her face. But she continued to gaze at me steadily while stroking the cat. "Though many wish I hadn't."

She gave me a look of warning as a priest and his acolytes entered the small church in preparation for the next Mass. Only when the men disappeared into the sacristy did she lean forward and begin to speak in a voice as soft as her cat's purring. "If you so desire, I shall read my book to you in its entirety."

I stayed with Dame Julian for the next seven days, only returning to the priory to sleep. Nell, meanwhile, suffered to sit at the back of the church and fetch ale and fish pies from the market for us. But Julian's words were my true sustenance. They made the outer world drop away.

When there was no Mass being sung nor none milling about the church who might overhear us, Julian read to me her entire long text describing her sixteen visions. She had first begun writing her book the same year I had nearly died bearing my first child, gone mad, and received my first vision. Julian's *Revelations of Divine Love* filled me with an inescapable sense of divine presence. Of hope and ineffable love and longing. Her words and phrases sang inside my heart as though they had always been there but I'd been too wrapped up in my own petty miseries to hear them until this moment.

Contemplate the Beloved with all your heart. It is by our longing for our Beloved that we are liberated. Know the truth—there is absolutely nothing separating the Divine Soul from the human soul. Know that you are never alone. How could we ever be separated from our Divine Mother? We are all holy creatures of endless life. There is really no such thing as mortal sin. We suffer from the consequences of grave error and then our Mother redeems us. Though we cannot know the ultimate reality with our limited five senses, in the next life we will see our Beloved face-to-face and all that has perplexed us on earth will suddenly become clear. All is well and all shall be well. All manner of things shall be well.

"Why should you have to hide a book of such beauty?" I asked her. "There's nothing unorthodox here, surely."

"Nothing at all," Julian said firmly. "My visions reveal nothing less or more than what my faith taught me. Three centuries ago, the Cistercian Brothers were already writing about Christ the Mother. But these are dangerous times. The bishops seem to think there's a Lollard lurking under every stone." Her voice turned grave. "Have you heard that John Oldcastle escaped the Tower of London?"

Stunned, I shook my head.

"Rumor has it he's conspiring with the Lollards to kidnap the King. He intends to establish a Lollard commonwealth."

Her words left me reeling. I tried to imagine this kingdom without a king. *Would we all be equal then?* I wondered. How seductive a cause this was, especially for the downtrodden. Little wonder that the authorities wanted to crush Lollardy at all costs.

"Many of Oldcastle's followers are women," I said uneasily. "One of the Bishop of Lincoln's men told me that venturing out into the world without my husband was enough to make me a suspect."

Julian nodded soberly. "The bishops are suspicious of any woman who thinks for herself. But more than anything, they fear a woman who writes."

Her words raised my skin. I recalled Master Alan's admonition that women who read holy texts in English risked being suspected of Lollardy. Dame Julian's book was written in our homely Norfolk tongue, so plainly expressed that any housewife or laborer could understand its message.

"Have you heard of Marguerite Porete?" she asked me. "The beguine?"

"What's a beguine?" I asked, recalling the women spinning and dyeing in their house on the square while their Sister read to them those words of unearthly beauty. "I passed a house of beguines on my way here, but I'd never before heard of such a thing."

"They are godly women who choose to live outside marriage and traditional life," Julian said. "Some are virgins, others widows. They welcome women of all ranks. They take no religious vows and may leave and marry if they choose. They may own property. They work together to support themselves and elect a grand mistress to lead their community, but they have no mother house, no common rule like the Rule of Saint Benedict that governs the nuns at Carrow. No superior of the order. Each community runs according to its own rules."

I contemplated this. What if I, as a young woman, had known that there was a middle way between marriage and becoming a cloistered nun, how might my life have unfolded?

"Marguerite Porete," Julian said, continuing her story, "was a beguine in France one hundred years ago. She had many visions of her soul merging with God. That in itself risked censure, but her fate was sealed when she wrote a book and refused to recant it even when they accused her of heresy. I once chanced on a forbidden copy a visiting pilgrim let me read before he took it away again for my own protection lest I be accused." Dame Julian sighed and rubbed her eyes.

"Her book was called *The Mirror of Simple Souls*. It's not so very different from my book. She wrote how in deep mystical union, we cease to exist. We become a piece of God—at least during that hallowed state of contemplation before our worldly duties claim us once more. There was not a single unorthodox word to be found in those pages. Yet she was considered dangerous. How dare a mere woman look to the authority of God within her heart rather than in those flawed men who would be her superiors?"

My palms began to sweat to even imagine Mother Julian under such interrogation.

"What happened to her?" I asked.

"She was burned at the stake in Paris." For the first time in our conversation, Julian looked truly old and weary, her eyes hooded. "Then many of the beguinages in France were forcibly dissolved."

"Do you fear they will condemn you?" I whispered. I wanted to reach through the bars and take her in my arms. Keep her safe.

Julian smiled ruefully. "Don't trouble yourself, sweet Margery, for the safety of my person. They tolerate me because I'm old and frail, but mostly because I'm enclosed. They think they can contain me in this cell and that my writings and revelations will die with me."

I shook my head to think of all that radiance extinguished from this world, as if it had never existed. After she departed this life, her message would disappear like a puff of smoke into a vast sky, her life and labors rendered meaningless.

"The friars and priests only preach of purgatory and hell," she said. "How should they be expected to suffer my little book that tells people to place their absolute trust in divine love?"

"They want to rule us by fear," I said, lurching at the memory of my horrors of hell after giving birth to my firstborn, of being too terrified to confess my sins. My conviction that I was forever damned had driven me to lunacy and very nearly destroyed me. What if I had, in fact, been deluded—not by my visions but by Father Spryngegold's sermons of hellfire and eternal torment? His preaching that women were evil by their very nature. What Julian revealed was that God was love. Not wrath. Not punishment. God is lightness and joy. And women were created in Mother God's own image. No one was defiled or outside of divine grace.

Now I understood why Julian had chosen this slum church as her anchorage. This was the only way she could mingle with those, like the young prostitute, whom respectable folk shunned. She had sacrificed her own freedom to give them counsel and solace.

"I am enclosed in a house of stone," Julian said. She reached through the bars and took my hand as though I were her lifeline. "But you, my sister, wander free. That is why I must ask for your help."

I blinked, dumbfounded. How could one as bumbling as I be of any help to one as reverend as Dame Julian?

"Margery, I am old and have not many years left in this world. I beg you to keep my writings safe."

I caught my breath, the weight of her summons settling on my shoulders.

"You might secretly carry my book with you on pilgrimage and share it with those you meet on your way." Her voice caught, poised between hope and fear. "If you sail from Yarmouth, you shall land in Zierikzee in Holland. Perhaps I might even ask you to carry my book to the beguinage there so the beguines might copy it. Our beguinage in Norwich is small, but in Zierikzee and elsewhere in the Low Countries, you'll find great flourishing beguinages, with a hundred or more women living together."

She broke off then, as though fearful she had asked too much of me. That I would refuse. I even saw the glint of tears in her eyes.

Moved beyond speech, I gazed at her. At Julian with her eyes as wide as heaven, her mind as sharp as a bodkin, her speech more intoxicating than honeyed claret. All my longings, all my prayers, all my visions had led me to this place, this eternal moment with the sun pouring through the stained glass to wash our clasped hands as red as the blood of the passion. My lonely path converged with hers.

"Yes," I whispered fiercely. "I will carry your book."

I felt as though I were Ruth pledging my troth to Naomi. *Wherever I go, your book shall go. Your wise beguines shall be my people.* I knew I would find the strength to endure whatever happened to me from that moment onward. For now I knew that my life mattered.

9

HERE WAS STILL THE matter of my white clothing and the golden ring to mark my vow of chastity.

When I told Mother Julian that the Bishop of Lincoln had refused to give me leave to wear white but instead ordered me to go ask the Archbishop of Canterbury, she smiled shrewdly.

"Would my blessing suffice?" she asked. "I've no white clothes for you, but you can buy the cloth in the market. Norwich, after all, is a city built on wool. But I can give you this."

Her face softened as she took from her own finger a golden ring, the symbol of her marriage to Christ. She would have received this ring when she professed her vows as a Benedictine nun. Before I could blink, she placed it on my finger where I had once worn John's ring. Holding my hand up to the light, she read aloud its engraved inscription.

"*Ihesus est amor meus.*" Jesus is my Beloved.

"I can't possibly take this from you," I said. "It's too precious."

I had never forgiven myself for taking Martin's Saint Christopher medal all those years ago. How could I accept Julian's ring? I removed it and handed it to her. But Dame Julian blessed the ring, sprinkled it with holy water, and placed it back on my finger, saying, "*Accipe, famula Christi, anulum, fidei signum, connubii indicium, quem devote deferas, costa custodias, quoad amplexus divini sponsi coronanda pervenias.*"

The precise words the bishop would have used had he deigned to perform the ceremony marking me out as a vowess.

I wanted to fall to my knees and kiss Dame Julian's hand, but she went on speaking so urgently that I could only remain upright and pay attention.

"There's a ship departing from Yarmouth to Zierikzee in five days, so Alice tells me. You must be prepared to sail with that ship, Margery, before the autumn gales begin."

Alice, Julian's servant who came to bring her food and drink, wash her linen, and remove the waste in her chamber pot, also kept the anchoress apprised of the news of the outer world. Julian trusted Alice implicitly. Alice, who had been sitting with her mending at the far end of the church, now stepped forward at Julian's call.

"Alice, please take Mistress Margery to Master Thomas's market stall," Julian told her, before turning to me. "Master Thomas is a loyal friend. He shall sell you the cloth and stitch your clothes for a good price. And he shall give you your pilgrim's staff."

Alice lowered her eyes and Julian squeezed my hand.

"A special staff," Julian whispered, "with a hollow compartment within. Perfect for concealing pages of scrolled parchment."

Master Thomas would take no payment from me whatsoever.

"White clothes," he said, nodding. "With God's permission."

It seemed the very fact that Julian had sent me convinced the man of my worthiness. After Alice took my measurements for him, he told me to come back the following evening.

The next day, after my many hours with Julian, I stopped by his market stall on my way back to the priory. This time Nell accompanied me.

"Mistress Margery," Master Thomas said, greeting me with great respect. "Your new clothes are ready."

He presented me with the staff, then held up the white gown, hood, kirtle, and cloak for my inspection.

Nell looked on slack-jawed, as if not knowing whether to laugh or sputter.

"White clothes for *you*, Mistress Margery?" she exclaimed so loudly that half the people on the market square turned their heads to gawp.

My nape prickled when I realized that Nell with her loose tongue wasn't just an annoyance but a liability. If she had even an inkling of what Julian had asked me to do, how easily she could betray me and Julian both. Yet I needed Nell, for no honorable woman could travel without a female companion.

Though Master Thomas had a curtained booth at the back of his stall where I might have changed at once into my new attire, a small voice at the back of my head warned me not to put on the white clothes just yet. Instead, I carried them back to the priory in a plain hessian sack. In my other hand, I bore my pilgrim's staff.

Blessedly, my maid fell silent and was yawning extravagantly by the time we arrived at the priory just before they locked the gates for the night. The portress glanced briefly at the pilgrim's staff and hessian sack I carried, but neither appeared to arouse her suspicion.

I didn't change into my white clothes until the next day at Saint Julian's Church. In between Masses, when the nave was empty and quiet, I sent Nell out to buy pies. Once she was gone, Alice ushered me into the sacristy and stood guard outside the door. There in that hallowed room, among the priests' silken chasubles, altar cloths, and the silver communion cup and tray, I shed my worldly garb and donned my new clothes. It was as though I had become a maiden again, bequeathed with a second virginity and the freedom I had yearned for my whole life. Arrayed in purest white, I was a bride united in body and soul with my Beloved.

Still, doubts clamored in my head. Was I even worthy of Julian's summons or should I go home to my children before I became an utter stranger to them? Then, as a shaft of sunlight pierced the stained glass to bathe my face in its radiance, my heart tremored with the stark truth that I had come so far that there was no turning back.

I knelt outside Dame Julian's window to receive her benediction.

"Margery Kempe," she said, her eyes shining like stars. "Know that you are my other half."

She passed me a leather cylinder filled with her precious pages and showed me how to hide it in the secret compartment in my staff. She took the pilgrim's map I had inherited from Father and showed me the foreign cities where her friends and sympathizers lived. These friends would rejoice to see her manuscript. As well as the beguines of Zierikzee, there was Christopher Hope, an English papal legate residing in Constance.

"Because you wander free, you will arouse suspicion," Dame Julian said. "Play the fool if you must but know that you are God's fool. Play the ignorant, unlettered woman or else they might call you a heretic. If you find yourself under interrogation, call upon your gift of tears as your shield."

Dame Julian set me on my quest to not only be a pilgrim but also a living reminder of the divine love that we both had witnessed.

"Remember this," she said. "'The words 'You shall not be overcome' were said in my visions very loudly and clearly. Our Lord did not say, 'You shall not be tormented, or troubled, or grieved' but 'You shall not be overcome.'"

On the eighth day of our time together, I walked out of Saint Julian's Church a new woman. Forever after, I would know I was not alone even if I traveled to the edges of the known world. I carried Dame Julian's book, her precious words that were my balm and courage. If she had been my Mother Superior, I would have gladly sworn obedience to her, but that was not what Julian wanted from me. She wanted me to be free, a woman in the world.

Nell and I caught a ride to Yarmouth on a passing beer wagon.

The driver's eyes fairly bulged out of his face at the sight of me. "God's blood, I've never seen a woman of *your* years dressed all in white!"

Nell stifled a laugh and winked at him, as though tempted to forsake me altogether and try her luck with this handsome drayman.

But still on fire from Julian's blessing, I held on to my dignity.

"Mind your tongue, sir!" I told him smartly as I hauled myself aboard with no help from my useless maid. "Surely you know it's a sin to swear."

When our ship lifted anchor in Yarmouth Harbor and set off over the rolling gray waves, I watched Norfolk receding farther and farther in the distance. The flat humble landscape that had been my home. In a blink it vanished away. A swell lifted the ship, then there was only water on all sides and the gulls that screeched and soared. I trembled as both freedom and fear coursed through me. No one would know me as John Kempe's wife anymore. I was simply Margery, consecrated by Julian, secretly carrying her book out into the great world.

II

The Gift of Tears

IO

HE PREVAILING WINDS WERE kind, the weather clement, and by God's grace, we reached Zeeland the very next day, those islands situated at the mouth of three great rivers—the Scheldt, the Meuse, and the Rhine. Alight with wonder, I clung to the rail as the ship navigated around the Isle of Schouwen and entered the broad canal lined with windmills and pastures where fat glossy milch cows grazed. Behind us trailed another English ship, this one from Ipswich, while ahead the prosperous port of Zierikzee beckoned. We sailed at a slow and stately pace through the water gates before anchoring in the harbor in the pulsing heart of that town. Those gabled brick houses and cobbled quays glittered and gleamed in golden noontide light. Before me lay a brand-new world where I might become a wholly new person, all my encumbrances and past humiliations left behind. *Everything will be different now.*

Disembarking, I tried to steady my sea legs on solid earth. I had only taken ten steps from the quay when a pimpled youth blocked my path.

"You come to my inn, *mevrouw*. I give you good price," he said, his eyes darting from my golden ring to Nell's bosom. "Come, I carry your things."

His huge grubby paws reached to snatch my satchel from Nell's arms.

Before I could even think, I let loose the most bloodcurdling shriek, one I had perfected over twenty long years of trying to be heard over the racket of my children. Everyone within fifty paces jumped and skittered. A dockworker dropped a crate on his foot and yelped, *"God-verdomme!"* But his shouting was like a whisper compared to my roar.

"Away from me, false deceiver!"

I'd heard tales of tricksters like him who lured unsuspecting newcomers just off the boat with the promise of decent lodgings only to lead them into some alley where they would beat them senseless and strip them of all possessions, even the clothes on their backs. Women and girls, left mother-naked and unconscious, would then be forced into servitude by some pimp.

Seizing my pilgrim's staff, I struck the youth's hands away from my belongings. Grabbing Nell's arm, I shoved past him and charged forward as though I knew where I was heading. For all my bold moves, I shook in fear and asked myself why I had ever left the safety of my old world, stifling though it had been. Back in Lynn, I'd been a figure of public ridicule yet no one had ever dared to threaten my safety on the streets, owing to my position as the mayor's daughter. But here, it seemed, Nell and I were fair game. Nell's eyes shone stark with dread, and she clung to me as though she were my daughter.

"Fear not," I told her, trying to sound braver than I felt. "We'll be safe once we reach the beguinage."

But how would I even find the place in this maze of unfamiliar streets? The best I could do was head toward the cathedral, easily identified by its soaring steeple. I marched on as briskly as I could without breaking into a run. The sense of peril did not relent. Had I been accompanied by at least one man or boy, I think our way would have been easy enough. But as two foreign women, we stood out, as tempting as a sack of gold left unguarded. We couldn't walk more than a dozen steps without rough-looking men calling out what I clearly recognized as obscenities. The Dutch word *hoer* sounds nearly the same as the English "whore."

A prostitute called out to us in broad Norfolk English. "Come and make friends, my sweetings. You'll soon be working with me."

The Bishop of Lincoln had lectured me that there was scarcely a town in Europe that didn't have a score of English prostitutes — female pilgrims who had lost their virtue, according to his reckoning. *Not of their own choice*, I thought bitterly, *but because wicked men viewed them as theirs for the taking*. My most bitter disappointment was that neither my age nor my white clothes had the power to repel such lewd appraisal. The only way to be left in peace if I traveled without male escort would be to play the part of a mad gibbering religious fanatic muttering utterances of impending doom.

My knuckles white, my hand cramped and clenched, I clung to my staff as though it were my lifeline. I couldn't even take pleasure in the lively market where merchants traded for salt and Zierikzee's famous madder root that was used to make brilliant crimson dye—I was too painfully aware of the many staring, leering men. My forehead throbbed. If I was already so far out of my depth in Holland, how would I fare in Palestine among the Saracens?

Then the most foul of English voices assaulted my ears. "By the dugs of Our Lady, isn't that John Kempe's wife, dressed all in white? A bigger hypocrite than all the Pharisees!"

My shock froze into panic when I saw it was Hugh, the driver formerly in my employ who had beaten to death my two mares and so ruined my grain mill. I hadn't seen the cursed man on my ship. He had probably sailed on the Ipswich vessel.

"At least poor John's finally rid of you," Hugh said, glowering down from his great height. "What kind of woman tries to turn her lawful husband into a monk? If you were my wife, I'd have beaten you blind."

A prudent woman would have kept her head down and scurried on her way. But, for all my terror, I couldn't hold my tongue.

"*Your wife,*" I said hotly, "could take no more of you and ran off with the rat catcher. You can't be trusted with horses, let alone a woman."

Hugh flushed fiery red and the look he gave me was murderous, but I had managed to render him speechless.

"Come, Nell! To the cathedral," I said, hoping to leave him there, momentarily stupefied.

But my maid would not be moved. Her face had gone bright pink. As if utterly deaf to my condemnation of the man, she gawped at him with huge moist eyes, as though she were some besotted heifer. He, likewise, rallied to notice her.

"Well, if it isn't Nell," he said in an altogether different tone. Indulgent and familiar, as though the witless creature had once warmed his bed.

The thought was so revolting, I could only grab my satchels off her and stalk away, banging my pilgrim's staff into the cobbles. Even if I had to walk alone, I would not linger anywhere near that man. Somewhat reluctantly, Nell sprinted after me and was persuaded to carry our satchels again.

Rage ripped through me. To think I had believed I could leave my past behind! Yet the most hateful man in Lynn was here in Zierikzee. When I entered the cathedral, my hands were still shaking even as I knelt before the altar of the Queen of Bliss and lit a wax candle. As white as hope, it was.

Blessed Mother protect me. I tried to lose myself in her sweet serenity. But dark thoughts plagued me. What was Hugh doing here? My heart seized at the thought that we might be bound for the same destination—Jerusalem. Though he was the last man on earth I'd expect to meet on pilgrimage, perhaps his priest had sent him on this journey as penance for his countless wicked deeds. If that was so, this probably wouldn't be our last encounter.

Before leaving the cathedral, I asked one of the priests who spoke passable English the way to the beguinage. It was located in Sint Anthonis Straat, I learned. Just behind the cathedral. I'd recognize it by the image of Bridget of Sweden over the door.

I fairly bolted down the cobbled streets in my eagerness to find kindred souls and a safe haven. But when I had at last located the place, my spirits drooped. Though the image of Saint Bridget was brightly painted, the edifice itself with its windowless flint walls seemed so forbidding, more like a prison than anything else.

Plucking up my courage, I rang the brass bell at the gate. After a minute or so, it opened and I found myself staring up at a tall, strapping young Dutchwoman. Clutching an ax in one hand as though she'd been chopping wood, she addressed me sternly in her language, which left me tongue-tied. Of course, a house of chaste women would have to keep their gate locked and exercise caution as to who they let in, but this young woman was terrifying. She looked powerful enough to pound the likes of Hugh into the ground.

Remembering that Julian had said I must ask for the Grand Mistress, I cleared my throat and clasped my hands.

"I have come from England to see Dame Godelieve," I said haltingly. "I bring news of Dame Julian of Norwich."

Julian's name was a magical key. The girl's face brightened. *"Welkom, mevrouw."* She pointed at herself, and said, "Annemieke."

I pointed at myself. "Margery."

"Margriet," she said, beaming. *"Kom met mij, Mevrouw Margriet."*

Nell and I followed her through a narrow passageway that opened into a lush garden with its own well and orchards. Surrounding the garden on all four sides were tidy terraced cottages and, at the far end, a chapel. Everywhere I looked there were women in simple gray gowns. Some picked apples and pears. Some hoed in the garden or harvested herbs. Many sat on their stoops with their distaffs and spun flax while others perched over their embroidery frames. Through the open windows of the cottages, I saw women working at looms, weaving spun flax into linen.

Annemieke took us to a small guest room above one of the loom cottages where I left Nell and the baggage behind. Mindful of my mission, I held fast to my pilgrim's staff as I followed Annemieke across the garden to the leafiest and most hidden corner of the beguinage where Grand Mistress Godelieve dwelled. The wealthier beguines could bring their maids with them and it was her maid who opened the door to us. She and Annemieke conferred in hushed tones.

"Yulian van Norwich," I heard Annemieke say.

Godelieve's maid nodded and led me up two dizzyingly steep flights of stairs. We emerged in an attic. The sun pouring through the large glass window on the gable end was enough to blind me. Her back to us, Godelieve sat at her desk in the full flood of light. She seemed too absorbed in her task to notice our presence. The only sound in that room was the scratch of her quill. Glancing round, I saw books and maps everywhere. Such a high-learned woman. No wonder Julian had sent me here.

The maid spoke softly, announcing my visit. Just as quietly, the lady turned on her stool, the sun blazing behind her like a halo. She looked to be about my age.

"Welcome, Margery," she said in English, rising to take my hand. Her fingers were mottled in ink. "I rarely receive guests up here, but any friend of Dame Julian's is a friend of mine." Noting my astonishment to hear her flawless English, she smiled. "My mother was born in Dover, so English is truly my mother tongue."

Godelieve's maid departed, leaving her mistress and me alone in this attic that was at once a scriptorium and a library, a refuge of the mind hidden away. Like Julian, Godelieve was clearly a woman who guarded her secrets. I soon saw why. Upon her desk lay a Bible open to the Gospel of John. Though I wasn't learned in Latin, I recognized the opening line, which I had heard often enough in Mass.

> *In principio erat Verbum, et Verbum erat apud Deum,*
> *et Deus erat Verbum.*

But the words Dame Godelieve had copied on her page were not in Latin nor even in Dutch but in English.

> *In the beginning was the Word, and the Word was with*
> *God, and the Word was God.*

My heart stopped. This was the first English translation of the Scriptures I had ever seen.

"We sell my Dutch and English translations of the Gospels in the bookshop across from the cathedral," Godelieve said. "Would you believe that my English translation is one of the beguinage's main sources of income? That and the badges we embroider and the linen we weave."

"In England they would burn you," I said, my throat tight with fear. *They might even burn me,* I thought, *for merely laying eyes on the manuscript.*

She nodded sagely. "I know very well. But in Holland the rules are different. There is one thing you must understand about the Dutch. They're prepared to tolerate all manner of business as long as they can make money off of it. The bookseller takes a goodly cut of the profits, and he's quite cozy with the bishop."

The aura of the forbidden seemed palpable enough to grasp in my hands — anyone could possess their own translation of the Gospels simply by crossing the sea to Holland. Examining the copied page more closely, I saw that it was not parchment but some other, thinner material.

"This is paper," Godelieve said, running her hand along the margin. "Made of linen rags. It's far cheaper than parchment and makes the books more affordable, too. But come, tell me of Dame Julian."

Godelieve drew me to a cushioned bench where we could sit together, surrounded by her books. Her maid tiptoed in with a tray of honey cakes and two cups of buttermilk.

I waited until the maid had left before reaching for my pilgrim's staff. "Dame Julian sent me here to bring you this." I carefully upended the staff, removed the false bottom, and took out the leather cylinder containing the scrolled manuscript of Julian's *Revelations of Divine Love*. "She asked that you might make a copy of it and keep it safe in your library."

Julian's handwriting was small and economical, allowing her to squeeze as much text as possible on each page. It would take Godelieve weeks to copy the manuscript, but I was happy to linger here for as long as it took her to complete the task.

"Sweet Julian," Godelieve said, carefully setting the manuscript on her desk before wiping the tears from her eyes. "I'm so happy to hear that she still lives. Once, many years ago, I went on pilgrimage to Our Lady of Walsingham. I stopped in Norwich to visit the anchoress — she's famous even here. She had only just begun to write her book and now you have delivered it to me." Godelieve pressed my hand. "Bless you, Margery. Bless you a thousand times."

"It's my greatest joy to be here," I said. "How wonderful to live like this, in such freedom."

Godelieve smiled wistfully. "It's no easy existence. The town tolerates us but ever more grudgingly. We live simply and work very hard to earn our keep. The linen we weave is the finest in Zierikzee. Our embroidery is even finer. The guilds aren't happy to have us as competition." She set down her cup and sighed. "Last summer the emblem embroiderers' guild tried to force their way in and destroy our work. It took all my powers of diplomacy to persuade them to leave us in peace. Then the linen weavers complained so loudly that the mayor has limited us to six looms lest we threaten their business."

Godelieve's story made me reflect upon my own fraught and ultimately futile attempts to support myself in the world of commerce — first with my brewery, then with my grain mill. I had been just one woman. This was an entire community. To think of the courage and vision Godelieve and her sisters possessed to persevere and even thrive in the face of such hostility.

Three weeks I stayed in the beguinage while Godelieve copied Julian's manuscript, using cursive script instead of book script in order to copy it faster. Meanwhile, I repaid the beguines' hospitality by sharing their labors. I cooked turtle broth for the sick, helped wind linen thread, and took my turn brewing the beer that accompanied our meals. I sat with Godelieve in her scriptorium and told her everything I could remember of Julian — her counsel and comfort. In the evenings when we supped in the refectory, Godelieve read aloud from her Dutch translation of the Scriptures.

The beguinage gates remained locked at night, but during the day, the beguines were free to come and go as they pleased. The women went to the market to sell their linen cloth, embroidery, honey, and the surplus apples and pears from the orchard.

One morning, accompanied by fierce Annemieke, I set out for the cathedral only to let my curiosity get the better of me. I asked my new friend to show me around the long row of stationers facing the main cathedral entrance. The shopfronts were crammed with signboards advertising the services of binders and illuminators. Scribes hung large sheets outside their doors with writing samples to display the scripts they had mastered.

Canons, clerics, pilgrims, and merchants crowded into the book vendors' shops to place their orders. One could commission a book of hours, a Bible, an atlas of the world, or even an obscure treatise on medicine or the planets. The vendor then inquired whether the buyer preferred book script or cursive script, paper or parchment, illuminations or plain text, and whether the book should be bound and with what materials. Every embellishment, of course, added to the price.

Some even sold finished copies, mostly used ones. I had to pinch myself when Annemieke proudly pointed to Godelieve's English Gospels set out on the table where anyone might pick it up and examine it. When the vendor quoted the price, in English no less, it wasn't even terribly expensive, being an unbound paper copy with no illustrations.

Dare I? Under the vendor's sharp gaze, I carefully picked up the stack of pages. Although Father's legacy had been generous, my long journey to Jerusalem and back would cost me deep in the purse. I needed to be prudent with expenditures. Still, it wouldn't cost that much to have these pages sewn and bound — with heavy paper if not leather. The thrill of the forbidden rippled through me. But forbidden acts carry consequences. I was already risking so much carrying Julian's manuscript. I suspected that even here on the Continent the other countries I would travel through would not be as tolerant as Holland. Reluctantly, I made myself set the English Gospels back on the table.

In the three weeks it took Godelieve to copy Julian's manuscript, I came to love my life in Zierikzee. The beguinage had become a dearer home to me than any I'd ever known. I shared a true sense of sisterhood with the beguines, singing with them in the chapel and pitching in when it was my turn to help with the laundry. I learned enough Dutch to understand most of what was being said and to speak enough to muddle along. I could imagine staying here for the rest of my days, spending each evening listening to Godelieve read from the writings of the German beguine Mechthild of Magdeburg, whose poetry I had first heard when walking past the beguinage in Norwich.

But the time had come to continue on my pilgrim's way. I had learned from bitter experience that it would be a veritable death wish to attempt this journey alone — I absolutely needed to find trustworthy travel companions. However, precious few women made the pilgrimage to Jerusalem and most who did, according to Godelieve, were nuns in the company of other nuns. Thus, I would most likely have to settle for an all-male group, a prospect that nearly made me lose my courage altogether. Unless those men were truly honorable, it might prove as great a risk as traveling on my own. On the other hand, I might have to wait months or even years to find a Jerusalem-bound pilgrims' party that included a secular woman, such a rare and extraordinary thing it was.

Thus, when word went round that a band of English pilgrims, including *two* women — a wife and a widow — was staying in the hostelry up the street, I rushed over at once to introduce myself, accompanied by Godelieve and her priest.

"Well met!" I cried out heartily. "I am Margery Kempe of Lynn."

For all appearances, these people seated around the refectory table seemed decent and respectable. The widow, who looked to be in her late thirties, was joined by her brother, a yeoman farmer. The matron, some ten years younger, traveled with her husband, a tax collector. As for the rest, there was a baker, a blacksmith, a shipman, and a learned clerk who had studied at Cambridge. The highest-born of them all was a squire's son turned ascetic holy man. His name, I learned, was Ignatius, and he wore the coarse woolen tunic of a penitent and fasted on bread and water while the others shared meat and wine.

But the spiritual leader of the party was a Franciscan friar named Timothy who had no such inhibitions about making merry. At first, I didn't even recognize him as a religious man. His face was flushed with wine, and instead of a gray woolen habit and cowl, his rotund form was garbed with double-worsted sleeves and a cape of gray fur. When I inquired whether I could join the group and travel with them to Jerusalem, the friar's brow knit in suspicion.

"How do we know what kind of woman you are?" he asked sternly, while the others looked on in silence.

Even though Godelieve's priest was on hand to vouch for my honor, these people appeared puzzled over what to make of me, a solo woman pilgrim in her middle years.

"I'm the late Mayor of Lynn's only daughter," I was quick to inform him, my voice crisp with annoyance that even here, on pilgrimage, people would judge me according to whose daughter or wife I was. "I have twenty golden nobles to pay my way," I added, sharing a sly glance with Godelieve. "And a map of the pilgrimage routes to the Holy Land!"

With a flourish, I revealed the scrolled-up map I had carried beneath my cloak. The map itself was rare and precious, and proved that I hailed from exalted kindred.

To my relief, Friar Timothy brightened at once. "Well met, good mistress! Come join our table and share our wine."

The widow, Mistress Cecily, shifted on the bench to make room for me. A thin and sallow figure, she was clad in a dull black wool gown and hood with white crepe trim. But her smile was kindly.

"It's good to have another woman along," she said.

Meanwhile, the matron, Mistress Edith, eyed me quizzically. "Are you a nun or a wife?" she asked.

Plump and pink-cheeked, she stared at me in dismay. By my mere existence, I seemed to have run roughshod over every rule she had ever learned.

If I was going to survive this journey, I needed a quick and re-sourceful tongue. "I'm a faithful wife, madam. Just like yourself," I said. "My husband wanted with all his heart to accompany me on this most holy voyage. But, alas! His bunions stood in his way. And so I travel with his blessing. I wear white to protect my virtue."

I tried not to laugh at how ridiculous it was using John's bunions to explain away the oddness of my mission.

"Bunions," Edith echoed flatly. Then she shrugged and drained her wineglass.

"Good people," I said. "Might I ask the way you intend to go?" I unrolled my map and placed it in the center of the table.

Now Master Donald, the tax collector, spoke, for it seemed he was in charge of the logistics of the journey.

"The pilgrims' galleys to the Holy Land depart from Venice in the spring," he said, pointing on the map to that watery city ringed by ships and mermaids. "We must arrive in Venice with plenty of time to spare, for we've many preparations to make for the voyage—we must buy bedding and supplies and change our money. The date the galleys arrive is uncertain. Some years they come early and some years there is only one galley for all the pilgrims seeking passage. The earlier we arrive, the more likely we'll secure a berth."

I nodded, my eyes traveling across the sea toward Jaffa where the galleys would land. From there, we would travel overland to Jerusalem.

Donald went on to explain that tomorrow at first light we would board a ferry to mainland Holland, then proceed by barge up the River Waal and then the River Rhine. However, the Rhine, after the town of Bingen, was difficult and dangerous to navigate. Still, he hoped we would make it at least as far south as Strassburg then continue overland to Constance.

"Bingen!" I said brightly. "Where the Holy Hildegard lived!" Master Alan had told me of the visionary abbess who had lived three centuries ago. Poring over my map, my eyes lit on the fabled cities along the Rhine — Cologne, Mainz, and Worms — far-famed for their great cathedrals housing countless relics.

"At any rate," Master Donald said. "After Constance, we shall cross the Alps and head for Milan. If we have enough time, we might visit Bologna, though that is a detour. Otherwise we'll press on from Milan to Verona to Mestre where we board the ferry across the lagoon to Venice."

Those painted rivers, cities, and mountains on my map seemed to come to life before my eyes. Crossing the Alps! Born and bred in the lowlands of Norfolk, I could hardly imagine such a thing.

"As for Rome," he added. "We shall visit it after we return from Jerusalem. Our last great site before we return to England."

"I shall be ready at dawn to join your travels," I said, smiling at everyone up and down the table.

When I met Ignatius's eyes, the holy man averted his gaze and grimaced, as though his penitent's vows forbade him to so much as glance at a woman. But even he couldn't dampen my good cheer. I must have looked too blithe for my own good, for then Master Donald proceeded to warn me of the many perils we faced. Bandits might rob us of all our belongings, slit our throats, and leave us to die unshriven. In the Holy Land, pilgrims were regularly kidnapped and sold into slavery to the Saracens, he said. That was why he'd brought his sword to protect us all. Likewise, the shipman and blacksmith, who had once served in the King's army, came armed with crossbows. Master Donald then offered to take my gold and map for safekeeping, as he had done with the other pilgrims' money and valuables.

That evening I bade my loving farewell to Godelieve and her sister beguines. In the privacy of Godelieve's library, I scrolled Julian's precious pages into the leather cylinder and slid that back into the secret hollow of my pilgrim's staff. The following morning, I rose at dawn and set off with my fellow English travelers.

II

Y NEW COMPANIONS AND I traveled in a heavy flat-bottomed barge made of solid slabs of oak, with oars forward and aft. The craft was laden with Flemish linen, Dutch herring, and Frisian wool. As we forged upriver, the flat lands of Holland with their ancient towns and churches gave way to the pastureland and forests of Germany.

I did my utmost to befriend Edith and Cecily and thus found myself squeezed in a tight circle with them in the cabin Cecily and I shared. With great ceremony, Edith opened a carved chest she carried with her everywhere and took out a painted wooden doll intended to be the likeness of Baby Jesus. Reverently, she set it upon her lap while inviting Cecily to choose a shirt to dress it in. I watched my companions kiss the doll as if it were God himself.

I had to remind myself that behind Edith's pious display was deep abiding pain, an emptiness longing to be filled. She'd been married twelve years without conceiving and had begged her husband to take her on pilgrimage in hope of curing her barrenness.

When it was my turn to hold Baby Jesus, I silently wondered why Edith didn't take in some poor orphan and raise that child as her own if she so longed to be a mother. To me, that seemed a much holier thing than lavishing such attention on a doll.

Noticing my awkwardness, Edith frowned and took the doll away from me.

"Do you think this is a silly game I play?" she asked irritably. "But how could I have expected otherwise from a woman who abandoned her babies?"

A few days ago, Nell had let slip that I'd borne fourteen children. Edith seemed to take my overbountiful fertility as a personal affront.

"God blessed you with healthy children!" she blustered on, as if to put me forever in my place as a wicked and unnatural woman. "And you *spit* on his gift!"

"Peace," I managed, my voice shaky. "Let us not be enemies."

Edith glared at me, as if willing me to disappear, while Cecily, her eyes downcast, appeared at a loss for words. Like Julian and countless others, Cecily had lost her children and husband to the plague. A widow of some means, she had embarked on this pilgrimage to mend her unspeakable grief and pray for their departed souls. Though she confessed that her husband had been harsh to her and beaten her, she seemed at a loss as to how to live without him. She'd married at fifteen to a man nearly thrice her age. She hardly seemed to know what to do or feel or think now that she had her freedom and no longer lived under his shadow. If Edith couldn't forgive me for leaving behind my children, Cecily seemed flabbergasted that I could seize my liberty and travel the world even though I had a husband still living. Both Edith and Cecily had men with them—Edith's husband and Cecily's brother—to watch over them and uphold their honor as they traveled through foreign lands. While I had no one, only my own sharp tongue to defend myself. I was truly the outlier in every way.

Mumbling an excuse, I wriggled out of the tight cabin. In truth, I couldn't clamber out of that stuffy little chamber fast enough.

Heading down the side deck, I took a deep breath before wondering where Nell was keeping herself—I hadn't seen her since breakfast. I came round a tight corner and nearly tripped over Ignatius who knelt bare-kneed on the splintering deck where he had been deep in prayer since dawn. He didn't sleep in a cabin like the rest of us but on the deck regardless of the weather God sent. And if that wasn't sufficient mortification of the flesh, he regularly scourged himself.

Yet for all his studied abstinence, he was no monk but a married man and father of nine. Once he'd lived a life of wealth and ease until the death of his only son had plunged him into a maelstrom of grief and repentance, so Cecily had told me. Blaming his son's demise on the many sins he'd committed in his former life—drunkenness, lechery, and gambling — Ignatius had left his ancestral manor house, joined a lay order of penitents, and gone on pilgrimage.

Ignatius broke off his silent prayer to scowl at me.

Keeping my mouth firmly shut, I moved on. I'll confess that although Ignatius must have been as undone with loss as poor Cecily was, the man was such a self-righteous prig that I was sorely tempted to burst out singing a ditty about beer-drinking nuns just to annoy him.

Like me, Ignatius had left his family to go on pilgrimage and follow God's call. Unlike me, no one faulted him for it or called him selfish. Quite the contrary — we tiptoed around him as though he were a living saint. Even Nell took great pains not to disturb him. When he deigned to eat with us, Friar Timothy gave Ignatius pride of place at the head of the table.

The other men in our pilgrims' party were decidedly less somber. I discovered the baker, the shipman, and the blacksmith balanced on the edge of the stern. The three of them pissed loudly into the Rhine while bragging what a marvelous waterfall they made.

I finally found Nell, who seemed to be having a right jolly time with Friar Timothy. Before my unbelieving eyes, the friar handed my maid a brimming cup of wine and pinched her rump. Throwing back her head, the girl squealed, which left me wondering how much she had already imbibed.

"Oh, sir!" she cried. "You do love to jape and jest!"

Her smile froze, however, when I marched up, wrenched the cup from her hand, and shoved it back at Friar Timothy. Alas, I chanced to spill half the contents on his fine fur cape.

"What are you *doing?*" I asked Nell as I pulled her away.

I thought of the many dangers that could befall a comely young woman traveling among strangers. While I gathered from her history that she wasn't some untouched maiden, it was still my duty to protect her from those who would use her for their pleasure then throw her away. What honorable intentions could a friar, of all men, possibly have?

"What if he ruins you?" I asked Nell with desperation. "What if you find yourself pregnant and forsaken?"

My maid's eyes glazed as if I — not she — was the bigger fool in the ways of the world.

"He said if I kept him in merry company, he would pay for my dowry," she said smartly. "He gave me *this.*"

She opened her hand to show me a cloak pin that glittered brightly enough though it was only cheap and thinly gilded pewter.

"I'll wager this *friar,*" I said, my voice thickening in scorn, "has arranged many a young woman's marriage at his own cost." I'd heard tales of clergymen, low-ranking and high, who used this ruse to marry off their pregnant concubines. "But when he discovers you're no maiden, he won't pay you a farthing, only call you a whore."

Nell clenched her jaw, but before she could say a word, Cecily came running, her eyes wide and fearful. "Mistress Margery, did you not say you had a pouch of physick herbs with you? Poor Master Rupert's been taken by fever."

I found Rupert, the young clerk from Cambridge, awash in cold sweat in his narrow berth. As I touched his hot brow, his eyes flickered in apology as if he were sorry for my trouble. Truly this boy was as gentle of manner as he was delicate of constitution. In my satchel, I'd a pouch of willow bark, which I brewed to lower his fever. As I supported his head to help him drink it down, I felt a pang for my own son Jack, Rupert's same age, in faraway Danzig. Was he healthy or did he suffer illness as this young man suffered?

After Rupert had swallowed the last sip of willow bark potion, I sat by his bedside a long spell while he sweated and tossed. It didn't take me long to gather that there was more than the fever troubling him. He started speaking in fits and starts, revealing the secret pain oppressing his soul. He was making this pilgrimage, so he told me, on behalf of his widowed mother who had recently died.

"I swore to her on her deathbed I would go to Jerusalem to shorten her time in purgatory," he said. "But what if I don't even make it as far as Cologne?"

I folded my hands and sank deep into contemplation. Colors and fleeting pictures danced inside the blackness of my closed eyes. The radiant image of a woman slowly took form. Gleaming with benevolence, she had Rupert's kind eyes and thoughtful air. I could feel the full force of her mother-love as she gazed down at him from a great height. She didn't speak in words but in pictures that were like a tableau of moving illuminations, revealing Rupert's progress to a sunbaked land where the golden Dome of the Rock glittered beneath the dazzling sky. There I saw Rupert restored to full health and effulgent with joy and purpose.

Sometime later, I emerged from my reverie more serene than I'd been since leaving Zierikzee.

"Our blessed Lord showed me the vision of your mother in paradise," I told him. "So you've no worries at all on her account. As for your health, I saw that you shall indeed reach Holy Jerusalem and there find your heart's bliss."

This marked the beginning of our friendship. When Rupert was well again, I drew him out of his introspection by asking him to describe the scholarly books he had read. Many a delightful hour we passed conversing. But if the two of us spent too long in each other's company, we became the subject of the others' lewd mirth.

"A bit long in the tooth for you, is she not?" Friar Timothy asked Rupert. "I hope you like music, young man," he added with an extravagant leer. "For I hear there are no better drums than the skin of older women. If you touch them only once, they carry on making noise for an entire week!"

Friar Timothy, it seemed, could not forgive me for disrupting his attempt to seduce my maid. The dark wine I'd spilled on his fine cape had left an indelible stain like a mark of shame. And thus he appeared determined to make me pay for the humiliation I'd caused him. He mocked and denounced me at every opportunity and did his utmost to turn the others against me.

I'll confess the disdain was mutual—I had lost all respect for this man, who was unworthy of the office of friar. If he were truly living the life of Saint Francis, he would embrace poverty and simplicity in order to serve the poor and sick. Instead, he appeared to shun beggars only to prey on pretty young women or else cozen close to wealthy men like Master Donald who lined his pockets with donations. Timothy was a self-serving weasel who interpreted his religious office in a way that was most comfortable for him.

As for Nell, once she had sobered up and come to her senses, she avoided the friar, though she made free to flirt with others, such as the unmarried blacksmith, who took her fancy. The girl was incorrigible, attracting men the way a rose attracts honeybees.

Before we even reached the fabled city of Cologne, we could smell it miles downstream, for the city emptied its cesspits into the Rhine. Our barge battled its way through a sludge of human sewage, rotting raw hemp, dead fish, and the entrails of slaughtered beasts. The stink drove us into our cabins.

Yet when we reached Cologne, the grandeur was enough to make me forget the horrors of its pollution. Our pilgrims' party wended our way to the great cathedral, still under construction, with countless stone masons at their noisy, dusty work. But there, amid the rubble and busyness, stood the great Shrine of the Three Kings housed in a reliquary made of bronze and silver that was gilded and encrusted with enamel and gemstones. As I lit my candle and knelt to pray, I reflected how these Three Wise Men had traversed the world following the star God sent them. What if we had all been given a star to follow? I vowed to follow my star wherever it led me.

A few days upriver from Cologne, we entered the Rhine Gorge with its rolling vineyards, dense forests, and towering cliffs spiked with castles and toll towers, the entire landscape awash in fiery autumn color. This stretch of the Rhine was as beautiful as it was dangerous with its blind bends and increasingly strong currents. We needed to be towed along in places by sturdy horses on the bank. Riverside shrines marked the memory of the souls who had drowned when their barges and ships had crashed up on the cliffs or rocky reefs.

We stopped at the ancient chapel of Saint Goar the Hermit to pray for preservation before our barge attempted the most perilous bend of all. Here the river snaked sharply around a massive rock face. Deep and narrow this passage was, with a roil of violent currents and a waterfall. The echoing of all that rushing water against the cliff made an eerie, otherworldly murmuring that rendered even stern Ignatius white-lipped with terror.

God's grace and the crew's efforts saw us safely past the bend. Even so, our way didn't get any easier. Just past Bingen, where the holy Abbess Hildegard had received her visions, we had to navigate yet another bottleneck with shallows, shoals, and reefs where ships regularly smashed up. From there, we progressed to the Upper Rhine where we battled increasingly mighty currents. It seemed a miracle that we made it as far south as Strassburg, the City of Streets, so named because it stood at the crossroads of the great trade routes crossing Europe.

From Strassburg, we ferried across the Rhine to Kehl on the eastern bank, where we would begin our overland journey to Constance. Coming up from the docks, we traversed the gauntlet of prostitutes from distant lands—stranded women fallen on hardship and doing the best they could to make a livelihood.

What chilled me far more as we approached the pilgrims' hostel were the scores of beggars, many of them women too old to earn their keep as whores. One such woman, probably only five years older than I, held out her bony hands while staring straight into my eyes, as if daring me to look down on her. Her fate could all too easily become mine. I gave her what coins I could spare before stumbling onward after the others. How vulnerable we were, women at large in the great world. All it would take was one robbery, one slip, one fall from grace, and I, too, could be left to beg and starve.

We intended to follow the trade road east, a well-traveled way that led not only to Constance but also to the rich cities of Augsburg, Ulm, and distant Prague. Many merchants, pilgrims, and other travelers followed this road, which made it a target for bandits.

We could have chosen to travel with a large and prodigiously armed merchants' caravan with many wagonloads of French wines and tapestries. Though this would have been the safest option by far, it would have slowed our progress considerably. Master Donald was confident that we could defend ourselves, armed as we were with his sword and our two crossbowmen. Besides, he reasoned, we were sure to join up with other travelers on the road. But we needed to buy swift horses in order to outride any pursuers.

Of course, the horse traders took full advantage of our plight. Though I used every bit of German I'd learned from my brother in my attempt to bargain down the price, the seller would accept nothing less than three golden nobles for a bad-tempered roan gelding with a tooth-jarring trot and a skittish mare for Nell to ride. I began to think that the horse traders were the biggest bandits of all, but what choice did I have? It was either lay down my gold or be left behind while the others rode off without me.

But I did feel a sense of guilty relief when I learned that Ignatius's penitent's vows forbade him from riding horseback. Instead, he elected to continue his journey on foot, penniless and left to beg his bread as a holy man without a scrap of anything valuable that a robber might wish to steal. Sitting on my newly purchased gelding, I watched the man, his back as straight as a spear, disappear down a forest track too thickly overgrown for us riders to follow. *What distinguished him from that downtrodden beggar woman?* I asked myself. Was it his air of sanctimony? The nimbus of holiness that everyone—apart from me—seemed to see around him?

Though a major route, the road we traveled was muddy, stony, steep, and ominously lonely, for it passed through wild and sparsely inhabited forests. On the first day's ride, I witnessed the specter of half a dozen abandoned villages. The red letter *P* painted on one of the doors indicated that most of the inhabitants had perished of the plague. We hardly met a soul and counted ourselves lucky to find an inhabited farmstead where we could shelter for the night.

These forests were deeper and darker than anything I had known in England. Dense pine boughs obscured the sun. Everything lay in green shadow. A savage land, this seemed. Barely civilized. Any number of thieves might be prowling among the trees, waiting to ambush us.

Master Donald rode at the head of our party with his sword at the ready while the two crossbowmen brought up the rear. Cecily, Edith, Nell, and I rode in a tight cluster surrounded by the men.

Following the main road all the way to Constance seemed a straightforward thing even if the forest was dark and frightening. However, after our second day's long ride, we discovered that a bridge had been washed away in a flood. The river being too wild to ford, we were forced to find an alternate route. My map suggested the wisest course would be to follow the river south where we would surely find a road to take us to a bridge or ford, yet the only track we came upon was hopelessly overgrown with brambles.

I had never seen Nell so frightened, her face as white as bleached linen. She rode close by my side as if I had the power to protect her from all the unspeakable harms that might befall us. In a half-strangled voice, she offered up her litany of fear.

"We shall be ravaged, then our throats shall be slashed, and we'll be left to die without salvation."

"Have courage, my girl," I said, trying to sound brave even as her horrors infected me. "We survived the most dangerous passages in the Rhine and we shall survive this, too."

Nell started at every noise, every rustle and twitch in the leaves. At the sight of sudden movement behind swaying branches, she let out a full-throated scream, nearly causing our horses to bolt to the far hills.

"Wisht, love!" I leaned sideways in my saddle to reach for Nell's hand. "See, it's only a few farm girls gathering mushrooms."

"Keep your voices down, both of you!" Master Donald hissed. "You'll attract every robber in twenty miles."

"Noisy, meddlesome females shall be left behind to their fate," Friar Timothy said, which made Nell go even whiter.

Though hate is a sin, I cannot describe how much I hated that man. Still holding Nell's hand as we rode forward, I endeavored to be as silent as the moss on the trees. Alas, only an hour or so later, both Nell and I lost our nerve and cried out at the racket of wild snorting and pounding hooves. My heart slammed against my breast. Even Master Donald looked like he would give way to panic when, just in front of us, darted a wild boar with a pack of bugling mounted hunters in pursuit. I nearly fell off my horse.

How far away from Lynn I was, beyond the bounds of anything that was familiar or comforting. Never had I known such terror. I wondered if my fear of all these unknown lurking dangers would be enough to slay me. Would I ever feel safe again? And poor Nell. At least I had freely chosen this journey, unlike this twenty-year-old girl dragged along at my behest. What if we did come to a bad end and I was to blame for her ruin? With all my heart, I wished I could protect her and give her fortitude.

As for my beloved map, so gorgeously painted and gilded, it soon proved to be of no practical assistance in negotiating this labyrinth of forest. Instead, we pressed onward and asked the way at each farmstead, but the people spoke an impenetrable dialect that even Rupert, the most learned among us, could not comprehend.

This was how we came to find ourselves benighted in the forest without shelter or food.

"All thanks to Margery and her ridiculous map," Friar Timothy said. "That will teach us to trust a woman to show us the way."

"We should have traveled with the merchants and remained in safety," I responded tartly, but neither Timothy nor Master Donald deigned to reply.

We managed to make a small fire and it was all I could do to keep the friar from using my map as kindling. The men agreed to take turns guarding our camp through the night while we women huddled in a heap, not daring to let one another out of our sight even though Edith had practically stopped speaking to me. Cecily was rigid with fear while Nell wept inconsolably in her terror that bandits would sweep down and murder us.

"I'm sorry," I whispered, curling up to my maid, trying to still her sobbing as she clung to me as though I were her mother. "Truly, I'm sorry."

The forest rang and echoed with all the sinister denizens of night. Owls hooted and wolves howled long and lonely, making me quail. Father Spryngegold's most terrifying sermons danced through my head with visions of demons teeming in the darkness all around. I slept with my fists wound tightly around my staff, prepared to use it as a weapon if needs must, to defend Cecily, Edith, and Nell, should any man or beast befall us. It seemed the very least I could do.

I was never so happy in all my days to see the light of dawn seep through the whispering boughs. Raising myself on one elbow, I rejoiced to find myself and my companions unscathed. Quietly rising and leaving the other women to their slumber, I crept off into the forest for my ablutions.

For the first time I saw this forest not as a thing of danger but exquisite beauty. Everything was so pristine, like the first day of creation, dew glistening upon each leaf, pine cone, and berry. Red-capped mushrooms bejeweled the mossy ground, as soft and luxurious as a Turkish carpet.

I came upon what appeared to be a suitably private place ringed by elder trees when the hairs on my nape stood on end. Footsteps rushed up behind me. Before I could even turn to confront my pursuer, hands shoved between my legs from behind.

"White clothes," a gruff voice said. "We'll see how pure you are."

The friar's voice. Thick with hate. It was not bandits I needed to fear but my fellow pilgrims.

However, the friar had not reckoned on my voice. My screams rent the dawn and set the birds flapping from the trees. He hadn't reckoned on my staff swinging out to knock him to the ground.

"For shame!" I thundered as I stood over him. "You're no man of God!"

At that, I set off running only to collide with Nell, Cecily, and Rupert who had come in answer to my cries. Nell wrapped her arms around me and held me fast while I wept loudly enough to awaken Adam from his grave. Oh, to think of the vows I'd made to God and Julian and the countless miles I'd traveled only to discover I must live in mortal terror of a friar who was meant to be the holiest soul among us, worthy of turning bread and wine into the body and blood of Our Lord.

The others soon appeared and looked at me in bafflement before turning their gaze on the friar who lay winded among the ferns.

"That friar," I told my fellow pilgrims, "is a wicked, *despicable* fornicator. No woman is safe around him."

Nell stared at her feet and looked miserable while the others, apart from Cecily and Rupert, exchanged uncomfortable glances, as if not knowing whether to trust my word against an ordained cleric.

With great effort, Friar Timothy hauled himself up from the ground. Brushing off his fine fur cape, now filthy with mud and crushed fern, he pointed at me as though unleashing God's wrath upon me.

"Margery Kempe," he said with great contempt, "is a lewd whore. It was she who attacked me! Woe betide the man who believes a single word she says."

He stalked away, his head held high, leaving me to quake in dread. I would never live this down — the man would stop at nothing to wreak his vengeance on me. No matter what I said in my defense, most would hold his word above mine. Edith stared at me in disgust, as though the friar had proved that her worst suspicions about me had been absolutely correct.

But Rupert remained steadfast, as did Cecily, who hugged me and whispered in my ear, "Next time you go into the woods to relieve yourself, I'll come along and stand guard."

By now we were muzzy-headed with hunger. I feared we might be lost in that forest for all eternity, but somehow we found our way to a road that led to a hamlet where we could buy food and drink. From there, we came to a place where we could safely ford the river, then we reached a town with a proper inn where we could spend the night.

Master Donald said we must give thanks for our deliverance by sharing a lavish meal in celebration. He paid for this feast himself, perhaps hoping to smooth over the enmity between Friar Timothy and me, and thus restore our group to harmony and good cheer. For my part, I was especially anxious not to offend Master Donald, for it was he who carried my gold.

But Friar Timothy declared he would not deign to join us unless I sat at the very foot of the table, far below the salt, as if I were the lowliest in our group. He wanted to signal my disgrace. He would have me sit below my own maid. Perhaps he thought I would make a fuss about this, giving him yet another excuse to condemn me. Yet I managed to outfox him by consenting without a murmur as though I were the model of Christian meekness. In truth, it served my purpose to keep as much distance from that hateful friar as possible. From my vantage point, I observed how successful he had been in turning the others against me.

"That will teach her not to slander an honorable man," the blacksmith said.

"And spare the rest of us the racket she makes," the baker said. "It's enough to make my teeth fall out!"

Edith laughed, but Cecily cast me a troubled glance. I lowered my eyes and tried not to let this vile talk get the better of me. These were just words, not the violence of a physical attack.

Meanwhile, the handsome young blacksmith kept filling Nell's wine cup.

"Think of what poor Nell must endure," he said. "Having to serve such a dreadful woman."

Nell froze. She was clearly besotted with the man, yet she looked at me helplessly, as though she were being torn apart by something too powerful to escape. At first she remained silent while the others degraded me, but as the blacksmith pressed more wine on her, she began to laugh along with them. To think that only the night before she had clung to me and wept in my arms.

The bitter truth dawned on me — Nell was playing a game of self-preservation. Now that I had become a pariah, she clearly believed that her safety and survival hinged on winning the men's favor. It seemed she feared that if she stood by me she, too, risked being cast out and left to fend for herself in a foreign land.

Cecily quietly got up and drew me away from the table.

"Come, my friend," she said. "We don't need to listen to them insult you."

Cecily and I retired to our room and gave Nell no choice but to follow us. Despite the humiliations of the dinner table, I was grateful beyond words to sleep in a proper room with a bed and a door that bolted. And a chamber pot, so I wouldn't have to risk going out in the night. All I wanted was to sleep in peace in the safety of other women. The rest of our party stayed up late to carouse, but even their racket couldn't keep me from my slumber, so exhausted I was by my ordeal in the forest.

Later, I awakened with a lurch to hear someone pounding on the main door. A late-arriving traveler, I assumed. I heard the landlady open the door and ask his business, then I heard the others, still at the table with their wine, shout his name as though they knew him. As though they were welcoming back a long-lost friend.

"Hugh! You've joined us at last!"

I stiffened, as though bracing myself for a blow. *Please let this be a horrible dream.*

Beside me on the pallet, Nell uncurled her slender body. She threw on her mantle and crept barefoot from the room. After she had left, I groped through the dark and bolted the door fast.

Hugh, Nell's old and true love, had now returned to her. I heard their muffled laughter as they climbed the stairs and entered an attic chamber directly above our room.

The next morning, having scarcely slept, I donned my white gown and descended the stairs to where the others had gathered for breakfast. Once again, I took my place at the foot of the table, hoping to remain as inconspicuous as possible. At the head of the table in pride of place sat Hugh, as smug as a swine with his snout in truffles. In his lap perched my maid. She slavered all over him and nibbled morsels from his plate. In the course of the breakfast conversation, I learned that Hugh was the friar's cousin and had grown up in the same village as Mistress Edith. Hugh, who had previously been laid up with some illness or other in a nearby hamlet, was now well. Having heard we were staying at this inn, he'd decided to join our party. So popular he was with the others, the blacksmith gracefully surrendered his own claims on Nell.

I did what I could to rein in Nell, reminding her that her duties and her pay were with me. The following night in the next hostel some fifteen miles down the road, I insisted she sleep with me and Cecily, and be present to attend me in the morning.

When I awakened after fitful sleep, I found Cecily had gone down to breakfast ahead of me. But Nell stood over the bed with an ugly smirk on her face. At this early hour, her breath stank of wine.

"Shall I help you dress, good mistress?"

From the other side of the door, I heard a snigger. No doubt Hugh was spying through the keyhole.

Nell held up my precious and dearly won white gown. The bottom of the skirt had been sliced off so it came to only my knees. I reached to grab my cloak to hide the shame, but it had disappeared. Instead, Nell held out a canvas made of shaggy sackcloth, rough and scratchy enough to raise boils on my skin. It was redolent of Hugh's foul stench. I imagined a priest had made him wear this sackcloth for some penance or other.

"Master Hugh and Friar Timothy thought you would look much holier in this," Nell said, before dissolving into helpless giggles while Hugh guffawed from his place at the keyhole.

Momentarily forgetting that I was supposed to be meek and humble and turn the other cheek, I opened the door with such speed and force that I knocked my tormentor to the floor. Gathered around him were the friar, the blacksmith, and the shipman, all of them roiling in laughter until they noticed that in opening the door so suddenly I'd bashed Hugh's ugly snout and given him a horrific nosebleed.

Standing as tall as I could in my wrecked gown, I looked every one of them in the eye.

"You vulgar blockheads," I said coldly. "You asses to crown all asses, screaming your hee-haws."

Before I could slam the door and bolt it, Hugh scrambled to his feet and lurched upon the threshold, forcing me back. I grabbed hold of my pilgrim's staff and clutched it for strength.

"The devil take you, Margery Kempe." He swiped at the blood gushing from his nostrils.

"Not only is she a lying whore," the friar said, squaring his shoulders and taking his place beside his cousin. "But she's a violent, unpredictable lunatic. I say we should banish her."

I couldn't speak, only stare at them in horror. Surely they couldn't just abandon me when everyone said how dangerous it was, with bandits lurking in the hills. And what about my golden nobles I had given to Master Donald for safekeeping? I seethed to think of the tax collector pocketing my father's hard-earned gold.

"I'm leaving your service." Nell wriggled past me to stand beside her bloody-nosed brute. "Hugh and me will be married at the next church door, won't we, my sweeting?"

"He already *has* a wife, you gormless goose!" I threw up my arms in exasperation. "But at least *she* had the brains to leave him for a rat catcher."

"I'll not be insulted by you, old bitch!" Hugh shoved Nell away and came at me. "Even if John Kempe wasn't man enough to shut you up, I will. The devil's death overtake you!"

He whipped my pilgrim's staff from my hand and raised it high overhead. I could already imagine my skull cracking from the blow. He would murder me so suddenly that I would die unshriven. Yet my thoughts were only of Julian. Of how I had already failed in my mission, which would end here ingloriously with my brains scattered on the floor. I imagined the secret compartment in my staff breaking open with the force of the blow, her manuscript pages fluttering out only to be trampled and shat upon by this thug.

Something moved inside me. Some power beyond my feeble human understanding seized me, and before I could blink, I had dived for the chamber pot brimming with the offerings of Cecily, Nell, and me, and flung it in Hugh's face. As he stumbled backward, I grabbed my staff and darted past him out the door and down the stairs into the crowded room below where Cecily awaited me at the table.

"Come, sit beside me," she said cheerfully, patting the space on the bench. "None of this nonsense of cowering at the foot of the table—"

She stopped short at the sight of my ruined gown.

"Margery!" she cried, leaping to her feet. "What in heaven's name?"

Friar Timothy stomped into the room and announced to all present that I was a dangerous madwoman who must be shunned.

"Just look at her," he said. "The slattern's wrecked her own clothing."

"Enough!" I slammed my staff on the wooden floor and appealed to Master Donald. "This friar tried to seduce my maid then tried to ravage me. Everything he says about me is a lie, but because he's a friar, you take his slander for truth. By all the laws of God, you must at least return my gold before banishing me."

"Ignore her," Friar Timothy said, as sly as any serpent. "How do we know the money's even hers? She might have stolen it or earned it by sinful means." He cast a withering eye at my shortened gown, inviting all the men and women present to view me as a harlot.

Panic hammered inside me. Could they truly ruin my clothing, cast me out, take my gold, and leave me stranded?

Master Donald appeared too dumbfounded to say a word though his wife tugged at his sleeve and whispered something in his ear that made his face harden when he looked at me. My heart sank to the pit of my stomach.

Cecily, her face as white as whey, then spoke more forcefully than I'd ever heard her speak before. "If you banish Margery, my brother and I will leave your party as well and take our gold with us!"

Across the table, Michael, her brother, shook his head furiously. "Are you out of your mind? Abandoning the others for the sake of that ridiculous woman?"

I was so astounded, I could not take my eyes off of her. The Cecily I had first met in Zierikzee would never have dared to be so defiant. In her twenty-four years of married life, her husband had chastised her with a birch rod whenever she'd presumed to speak out of turn. But now something steely shone in her eyes. She marched up to Master Donald and held out her hand to take back her gold.

While Donald hesitated, Rupert rose and spoke up in a mighty voice that belied his slight frame.

"There are dire legal consequences for banishing a mayor's daughter and depriving her of her gold," he said gravely, this young man who had studied with the finest scholars in England. "Her people would seek redress against you, Master Donald. They could ruin both your name and your fortune."

My friends' efforts to defend me gave me space to think, and now I stepped forward and spoke with as much dignity as I could muster with my knocking knees bared for all to see.

"At least let me continue with the group as far as Constance," I said, judging that we must be only a few days away if we kept to the main road and didn't get lost or waylaid. As for breaking away from the group and traveling with just Rupert, Cecily, and her brother, that would be putting my friends in unnecessary danger. I remembered that

Julian had told me to seek out one Christopher Hope in Constance—a papal legate. Surely he would be able to help me. "Once in Constance, I will seek out other travel companions."

Cecily appeared crestfallen. I ran to embrace her.

"Thank you," I whispered.

Back in our room, Cecily and I cleaned up the mess from the shattered chamber pot. After washing my hands, I rummaged through my belongings in despair. How on earth would I cope on the journey to Constance? I knew in my soul that Hugh would have murdered me if I hadn't hurled the piss pot in his face. On a more immediate level, how would I endure a long day's ride in my shortened gown? People would take me for a simpleton or a whore.

A sudden notion inspired me to drop down on my knees and peer beneath the bed where I found Nell's bundle. I tore it open to find my white cloak and the cloth she had cut off my skirt. Fetching my sewing kit, I stitched my gown back together.

The rest of our journey to Constance was fraught and tense. To insure my safety, Rupert watched over me by day and Cecily clung to me by night. I did my best to avoid even making eye contact with Friar Timothy. As for Hugh, he couldn't come within ten paces of me without having to be forcibly restrained by at least two other men.

12

Y FIRST GLIMPSE OF Constance four days later was enough to lift me for one fleeting moment far above my travails. How magnificent it was, that city of six thousand perched at the confluence of the High Rhine and a lake that seemed to stretch as wide as the sea. The vast water sparkled with fishing boats. Beyond the city, on the far horizon, rose vineyards, forests, and fields, and the foothills of the Alps.

To enter Constance, we first had to pay our toll to cross the bridge over the Rhine, the only one in many miles. The cost of bringing our horses was so expensive, we chose to sell them at the nearby horse market—for a much lower price than the fortune we had paid for them. I made sure to pocket the money—a pittance though it was—in case Donald refused to return my gold. Crossing the bridge, Cecily and I walked arm in arm toward the towering Rhine Gate leading into the city.

Instead of allowing our party to pass, the gatekeeper demanded to know our business. I panicked at the thought that we would be barred from entering, that I would be at the mercy of Hugh and Friar Timothy with no safe refuge in sight. Or was it simply that the gatekeeper expected us to grease his palms with silver before letting us in?

"We are but simple pilgrims," Rupert told the man. "On our way to Holy Jerusalem."

"You'll not find much in the way of accommodation here if that's what you're after," the gatekeeper said. "A great Church Council is underway. Bishops and cardinals and even the Holy Roman Emperor are in residence. The inns are full. But you might find room at Saint Jodocus's Soul House. Or else try your luck at Haus zur Katz."

Rupert duly translated for the group, adding, "The Soul House is what they call the Poor House."

Edith was aghast. "What? Bed down with beggars and invalids?"

"Perhaps this Haus zur Katz is more reputable," Rupert said, anxiously herding us through the gate before the gatekeeper changed his mind.

Somewhat unsettled as to what lay in store, I followed the others down the streets that heaved with an even denser crowd that I had seen in York during the Corpus Christi Mysteries. For fear of being lost in the press of bodies, I held on to Cecily and Rupert. At least I could take comfort in the fact that Hugh wouldn't be able to murder me here — there would be far too many witnesses.

As well as clerics of every rank, I saw more prostitutes than I could count. They spoke all manner of languages and had undoubtedly traveled from far and wide to profit from this commerce.

"Good afternoon to you, sweet damsels!" Friar Timothy called, making eyes at the women as they passed, but they shook their heads dismissively as though he was far too lowly and unkempt to be worth their while.

A free imperial city subject only to the Holy Roman Emperor, Constance was the richest city I had ever seen, situated as it was at the intersection of trade routes between Germany, Italy, France, and Eastern Europe. The market stalls sold fur, linen, and exotic spices from the Levant. The city was also the seat of a prince-bishop and an imperial elector. It seemed only fitting that an important religious council should convene here.

The bishops and cardinals had requisitioned a former granary as their meeting house, and it thronged with clerics and secular authorities passing in and out of the doors.

"They're going to elect a new pope to end the schism," Rupert told me.

Currently, there were three rival popes — one in Rome, one somewhere in Provence, and an antipope in Pisa. I hoped that this papal election would inspire a sense of unity once more and end the vicious talk of heresy and division.

Rupert, meanwhile, asked passersby the way to the Haus zur Katz. They regarded us most quizzically but pointed out the direction just the same. We crossed the fish market, then walked beneath a narrow arch into a street where I sighted a handsome stone building with an oriel window over the grand double doors. This might have been a guild house, it looked so respectable — a far finer accommodation than I had expected. But before I could take another step, I noticed how the residents of this quarter looked askance at us as if we didn't belong here. The men, I noted, were curiously dressed and wore their hair in long curling locks on either side of their faces.

Master Donald cursed. "The gatekeeper sent us to the Jewish quarter!"

He pointed to the street name painted on the side of a bathhouse —Judengasse.

I could only stare in astonishment at the people going about their business—I'd never before seen a Jew in all my life. They had been banished from England more than a century ago, yet they made their home here in this bustling street with its workshops, bake houses, booksellers, and apothecaries. I watched a group of women, their heads together as they laughed and gossiped. A midwife leaned out of a third-story window to hang her freshly laundered delivery cloths. A little boy chased a stray hen down the street. It was so commonplace and familiar and yet so different from anything I knew. My eyes rested on a churchlike building with five arched stained glass windows.

"Is that their synagogue?" I whispered to Rupert.

He nodded, then pointed out the small indentations on the right doorpost of every house in that street. Each held a piece of parchment.

"A profession of their religion," he whispered.

We were interrupted by Edith yammering that we couldn't sleep in a Jewish inn, for surely they drank the blood of Christians and would slit our throats in the night. Before we could cause further disturbance, Rupert hurried us back toward the cathedral.

The Cathedral of Our Lady's soaring spire of filigreed sandstone looked like the handiwork of angels rather than stonemasons. When we stepped inside, Cecily marveled at the ornate spiral staircase in the northern transept that looked as though it would lead to heaven itself.

But my thoughts were weighted by more earthly matters. I had to find Christopher Hope. Julian had said that he lived in the cathedral presbytery with the provosts. Since he was such an important man, I feared Master Christopher would be far too busy with the Council to have any time for me. Nonetheless, I summoned my nerve and asked the church warden where I might find him. The warden led me to the Lady Chapel where I saw my countryman praying. He seemed to have a troubled air, as if something pressed heavily on his soul. Cecily, Rupert, and I knelt and offered up our own devotions until Master Christopher had finished and saw me waiting to speak to him.

My friends stepped away to give me my privacy as I approached this eminent man, a doctor of philosophy as well as a papal legate. He looked to be about fifty, with grizzled hair and a careworn expression, but his eyes were kind.

"Good day to you, Reverend Sir." I dropped in a curtsy. "Dame Julian of Norwich told me to seek you in this city."

As in Zierikzee, Julian's name had the power of a secret key. Master Christopher's face transformed completely, blazing in joy and welcome.

"Well met, good mistress," he said, taking my hand.

"I have something from Julian to pass on to you." I dropped my voice to a whisper and wondered how I could take the manuscript pages from my staff without attracting attention. "Her book. She thought you would want to copy it."

A look of terror seized his face. "It's far too dangerous," he whispered. "Never mention it again while you're in this city, do you understand?"

While he spoke, he took my elbow and directed me to the shriving bench where I duly knelt as though to confess my sins.

"Is this thing you mentioned well concealed?" Master Christopher whispered.

I nodded.

He cut me off before I could speak. "Keep your secret to yourself. It's safer for both of us if I remain in ignorance. It will be dark soon, so you must spend the night in Constance. I shall ask the Dominican Sisters to find a bed for you in their priory. But tomorrow you will leave as early as possible and hurry on your way with all speed. Do nothing to draw attention to yourself."

"Good sir, if I am to continue my journey at all, I need your help." I spoke urgently, no longer bothering to whisper. "My traveling companions will no longer have me in their group. Two of them have even threatened me with violence. But I fear they won't return the money I gave them for safekeeping."

His brow furrowed. "I will do what I can. But you must promise to do as I say."

I nodded fervently yet couldn't resist asking why. "Surely if the Council is here to elect a new pope," I said, whispering once more, "they shall be far too busy to trouble themselves with an English-woman in her middle years."

His brown eyes clouded. "They're not just here to elect a pope," he whispered. "They've seen how Lollardy has spread through England, and they're fearful it could happen here—Wycliffe's writings have attracted many followers in the universities across Europe. The prelates are intent on uprooting heresy wherever they see it—or *think* they see it. There's an accused heretic—a priest from Bohemia—on trial in the cathedral chapter house as we speak. But enough of this. Let me talk to your companions."

"Welcome, pilgrims!" Master Christopher was the picture of warmth and ebullience when he went to greet our group. "Come, let me invite you to dine with me."

He led the way to his favorite tavern in the Haus zum Pilgerstab, the House of the Pilgrim's Staff. There, in an upper room reserved for distinguished guests, we sat together at a long table. Master Donald insisted that our host sit in honor at the head of the table whereas I, once again, sat at the foot despite Cecily's invitation to sit beside her. Master Christopher raised his eyebrows but said nothing.

My companions devoured the succulent roast goose, but I abstained from meat, as always, and ate from the other dishes—the barley pottage, the wild mushrooms cooked in butter, the bread, and the baked quinces. I kept my mouth shut while Friar Timothy and Master Donald fell over themselves to flatter Master Christopher and curry his favor.

"I hear there's a heretic priest on trial," the friar said. "Jan Hus, a goose farmer's son. Doesn't his surname even mean goose in his native tongue?" He pointed his knife at the mangled goose carcass on the table. "Soon he shall roast as well, no doubt."

A look of pain crossed Christopher's face, but he made no comment and changed the subject. "Why must that woman sit below all the rest of you and keep silent while you chatter freely?"

Nell had the grace to squirm and look uncomfortable, but Friar Timothy grew belligerent. "Good sir, she's a hideous claptrap. If we allow her to speak, she slanders and lies like the wanton harlot she is. And what a hypocrite! Look at her, making such a show of refusing good meat and it's not even a fasting day."

"We've wanted to be rid of her for some time," Master Donald said. Drunk on the good wine, he finally revealed his true intentions. Some struggle I'd have getting him to return my gold. "We've only kept her on out of Christian mercy."

I bit my tongue.

"That witch abandoned a good man and their children to wear white clothes and swan across Europe like some saint," said Hugh. "But she's as wicked and vile as any whore walking the streets."

Hugh would have gone on for some length, only Christopher held up his hand to silence him before looking down the table to me. "What do you say to this, good mistress? Do you wish to continue your travels with these people or will you allow me to help you make other arrangements?"

"Good sir," I said, straightening my spine. "I would be most grateful for your assistance."

"It would be my pleasure, dear lady." Christopher smiled. "By all the saints, I hope you shall soon find yourself in more honorable company than these crude drunken louts."

"Good riddance to her then," Master Donald muttered.

"There's still the matter of my seventeen golden nobles," I called out, rising from my seat at the bottom of the table.

Master Donald's face curdled, and I could tell a riposte was on his tongue. So he had indeed been plotting to oust me and pocket my gold. But before he could say a word, Master Christopher spoke with the full weight of his authority as papal legate. "Master Donald, you *will* return the lady's money. You have your purse with you now, I see. I bid you to count out seventeen golden nobles and return them to Mistress Margery. By God's grace, your ill manners shall never trouble this poor woman again."

As Donald begrudgingly counted out the coins, I marched to the head of the table to take what was mine.

"Anon, I must leave you," I told my fellow pilgrims. Not for one second did I trust to be left with them out of Master Christopher's sight, for these men would surely try to take my gold back by force. "This good man has offered to escort me to my lodgings."

"He found lodgings for *her* while *we* must sleep in the Soul House?" Mistress Edith seemed to view this as the greatest insult of all.

I kissed Cecily's cheek and implored Rupert and her brother to keep her safe. "Watch that friar as you would a snake!" I told them.

Seizing my bundle and staff, I then dashed down the stairs with Master Christopher. We darted down a series of alleys and rear passageways so we couldn't easily be followed.

When we emerged at the arched door of the Dominican Priory of Saint Catherine of Alexandria, he pounded breathlessly until the portress opened up with great reluctance, but her anger melted when she saw the pleading expression on Master Christopher's face.

He spoke to her in German before turning to me. "I've asked the good Sister to give you a bed for the night. I shall send a guide to collect you in the morning. God go with you, Margery Kempe."

At that, he vanished into the dark before I could even thank him.

Despite the late hour, Regula, the prioress, was gracious enough to receive me in her parlor. She served me caudled white wine spiced with white pepper and rosemary, and offered me a tray of sweetmeats.

"It's not every night that Christopher Hope comes pounding on our door to ask us to take in a stranger," she said mildly.

A high-learned woman of around thirty years, she was fluent in several languages, including English. All the Sisters here were expected to study and develop their intellect.

"You must be special, indeed, Mistress Margery," she said with gentle humor. "With your white clothes, you could be one of us."

Regula's Dominican habit consisted of a white tunic, scapula, and wimple. Only her veil was black.

I hesitated, wondering how much I should reveal. Master Christopher had indicated that I should tell no one of Julian's manuscript, yet it seemed I owed the prioress an explanation.

"I carry a book written by an English anchoress," I said. "Julian of Norwich. Master Christopher was worried I would be in great danger should anyone discover it."

I swallowed, aware that I was at the prioress's mercy. She could summon the authorities at once. Instead, she nodded in sympathy.

"English ideas have become incendiary," she said. "No doubt you've heard of that poor Bohemian priest on trial. He's not only spread the teachings of Wycliffe through his native land, but he's also expounded on them with writings of his own. This will not end well." She looked as distressed as Christopher had. "How unfortunate that your visit should coincide with this Council. It's not only Hus's fate up for discussion. The cardinals and bishops are debating whether the canonization of Saint Bridget of Sweden should be confirmed, owing to the controversy of the Bridgettine Order."

I shook my head in confusion. "How could enclosed nuns cause such controversy?"

"Their order welcomes reformed prostitutes," she said. "Some have even risen to the office of abbess. Some men in the Church think that such women have no business in holy orders and wish to force them back on the streets."

Regula and I both fell silent in somber contemplation of those women's uncertain destiny.

"But enough about the Council," Regula said. "How exciting that you're traveling to Jerusalem. Please tell me of your journey."

She smiled, her dark eyes keen and curious. A woman of such intelligence confined in these cloistered walls, Regula sounded both wistful and faintly envious. She listened as though spellbound as I described my adventures, particularly my time with the beguines in Zierikzee.

"This community was once a beguinage," she said. "Then it grew to have so many women and so much influence that the prince-bishop thought it best that we accept the authority of the Dominican Order and become enclosed nuns. That took place more than a hundred years ago. The Dominicans are the Order of Preachers—but only as far as our male brethren are concerned. They travel far and wide to spread the message of God. We nuns must support their efforts through our silence and prayers." Her voice rang with longing for the great world. "May I take a look at Dame Julian's manuscript? I give you my word I will keep your secret."

Aware of the risk this posed to us both, I removed the manuscript from my staff and told her of Julian, a humble woman whose visions had emboldened her to write of divine love.

Regula pored over the first pages. "A perilous thing for a woman to write a book in Latin, let alone her native tongue. This is exquisite! How I wish I could copy it and translate it into German. But Master Christopher is right. It's far too dangerous."

Her eyes looked haunted as she scrolled the manuscript and returned it to its leather cylinder.

"By the grace of God," she said, "I hope your travels will take you to Constance one day when there's no Council meeting here. But when you reach Venice, you must call on my dear friend, Sister Lorenza, at the Priory of Corpus Domini. She would not hesitate to copy Julian's blessed book."

The bells rang the hour of Matins.

"I must join my Sisters in the chapel," Regula said, rising from her chair. "But first let me show you to your room."

I followed her up a flight of stairs and down a narrow corridor to a cell facing the inner courtyard.

"I wish you a good night," Regula said before hurrying down to the chapel.

As I lay myself down in that narrow bed, my heart still pounding from my mad escape that night, I felt more alone than I'd ever been. Powerful people like Christopher and Regula might step in to help me, but ultimately my fate—and that of Julian's manuscript—was in my own hands.

The next morning I arose at Lauds and rushed down to the reception room where I anxiously awaited Master Christopher's guide. *Who*, I wondered, *might my new traveling companions be and how would Christopher find them at such short notice?* One thing was certain—I would have to leave Constance in a hurry to avoid being pursued by Hugh and Friar Timothy, who might try to waylay and rob me. As my tensions mounted, the hours dragged by, the priory bells tolling for Prime and Terce.

Just as Regula came down to inquire whether I wanted to join the Sisters for High Mass, we heard a knock. The portress opened the shutter and peered through before unbolting the massive oak door. When it opened, I saw neither Master Christopher nor a group of pilgrims but a barefoot penitent in a coarse woolen tunic. He was thin and wiry, his face taciturn, his spine as straight as a ship's mast.

My stomach flipped when I recognized Ignatius, the ascetic holy man and father of nine who had separated from our group at Kehl to make his solitary way on foot. How had he traveled so swiftly without a horse? It seemed a miracle. Unless, of course, he had made this journey before and could find his way through the forest without getting lost. Cold uncertainty washed through me. Who *was* this man?

Ignatius seemed just as unnerved to see me. But he addressed me with gruff urgency. "Madam, make haste to depart. Christopher Hope has asked me to guide you across the Alps to Venice."

"Where are the others in your party?" I was quick to ask, my mouth as dry as chalk. *Please let there be at least one other woman.*

"There are no others," he said shortly. "Only me. I bid you change into these." He shoved a pile of mud-colored garments at me. "Your white clothes attract far too much attention."

I stood there, frozen and dazed. Surely Master Christopher didn't expect me to travel alone with this mad zealot who clearly despised all womankind.

"How do I know this isn't some trick and you'll lure me back to Friar Timothy?" I asked.

"Friar Timothy?" Ignatius let out an impatient sigh. "I detest that viper—why do you think I left your group? Hurry, if you please. We haven't much time."

At wit's end, I turned to Regula who watched from the other side of the grille.

"I can't just put my life in the hands of a strange man," I told her.

"I know Master Ignatius and can vouch for his honesty," she said calmly. "I urge you to go with him now. Before it's too late."

While Ignatius stepped outside to give me my privacy, I changed into the roughly woven dirt-colored garments and packed my white clothes in my bundle. Lowering the hood of my cloak to better conceal my face, I seized my staff and set off with this grim man even as fear and misgiving surged through me.

"Why does everyone know you?" I whispered. I had to sprint to keep up with his brisk stride. "And why are you helping me? You don't even *like* me." He had made that much clear on the barge.

He let out a long breath as though I were the most tiresome woman he had yet endured. "I've been traveling these pilgrimage routes nearly twenty years," he said, not looking at me but at the way forward. "God has blessed me with the gift of wayfinding and I've taken it as my penance to guide travelers in need." He stopped short to look me in the eye. "No matter how irksome they might be."

The first thing Ignatius did was take one of my golden nobles and exchange it for a purse of smaller local coins.

"I'll carry this for you and pay for the expenses on our way," he said. "Keep the rest of your gold well hidden. It's best to appear poor and simple."

We had to cross the city to reach Schnetztor, the gate that opened out to the southern road. But the closer we came to the cathedral, the denser the crowd grew until we were caught up in such a throng of bodies pouring in from all sides that any further progress seemed impossible. We were shoved and jostled at the mercy of the mob.

"Stay calm," Ignatius told me.

No easy task, that was. Half the people seemed to be lamenting some terrible injustice while the other half reminded me of angry bay-ing hounds. I heard the word *ketzer* shouted again and again. Then the name *Jan Hus*. Jan Hus, the Bohemian priest and goose farmer's son accused of heresy.

I caught a glimpse of a middle-aged man being marched out of the cathedral. Ignatius forced our way through the crowd to get a better look. It was as if my guide could not help himself.

Jan Hus was clad in his priestly robes, but his hands were bound. A richly attired prelate stood before him and made some loud proclamation in Latin. The only word I understood was *haeresiarcha*. Heretic. The prelate seemed to be giving Hus a chance to recant whatever belief or opinion had condemned him. My heart in my throat, I watched the accused man fall to his knees and pray in Latin.

"What's he saying?" I whispered to Ignatius.

To my shock, Ignatius's face was glazed in tears—he was the last man I had ever expected to see crying. "He's praying for God to forgive his persecutors."

The words of Christ on the cross rippled through me. *Father, forgive them, for they know not what they do.*

The prelates handed Jan Hus over to the secular authorities, who made him stand. They tore off his priestly vestments, stripping him down to his braies, then shoved a paper crown of shame, some eighteen inches high, upon his head. The word *haeresiarcha* was written on it in huge letters, and there were pictures of devils tearing a soul apart. The condemned man endured this with quiet forbearance. I could not stop myself from weeping, for even if this man espoused beliefs that may have been different from mine, it was impossible not to see Christ in him. The more his captors tried to degrade him, the nobler and more dignified he became.

When the executioners slapped shackles on him and prepared to lead him away, Jan Hus looked at me. Looked directly into my eyes as though he could see into the depths of my soul. The way Julian had looked at me. The man smiled as if moved to see me weep for him.

"*Sancta simplicitas,*" he said, two Latin words so plain that even I could understand them. Holy simplicity.

I wished with all my heart that I could summon words to comfort him, but it seemed my tears were enough for him. Then he was wrenched away and marched off toward Schnetztor.

The acrid smell of smoke filled my nose. I turned to see a cloudy black column rising from behind the cathedral.

"Ignatius!" I cried. "The city's on fire!" I imagined all of us in the crowd burning to death along with the condemned man, sharing his passion.

Ignatius shook his head. "No, they're burning Hus's books in the cemetery."

I grabbed my guide's arm as we were pushed along in Jan Hus's wake. It was that or lose him in the fray.

"What did he do to be branded a heretic?" I asked.

"He agreed with Wycliffe on the primacy of the Gospels. He openly preached against the sale of indulgences. He believed that the laity — not just the clergy — are entitled to drink communion wine. He argued against the whole notion of pilgrimage and holy relics. But most dangerously of all," he added, lowering his voice. "He refused to submit to the prelates. He appealed to Christ alone as the supreme judge."

Hearing this, I felt a shock of recognition so sharp that I stumbled. I would have fallen and been trampled to death had Ignatius not yanked me upright. My heart thudded, for Jan Hus's ultimate error was one I, too, was guilty of. I remembered when I had faced down Bishop Repyngdon in Lincoln and called upon Christ's authority above his own in front of all the canons at his table. And this was what Julian had done, writing her book on the primacy of divine love, placing her absolute trust in that love over all her superiors' talk of hell and purgatory. How easily I could be convicted if any of these clerics discovered I carried her writings. But worse, far worse, if I was arrested and sentenced to burn, Julian most likely would be doomed to burn as well even though she was a holy anchoress who had offered up her body and soul to the Church as a living sacrifice. It was only the fact that most people dismissed me as a silly, hysterical woman that had kept me safe thus far.

The guards marching behind Jan Hus carried a great wooden post half a foot thick. Three wagons loaded with firewood and straw trundled behind them. Swept along in the crowd, we squeezed through Schnetztor. Onward this gruesome procession snaked, past farms and pastureland until we reached a meadow halfway between Constance and Gottlieben Castle, seat of the prince-bishop.

Though it was late October, it felt as warm as summer. The sun illuminated everything in her radiance. The harvested fields and vineyards. The orchards and pastures of well-fed cattle and horses. The snowy Alps rose against the southern sky.

In that green meadow starred with gentians as blue as heaven, the men drove the stake into the ground and bound Jan Hus to it with a giant sooty chain that looked as if it had withstood many heretics' burnings. At first, they positioned him so he faced east, the direction of the resurrection, until someone deemed that too good for a man damned to hell. He wasn't even allowed a confessor to give him the last rites. They just shoved him around so he faced west. Hus, meanwhile, calmly called out to the crowd.

Ignatius translated his Latin. "He says, 'Our Lord was bound by a heavier chain than this and I am not ashamed to be bound by this one in his name.'"

Two of the wagonloads of wood and straw were piled around him as high as his neck. But before ordering the fire to be lit, the imperial marshal stepped forward and gave him one last chance to save himself. Jan Hus refused to renege on his convictions.

With grisly efficiency, the executioners kindled the flames, orange and red tongues leaping high. I cried out in horror to see that the men had not even granted Hus the mercy of strangling him before burning him. Still, he remained unbowed. In a clear and beautiful voice, he sang the Kyrie from Mass. *Kyrie eleison. Christe eleison.* Lord have mercy. Christ have mercy.

I broke down sobbing. How could any human being bear such torment, the fire consuming his living flesh? His paper crown and his hair became a halo of flame. As the wind blew the fire into his face, he fell silent, but I swore I saw his lips moving. *He was praying within himself,* I thought. He made no noise. Then he went so still, I could not tell whether he was already dead. Julian's words describing the writings of Marguerite Porete came to mind. *In deep mystical union we cease to exist. We become a part of God.* Marguerite Porete, too, had been burned for daring to trust the authority of God within her own heart. *They can burn me,* she had written. *But they will never burn the truth.*

When the wood burned to ash, Jan Hus's charred remains hung by the chain round his neck. But the executioners were still not finished with him. Using the third wagonload of wood and straw, they set alight his corpse. Circling the fire, they smashed apart Hus's bones with clubs so his corpse would burn more quickly. Finding his head, they shattered it to pieces. When they dug out his heart, they impaled it on a sharpened torch and pierced it with swords until its entire mass burned to ash. Then they loaded Hus's ashes on a cart to dump in the Rhine.

"Lest his followers venerate his remains," Ignatius said, rubbing the tears from his eyes.

Shaken to my depths, I swayed, weak and light-headed. As long as I lived, I would never forget the terror, the smell of burning human flesh.

My breath was labored as I struggled to keep up with Ignatius on a narrow forest path skirting the shore of Lake Constance. We hastened along with none to overhear us but the birds and wild deer.

"What have they done?" It seemed he needed to speak or he would burst. "They invited the poor man to the Council and guaranteed his safety only to arrest him and do *that*."

I bowed my head and crossed myself, too choked to say a word.

"Jan Hus was just one dissenting priest," Ignatius said. "Now they've made him a martyr. Now he will never die."

We reached a lonely farmstead where a fisherman sat on his dock and mended his nets. Looking up, the man greeted Ignatius.

I watched the two men confer in the local dialect. Ignatius opened his purse to pass some coins to the man before turning to gesture for me to follow as he clambered into the boat tied to the dock. The fisherman unmoored the vessel and rowed us out into the blue expanse. Then he lifted sail and the wind, like the breath of God, blew us swiftly eastward.

The three of us sat in mournful silence — it seemed Ignatius had told the fisherman about the execution. Meanwhile, I contemplated the vast blue lake mirroring heaven. How could such evil and brutality exist alongside such heart-stopping splendor?

We traveled a great distance until we came to what appeared to be the lake's southernmost point. In the distance I saw a castle and a fortified town glimmering pink in the evening light. But the boatman moored in an isolated stretch of forest. Ignatius and I clambered ashore, and the boatman sailed silently away.

Up the steep path we scrambled into that forest of massive pine and spruce that looked as if it had never known the bite of an ax. Beneath the densely woven branches, I could hardly see. Daylight was fading fast. Ignatius's cloak blended into the gloom and darkling leaves, which caused my heart to pound in panic that I would lose sight of him and become hopelessly lost in this wilderness. Creatures rustled unseen through the underbrush. I began to fear each shadow was a bear or wolf.

Ignatius took my arm and guided me forward, as though I were a blind woman. His night vision, it seemed, was far better than mine. How perplexing my circumstances had become. I barely knew this man and hadn't a clue where we were going. I didn't know where — or even if — we would be sleeping that night.

I opened my mouth to ask him this question when the trees gave way to a clearing and a house with a candle in the window. Ignatius knocked on the door and a stout woman answered. Like the fisherman, she greeted him by name and opened the door wide to let us in.

It was difficult to make much out by the light of a single candle, but the woman gestured for us to sit at her rustic table, where she served us pottage and heavy black bread. In the dim light, I saw the rest of her family. A thin older man, seated beside the hearth, whittled at some wood while a young woman spun at her distaff. The strong smell of cows came through from the byre built onto their house.

The woman showed me to a bed built into a niche in the wall.

"You'll be sleeping with her and her daughter," Ignatius told me. "I told them you're my sister so they won't think ill of you. We'll set out tomorrow at first light."

"Where are you going?" I asked in alarm when he opened the door.

"I sleep under the sky," he said.

I nodded, remembering how he had slept on the barge deck whatever the weather. I imagined him lying in the grass, staring up at the countless blazing stars. Would either of us sleep after what we had witnessed that day?

13

FTER A SLICE OF dense black bread and a cup of buttermilk, Ignatius and I were out of the farmhouse and on our way before the sun had climbed above the horizon.

Although Ignatius had proven himself trustworthy thus far, I could not get over my sense of unease, traveling alone with a man I barely knew, especially one as brooding and unfathomable as he. If only he would talk more, I might have come to know him better. But he spent most of his time in silence, speaking only when necessary. When I tried to strike up a conversion, he revealed himself only sparingly. Yet what I did come to learn struck me with awe. In his years of wandering, he had traveled the length and breadth of Christendom, from Santiago de Compostela to Jerusalem, Mount Sinai, and Alexandria. He'd traversed the Alps more than two dozen times in every season and all weather.

"Will you ever return home to England?" I asked as we forded a brook.

He winced as though I'd wounded him. "I've no home left in England. The path I walk is now my home."

I remembered the story Cecily had told me of how he'd blamed himself for his young son's death—surely that must have transpired many years ago if he'd been walking these pilgrimage paths for two decades, as he claimed. I thought of the wife and daughters he had left behind. Even I, for all my waywardness, couldn't imagine not seeing my children for twenty years.

We didn't travel by the main roads or well-traveled pilgrim routes but by the obscure and narrow ways he knew by heart.

I had never walked over such steep terrain or at such a pace over such a distance in my life. If I complained of blisters, he made me remove my shoes and plunge my bare feet into an icy mountain stream until they were numb. Then he bandaged my feet in clean rags, I tugged on my shoes, and off we trotted.

"This ordeal is our penance," he said sternly as we clambered up an impossibly steep slope that sparkled with mineral-threaded rock. He was so self-punishing, he climbed up that sheer rocky expanse barefoot.

As the days wore on, the journey did not get easier, only steeper and colder. Snow fell and made the paths ever more treacherous. I was perpetually exhausted, my every muscle shrieking in pain even when I lay down to sleep at the farmhouse or hospice where we sheltered for the night. Everyone we stayed with knew Ignatius from his previous journeys, and because of this, they treated us well. But there was no rest, just one long hard march after the next, for Ignatius was determined to get us through the mountains before the worst of the winter weather blasted down. I was grateful that he at least slept indoors when it snowed so I wouldn't have to fret about him perishing.

One icy night high in the mountains, I dreamt I was back home in Lynn, cuddled in bed with little Juliana in my arms, and I was just as content as that sleepy little girl, all my restless longing to travel lulled into stillness and peace, as though God were singing me a lullaby. I was utterly safe. John respected my calling and troubled me no more. There was nothing to flee. I kissed my daughter's sweet brow, which smelled just like freshly baked bread. Then an awful noise wrenched me from my sleep.

I awakened in the pilgrims' hospice in Bivio, where I was the only female guest. The noise sounded again and again as if there would be no end to it. The crack of a whip splitting flesh, yet no cry followed, either human or animal, and that terrified me even more.

With shaking hands, I opened the heavy wooden shutters, then shivered as bitter cold air flooded the already frigid room. But what I saw through that open window chilled me to my core. Ignatius knelt in the stained snow. Stripped to his waist, he scourged himself over and over. In the moonlight, the blood cascading down his scarred back looked as dark as ink.

I laced up my boots and threw on my cloak before unbolting the hospice door and floundering through the deep snow.

"Ignatius!" I cried. "For the love of God, please stop."

Blind and deaf to me, the man went on flagellating himself, his mouth clamped shut so he could utter no cry. A penitent's whip is normally made of rope or string with seven knots for the seven deadly sins, but Ignatius's was made of cruel, sharp leather. I feared that if I didn't stop him he would either bleed to death or freeze.

With a strength I didn't know I possessed, I wrenched the cursed whip from his hands. Only then did he open his mouth. How he cursed me, his face a mask of fury. But I was swift on my feet and tore away from him, heading straight for the precipice on which the hospice was built. I hurled that whip over the cliff edge where it would be lost in the ice and snow. Clutching the stone wall for support, I tried to catch my breath.

Like a man possessed by demons, Ignatius railed and bellowed at me. He sounded so fearsome, I didn't blame the few other guests for cowering in their beds instead of venturing out to investigate. Gulping down a prayer, I grabbed Ignatius's shoulders and shook him until his head snapped back and he stopped shouting. Now it was my voice that rent the night.

"What kind of ungodly priest inflicted such a penance on you?" I asked, my voice raw with rage.

His face crumpled. "No priest. I have taken this on myself."

"But why?" I seized his hands before he could find some other way to punish his flesh. "If God can forgive all, why do this to yourself?"

"God might forgive my sins," he said in a choked voice. "But I can't."

I led him back inside and sat him down before the fire where I cleaned and bandaged the bloody welts that crisscrossed his back like the countless paths on which he had guided pilgrims.

"You blame yourself for your son's death," I said. "But surely that innocent child is with God."

Still weeping, he confessed how in his old life, when he'd drunk to excess and lived only for pleasure, he had taken his ten-year-old son hunting even though the boy was afraid of horses and terrified of jumping hedges and walls. Ignatius had insisted the boy ride along, thinking to make a bold man of him, only his son's pony shied at a deer and the boy fell to his death, breaking his slender neck. His wife's hair had gone white with grief. She barred Ignatius from her chamber and his daughters shunned him, too. Filled with self-loathing, he had set off on his penitent's journey, never to return.

"If I were your priest," I said, shocking myself with my blasphemy for daring to say such a thing as a woman, "this is the penance I would give you."

Ignatius lifted his sorrowful eyes to mine. "Tell me, Margery."

"You must forgive yourself," I said. "Just as God has already forgiven you."

I insisted that Ignatius give himself at least one day to recover from his self-inflicted wounds. The following morning, we set off to cross the Septimer Pass.

The sky was still black. The waning moon illuminated our way as we hiked up the white road, which was indistinguishable from the snowy meadows flanking it. Only wooden stakes set a spear's length apart marked the route. If we lost our way at this elevation, not even Ignatius would be able to save us.

Up and up we marched, climbing the mountain's rugged brow. The wild summit loomed before us. The fiercest wind I'd ever known scoured my face and threatened to knock me down. Yet I didn't cower or lag behind but kept pace with Ignatius, walking shoulder to shoulder with him as though I were every bit as intrepid as he. Lurching along, I entered a realm where cold, pain, and strenuous effort blurred into one. Ignatius had said that our pilgrims' journey, with all its perils and hardships, was our penance. But even more so, I thought this pilgrimage was our redemption. While still a wife in Lynn, I had never dreamt of scaling such heights. It seemed we were approaching the top of the world. Moonlight washed the snow in silver radiance, suffusing everything in an eerie, unearthly beauty. *Angels could live here.*

By and by, the road flattened. We had reached the top of the pass. Lifting my face to offer a prayer of thanksgiving, I cried out to see an ineffable burst of radiance appear over the white mountain. The rising sun. We carried on around a snowy bend.

What I saw next made me clutch Ignatius's sleeve. The road descended into a long forested valley. Beyond that rose a ring of the tallest mountains I had ever seen, jagged granite spearheads that looked as though they touched heaven. Surely seraphim danced on those peaks. I had never imagined that such beauty existed. Even the sun seemed to shine more brightly on this side of the pass.

Ignatius's smile was almost as blinding. "That's our way to fair Italy. It's all downhill now. We don't have to cross the other mountain chain but only follow the valley to Milan."

The descending path was so steep, it hurt my knees. Ignatius made sure we went slowly and that I was tethered to him by a rope around my waist in case I slipped and fell. He told me tales of entire trains of pack mules tumbling to their deaths on trails like these. We clambered down a stony gully beside a frozen waterfall, then entered a pine forest that sheltered us from the wind.

In the mellow light of late afternoon, we reached Casaccia.

14

N THE JOURNEY, I had passed as Ignatius's sister for propriety's sake. Now I had come to feel a true affinity with this man, as if we were indeed blood kindred. Our travels had left me just as lean, sinewy, and weather-beaten as he. I might have gained a few wrinkles and gray hairs from the rigors of our alpine crossing, but my body felt younger and so powerful. The freedom of the open skies and the endless vista of the unfurling road nourished me deep into my bones. I grew accustomed to sleeping on hard ground—more than once Ignatius and I sheltered for the night in lonely wayside chapels where roughhewn statues of saints watched over us. I could effortlessly walk fifteen or more miles a day, up and down hills. Could hitch up my skirts and ford bitterly cold streams. Ignatius taught me how to kindle a campfire and chew on herbs if that was all we had to still our hunger.

Despite the many hardships, I had come to savor this wanderer's life. I thought that John and my children would no longer recognize me, my face burned brown by the sun reflected off the snow. After crossing the Alps, Ignatius and I pressed on toward Venice.

Many a tale Ignatius had told me of how beautiful Venice was, that mirage of a city rising from the lagoon, that fabled republic with canals for streets and waves for ramparts. When our ferry approached San Marco, ghostly white fog shrouded the grand churches and palazzi. Clinging mist muffled and distorted the murmur of ever-flowing water.

The Venetians themselves were as stunning as angels. The ladies' headdresses, fashioned of the sheerest silk, seemed to only accentuate their elaborately dressed hair that was meant to be hidden beneath. Such rare perfumes they wore. Though we were in the depths of winter with a bitter wind whipping off the lagoon, they smelled like a garden in high summer, redolent of rose and myrtle.

After I had found lodgings at the guesthouse of the Dominican Sisters of Corpus Domini, I had expected to bid farewell to my dear guide, but Ignatius stayed on for several days to show me around the city's churches, which housed some of the most precious relics in Christendom. We knelt in reverence before the grave of Saint Mark the Apostle, the arms of Saint Lucy and Saint George, the heads of Saint Cosmos and Saint Damian, Saint Nicholas's pilgrim staff and molar, and the feet of Mary of Egypt. But the images of so many pagan gods on the doges' tombs bewildered me.

"What could be the purpose of such art?" I asked Ignatius. "To create confusion in people's minds?"

"You had better get used to the unfamiliar," Ignatius said gently. "Once you reach Jaffa, you'll leave Christendom behind and enter the realm of Saracens."

I couldn't get over the exoticism of Venice. Though a Christian city, it was a window into the East where Christendom ended. Here young wives adorned themselves in precious stones and jewels, and wore low-cut dresses baring their shoulders for the first two years of their marriage, but ever after, they veiled themselves entirely in black, even hiding their faces from view, as though they were widows, though their husbands still lived. What was I to make of this wondrous but riddling city surrounded by waves whose citizens were forced to pay for drinking water, which had to be imported from the mainland? There were no wells in Venice, only cisterns to collect rainwater and these were kept under lock and key.

Ignatius and I walked together along the Piazza San Marco where the pilgrim ships would dock come spring.

"Remember," said Ignatius. "When the time comes to sail, you must choose the best ship. Some of those tubs are wrecks, so take care.

Be sure to bring enough fresh water, because if you run out or if you have to drink polluted water, you could die. I will pray for your safe travels."

My throat tightened to think that this was our last farewell. "Will you not travel to Jerusalem with me?" I asked, hoping against hope. How I had come to trust this man.

Ignatius sadly shook his head. "Every mortal has his weakness and sea journeys are mine. The last time I traveled in one of those galley boats to the Holy Land, I contracted the bloody flux and nearly perished." His face turned green at the memory.

I trembled, for if such a journey had nearly killed one as stalwart as my friend, how would I fare? Then I remembered my manners, gave Ignatius my hand, thanked him for all his kindness, and wished him well.

Back at the priory, I requested an audience with Suor Lorenza, the high-learned scribe Regula had told me about back in Constance.

The portress beamed. "An Englishwoman has heard of our Lorenza! She is our pride. Such a scholar! She translates Latin texts into Italian so the less educated Sisters can read them. She writes poetry. Our bishop calls her 'our Sappho.'"

"Who is Sappho?" I asked, utterly mystified, thinking this must be some important local saint.

The portress blushed. "She was a pagan poet who lived long ago, the greatest woman to ever hold a quill. Until our Lorenza."

The portress showed me into the library, the biggest I had ever seen, all those leather-bound tomes in Latin and many other languages, some in alphabets unknown to me. The library's desks and tables were crowded with Sisters diligently reading, an essential part of their vocation. Never had I been in the company of so many high-learned women and girls. Such a rarefied place this was — it was as if they lived and breathed scholarship. They seemed to inhabit a different universe from the close-minded prioress of Carrow to whom my poor daughter had sworn fealty. My heart caught to think of Anna. How I wished she were here with me.

The portress led me into the scriptorium, which was swathed in silence but for the scratching of quills on parchment. We found Suor Lorenza scoring a large piece of parchment in preparation for writing. The portress whispered to her, then Lorenza looked up and smiled.

"Welcome, Mistress Margery," she said in English. "Let's go to the refectory where we may speak without disturbing the others."

"How kind of Regula to send you my way," Lorenza said once we were seated in the refectory. "She's a dear friend, though we've never met face-to-face. Instead, we exchange letters and send books back and forth."

What struck me most as I gazed across the table was Lorenza's beauty. She looked no older than twenty-five with full red lips and dark eyes with flecks of amber floating inside them. She was clearly from an elite family, judging from her manners. As a girl, she must have been thronged with suitors.

As we sipped cups of frothy spiced milk, Lorenza told me her story. Her mother had died when she was only three, so Lorenza had been brought up in this priory where her rich and highborn father had placed her, like a jewel in a vault, to keep her pure and unworldly while he hunted down the most prestigious husband for her to advance their dynasty. To Lorenza, the nunnery had always been her home. She had several aunts and cousins who were Sisters here. As a little girl, she could imagine no other life. She was only ten when she learned that her father had betrothed her to marry an English nobleman. A tutor was sent to teach her English. Another tutor taught her courtly dances and the art of falconry. She learned to play the gittern. Meanwhile, the nuns taught her to play the psaltery. They taught her to read and write in Italian, Latin, and Greek. To think and discern. On her fourteenth birthday, her father took her from the priory to their palazzo where she met her bridegroom for the first time.

"He was forty years old," Lorenza said. "He was hideous and had a cruel, spiteful mouth. I burst into tears and said I would never marry him. My father and brother beat me until they broke two of my ribs and I still refused to take that man as my husband. Thinking to punish me, Father threw me back into the priory and said that if I didn't marry the man he'd chosen for me I'd have no other husband but Christ."

My father had given me a similar ultimatum, I reflected, but at least he never beat me.

"Little did Father know that returning here was exactly what I wanted." Lorenza smiled triumphantly. "Living with the Sisters and spending hours in the library. Some lovelorn girls, it's said, elope *from* the nunnery, but I wanted to elope *to* this life. My brother is now a famous architect and philosopher who teaches at the University of Bologna. *This*," she said, stretching out her arms as if to embrace the entire stone-built priory, "is *my* university."

After hearing Lorenza's story, how could I not trust her with Julian's book? I retrieved the leather cylinder containing the manuscript that I now unfurled and laid upon the refectory table.

"Sister Regula in Constance thought you would like to see this," I said. "A book by a holy English anchoress."

I thought how plain Julian's life was compared to that of the Sisters at Corpus Domini. Julian would be astounded to see such achievement, so many books and so much parchment at their disposal. Yet for all my friend's poverty and simplicity, what wisdom flowed from her pen.

"I'll ask the scribes to help me copy this so we can finish before you sail to Jerusalem," Lorenza said. "I shall translate it into Italian later. And I shall have a special copy made as a gift for Regula of Constance."

"Please allow me to help," I said, suddenly inspired. "I'm no scribe, but give me a quill and paper. Surely I can copy a chapter or two."

I spent the better part of winter in the scriptorium bent over the desk until my neck ached and my hand cramped around the quill. Though silence pervaded our scribing, it was not the silence of repression but of deepest concentration. I shall never forget the joy and feverish hunger for knowledge on the Sisters' faces. These were not women who had renounced the pleasures of the world but who had rejected the hell of dynastic marriage and bearing countless babies to men they didn't love. Their holy calling had elevated them to this sanctuary where their intellects could flourish.

15

HIRTEEN WEEKS I STAYED with the Dominican Sisters at Corpus Domini, during which time my Italian was much improved. I could converse with the Sisters and understand most of what they said.

As winter waned, countless pilgrims poured into Venice. The spring processions commenced. I witnessed the doge parading on a fine stallion. Children followed, clad in cloth of gold and carrying chalices of gold and silver. Behind them marched the members of the five city guilds.

At long last, the galley ships arrived. In anticipation of my upcoming journey, I changed my money. When I returned to the priory with the ducats used as currency in the Holy Land, Lorenza greeted me with great excitement.

"Margery, we have such good news! A group of English pilgrims has arrived in our guesthouse. You may travel with them to Jerusalem!"

With rising apprehension, I followed her into the guest parlor where I found a number of my erstwhile companions looking all the worse for wear. My former tormentors, Friar Timothy and Master Donald and Edith, his wife. The baker, shipman, blacksmith, and Master Michael, the yeoman — Cecily's brother. Their mouths flapped open at the sight of me while I could only gape at them in alarm. At least Hugh was conspicuously absent. As was Nell, which made me fear for the poor misguided creature.

I was about to back out of the room and warn Lorenza about the friar's vile ways when, out of an alcove, Cecily came running to embrace me. Rupert followed at her heels.

"God be praised!" she cried, hugging me so hard that she nearly squeezed the air out of my lungs. She took a step back to look me up and down. "How well you look!"

Alas, I could not say the same of her or Rupert. Even when I hugged her, I'd felt how thin she'd grown. Rupert's young face was haggard, as if he had experienced unspeakable hardship. I noticed he wore his plainest clothes, which had grown ragged and threadbare.

"What happened to you both?" I asked.

"We were attacked by bandits crossing the Alps," Cecily said, turning a bitter eye at Master Donald on the far side of the room. "He said that he and the crossbowmen would keep us safe, but the bandits were better armed and they stole his purse with everyone's gold." Then she gave me a secret smile. "Except mine," she whispered. "I sewed it into my hem."

"How clever," I said, vowing to do exactly the same for my onward journey.

"I was not so fortunate," Rupert said mournfully. "I had to sell my books."

Only then did I notice that the others, likewise, had been forced to sell their finery to afford to continue their pilgrimage. Edith's elegant headdress and girdle were no more. Even the friar's considerable girth had dwindled. Gone were his fur cape and double-worsted sleeves. Instead, he wore the simple gray tunic and cowl of the Franciscan order. I'll confess that the sight of his humbling gave me a grim sense of vindication. An ugly scar ran across Master Donald's face from his unsuccessful attempt to ward off the thieves. I almost pitied the man.

When I asked after my truant maid, Cecily turned scarlet and told me of the terrible mischief that had transpired some months back. Hugh was gambling with dice one night and lost all his money. Never one to admit defeat, he accused the other man of cheating. A terrible brawl ensued, resulting in the other man's death. For fear that he would be hanged for murder, Hugh ran away. Nell, the witless cow, went with him. My heart dragged to think of her so far from home and saddled with that thug. If indeed she was still alive. Perhaps in a fit of rage, Hugh had murdered her, too.

My thoughts were cut short by Mistress Edith's noisy, anguished vomiting. Trying to put aside my bitterness at the way she had betrayed me, I rushed to her side.

"What ails you?" I asked. "Did you eat something foul or is it some ague?"

When she jerked upright and I saw her pale, resigned face, I deduced the truth at once. After twelve barren years of marriage, Edith, who had so pined for a baby, was pregnant at last.

"Blessing of blessings!" I cried. "Oh, happy day!"

Edith dropped her head and spewed again, this time on my shoes.

"Never mind that," I said cheerfully. "The Sisters in the infirmary have cat mint and galangal to treat your morning sickness and pickled octopus for your cravings. They'll look after you."

"Fine talk from you, Margery Kempe," she spat tearfully. "*You'll* go gadding off to Jerusalem while I'm left here on my own."

She was certainly in no state to endure the five-week sea journey to the Holy Land.

"But isn't this what you wanted—a baby of your own?" I asked, recalling the kisses she'd lavished on the Baby Jesus doll.

"To be left behind in a foreign nunnery while my husband and everyone else sails off without me?"

I cast a glance at Master Donald, who studiously ignored his wife —tears, vomit, and all—while he played chess with the friar. Edith's self-pity, I conceded, was not entirely unfounded.

Later I convened with Cecily and Rupert in my private quarters.

"I will gladly travel with both of you," I said, while pouring them cups of pale Veneto wine. "But not with that friar. Or Master Donald."

"When you fled that night in Constance, I wanted with all my heart to follow you out that door," Cecily said, tears in her eyes. "My brother said it was too dangerous. But now I swear I'll go with you even if I must part ways with him."

"Is that wise?" I asked, not wanting to come between siblings.

"God favors you," she said. "*You* weren't attacked by bandits."

"To the three of us," Rupert said, lifting his cup. "Maybe even four if Cecily can persuade her brother to join us."

"I think she might persuade him yet," I said, smiling shrewdly at Cecily. "She's the one who carries the gold in her hem."

The following morning, Cecily had not yet worked up the courage to tell her brother that she intended to break ranks and travel with Rupert and me instead of the larger group. But she had managed to convince Michael to come with us to the Rialto markets.

"Margery knows better than any of the rest of us what supplies we need," she told him.

I explained that we each required a sleeping mat for the ship, a blanket, a sheet, and a rope to tie up our bedding during the day. Ignatius had advised me to buy everything new despite the expense, for the bedding available on the ship was almost certainly crawling with fleas and lice.

Our newly purchased bedding in our arms, the four of us repaired to the Piazza San Marco to choose our ship. Dozens of galleys were moored at the edge of the piazza, each pilgrim ship displaying a white banner with a red cross. The captains, sumptuously dressed and displaying their finest manners, competed for our business. Each declared that his ship was the finest, swiftest, and most seaworthy, and that his competitors' vessels were plague-infested wrecks that would sink in the first squall.

"Step aboard, fair pilgrims!" one such captain called to us. "My ship is open for your inspection. I provide two meals a day, including bread, wine, biscuit, fresh water, cured meat, and eggs. You can even bring your own hens on board. Once we arrive in Jaffa, I shall provide donkeys for the overland journey."

The captain translated these words in a babel of languages while pilgrims from every corner of Christendom wandered on board to inspect his ship. My companions seemed to display the utmost confidence in this man and his promises, but I remembered Ignatius's warning of how such captains were prone to exaggeration and even lies. Many a pilgrim, he'd told me, complained of having been cheated and reduced to bribing the cooks to get any edible fare at all.

"This seems a fine vessel," Michael said, stroking an oak beam.

"Can you not smell how it stinks?" I asked him, shooting a worried glance at Cecily.

My father and brother had owned ships, so I knew a thing or two about them. While this vessel looked good enough to the casual eye, my nostrils caught the very distinct odor of vomit and excrement—from humans and also very probably from rats—that underlay the strong-smelling perfumes wafting from the pomander the captain wore round his neck.

But before I could convince Michael, Master Donald and Friar Timothy stepped aboard. Michael brightened at once to see that they, too, seemed to think this a worthy vessel. They all chattered at once so neither I, Cecily, nor Rupert could get a word in.

"So we're in agreement," Friar Timothy said, haughtily ignoring my existence. "We shall sail on this ship."

At once the friar began using his authority as a religious man to browbeat the captain to lower the fare from sixty to forty ducats for the round trip between Venice and Jaffa. I locked eyes with Cecily, wondering if she would choose to remain loyal to her brother even if Rupert and I sailed on another ship. Meanwhile, Master Donald and Friar Timothy promptly handed over their ducats to seal the bargain, then prepared to reserve their spaces in the dormitory. Before I could blink, Friar Timothy snatched away my brand-new sheet.

"What are you doing?" I demanded. "That's mine!"

He raised his chin and narrowed his eyes. "You accuse me, a man of God, of *stealing*? Before all these witnesses? For shame!" He gazed at the captain and mournfully shook his head. "Good sir, the woman is a flap-wagging liar. Don't pay her any heed."

I had, in fact, told Suor Lorenza all about this loathsome friar and she banished him from her guesthouse. Now he had a bigger grudge against me than ever before.

When the captain, now clearly regarding me as a troublemaker, held out his hand for my fare, I began to shout. "I shall never sail in this cursed tub! It reeks of vermin! Look, a great black rat!" I pointed to the space behind the friar.

While everyone shrieked and whirled about, I took advantage of their panic to seize back my sheet and storm off the ship. Rupert and

Cecily came flying after me, thus leaving Michael no choice but to follow his sister. But Friar Timothy and Master Donald had no choice but to stay aboard the smelly ship since they'd already paid their fare and couldn't persuade the captain to return their money.

Back on the piazza once more, I tried to ignore the tumult around me. Closing my eyes, I willed all my attention and senses to drop inside the inner sanctuary of my heart, that vast space hidden inside what seemed so small. The seat of that ever-burning flame that was the light of my Beloved shining inside me. *Guide me to the right vessel,* I prayed. My ragged breathing calmed and serenity stole over me along with a quiet certainty.

Followed by the others, I walked up the gangplank of a newer ship. Once we had paid the fare and reserved our sleeping spaces, my companions and I returned to the guesthouse for our belongings, then we went once more to the Rialto markets, this time to buy provisions, for none of us desired to be wholly dependent on the ship's captain for food. I purchased a keg of drinking water, a small barrel of red wine, hard cheese, dried figs, ship biscuit, dates, and almonds. I also acquired a chamber pot of fired clay.

Laden with our supplies, we returned to the ship where we would remain, living on board while we awaited a fair wind to sail.

Our galley, the *Spiritus Sanctus,* had three decks. The lowest was for the *galeotti,* the oarsmen who sat in rows of three. How I pitied those poor wretches who were little more than slaves, chained to their benches lest they try to escape. They were forced to work shirtless so their master could whip them whenever he pleased.

The second deck was for us pilgrims, with a tiny cabin for the few female passengers and a huge dormitory for the men. The third deck was for the captain and crew. Each galley carrying 170 pilgrims required 140 crew members, including twenty crossbowmen for defense. Ignatius had explained that pirates regularly attacked the galleys, resulting in many a pilgrim being killed, wounded, or sold into slavery. In the middle part of the stern was a common refectory where the meals for the pilgrims and crew were served, but we women were not admitted to the table and had to take our meals in our quarters.

Cecily and I shared our cramped cabin with the four other female passengers—two Italian widows and a French prioress and nun. There was just enough room on the floor to spread our sleeping mats. Our individual chamber pots were squeezed up against the wall. By mutual agreement, all pots were emptied before we went to sleep, and if one of us had to use the pot during the night, she then tipped the contents discreetly out of the porthole to keep the place from reeking. Each morning we rolled our sleeping mats and hung them up.

The space was so tight that we could hardly move in our sleep without disturbing the others. The prioress complained that I snored, so Cecily cheerfully offered to shove me onto my other side if I made too much noise. Though the mosquitoes were a nuisance, the nun insisted on sleeping with the porthole wide open, at least while we were moored, because she suffered from the night sweats. Otherwise we rubbed along quite well, at least compared to the 164 male passengers crammed into their dormitory down the passageway. Even with our door bolted fast, we could hear their curses and disputes that ran long into the night.

The next morning I met Rupert on deck. The young man had black shadows under his eyes as though he hadn't slept in weeks.

"Margery," he said dolefully. "I fear I have landed in the very bowels of hell."

He told me how he had been kept awake half the night by drunken Flemings. Then, just as he had managed to fall into a fitful sleep, an old man driven by urgent need had stumbled around in the dark to relieve himself and managed to knock over five chamber pots, spilling their contents, which soaked into the sleeping mats.

At least the men had the option of using the commodes near the ship's prow. Seeing them all queuing up for their turn on the throne reminded me of the lines for confession during Lent.

Out of the 170 passengers on our ship and the 140 male crew members, my five cabin mates and I were the only women on board. It was daunting to be surrounded by so many men. My female companions and I never let one another out of our sight. But even six women were too many for some.

Several German lords, candidates for the knightly Order of the Holy Sepulcher, complained how shameful it was that they were expected to share the ship with six women of mature years—none of us being the least bit comely to their eyes. We were fortunate that the ship's captain cared more for our ducats than he did for the Germans' objections.

After three days of waiting, we were blessed with a strong west wind to push us eastward out of the port. I gathered with the others on deck as the seamen unfurled the three sails to the fanfare of trumpets and bugles. When the first stroke of the oars broke the water, we joined in a joyous pilgrims' song. At long last we were sailing to Jerusalem the Golden, holiest of holies, the center of the world. Tears of gratitude streamed down my face.

"Oh, Margery, isn't this a marvel!" Cecily squashed me in her arms.

My heart exulted. To me, this seemed the very essence of freedom. Then I noticed Rupert, whey-faced and trembling at the sight of those frothy waves, as if he glimpsed the graveyard where his bones would rest. I crossed myself to banish the evil thought.

From Venice, we crossed to the Dalmatian coast, then headed past the islands of Rhodes and Cyprus on our way to Jaffa. I pointed out the way on the map to my friends.

Though I didn't suffer seasickness like Rupert did, the passage was nonetheless an ordeal. With so many people crammed together, there was no privacy, no peace. Not a second's silence.

If we weren't being tossed about in a tempest with half the folk spewing into their privy pots, then we were becalmed in searing heat and making no progress at all. I began to wonder if we would ever reach Jerusalem or just fester at sea while our supplies dwindled to nothing. Then again, at least I had provisions of my own. The water on ship was so bad, it made many people ill. The wine was sour and the ship biscuit so hard that it had to be soaked in watered wine, otherwise it would break our teeth.

Although we women were spared the worst of the squalor, it was so cramped and close that in the morning when we ventured out on deck I felt as though I had escaped a squalid prison.

With so many men sleeping cheek by jowl, the spread of lice was inevitable. Soon Cecily's brother had an entire colony of them breeding in his beard. Cecily borrowed a razor and shaved him clean — hair, beard, and all. For her trouble, he bitterly complained that his shorn head made him look like a galley slave. I spent my afternoons delousing Rupert.

As for the eminent German lords who had so scorned the very presence of women on board, they were forced to rue their arrogance when they fell ill with the bloody flux. Who but we women were called upon to nurse their lordships back to health and launder their soiled linens?

"In God, the meek are made strong and mock the mighty," I said jauntily while spooning broth into one such lordling's mouth. "By my troth, those shitty linens of yours are every bit as filthy as those of a hedge-born peasant."

A gleam in her eye, the French prioress, gifted in the knowledge of many languages, translated my words into German to drive the point home.

16

AWAKENED TO THE SAILORS' shouting. My throat tightened in panic—had they sighted pirates? I hastily dressed before making my cautious way up to the deck. The sailors exclaimed in a cacophony of languages. All of them pointed east. When I saw what they did, my eyes flooded. I sank to my knees. My first glimpse of the Syrian coast.

Jaffa emerged on the horizon, the closest port to Jerusalem. Clutching my Ave beads, I joined the others as they sang the Te Deum. *We praise you, O God.* This, my arrival in the Holy Land, was surely the pinnacle of my existence. My yearning set me on fire. Soon I would walk upon the holiest earth I could ever hope to tread, literally walking in my Beloved's footsteps. I would carry Julian's writings, hidden in my staff, all the way to the Church of the Holy Sepulcher. We would disembark in the very port where Saint Peter once preached and mended his fishing nets.

But as we approached the miserable little harbor, my spirits sank. Once Jaffa had been the proud stronghold of the Crusaders. Until the Saracens vanquished them a century and a half ago. What remained were the ruins of broken-down churches and crumbling fortress walls. The only creatures roaming the streets were skeletal stray dogs. The sole structures still standing were the Mamluk sultan's two watchtowers. Such a forsaken place.

Navigating the two treacherous rocks marking the port entrance demanded the crew's utmost skill to save us from running aground. Finally, I saw a flurry of activity as Mamluk officials and Franciscan monks emerged to meet us. The captain had to pay a landing tax for each pilgrim before we could disembark. When, after hours of haggling, we were finally allowed ashore, the Mamluks herded us into a dank cave where we would be penned up like cattle until the formalities of our overland journey could be arranged. The surrounding caves held other pilgrims who had sailed from Venice—we would have to wait until the last of the Venetian pilgrim galleys arrived before the authorities would allow us to continue on our way.

If the cramped ship had been purgatory, this cave was truly hell. With little fresh air and even less natural light, the cavern stank of the crude latrines built into the recesses. I feared my white clothes would be indelibly soiled. To further compound our suffering, the officials confiscated what remained of our wine since their religion forbade intoxicating drink. Every man who carried a sword had to pay a tax on it worthy of a prince's ransom. One of the German lords put up such a fuss, refusing to pay a single *denier*. The Mamluks then confiscated his sword, waving it aloft like a spoil of war.

The Franciscan Brothers who were our guardians counseled patience and forbearance.

"Don't blame the followers of Mohammed for our plight," one Brother said. "The Holy Land was lost to us through the Crusaders' sins and vainglory. We shall never win it back until we are truly worthy to rule this place."

The Franciscans, alone of all the Western monastic orders, were allowed to guide pilgrims under the Mamluks' watchful gaze—a privilege that might be revoked at any time. We were here on sufferance.

"Avoid any argument or conflict with the local people," the monk told us. "Pay any fee willingly and obey their rules. Christian women," he added sternly, casting his admonishing gaze at us few female pilgrims, "must never look a Saracen man in the eye lest she be mistaken for a wretched whore."

He went on to warn us that more than anything the Mamluks dreaded spies gathering intelligence for another Christian conquest. Any pilgrim found carrying materials of strategic importance would be arrested, beheaded, and denied Christian burial. These words left me quaking and cold.

Boys from a nearby village came to sell us bundles of grass to sleep on. They also sold us food—flat unleavened bread, apricots, olives, and tangy cheese made from ewe's milk. Later, a dragoman inscribed our names in a register. After pocketing our fees, he issued each of us with a *bulletta*, a document allowing us to travel through the Holy Land for five weeks. But we were still stuck in that cave.

As I bedded down for the night, I lamented that my visions of freedom and travel had come to this—being held captive in the bowels of the earth. We couldn't even get up in the night to relieve ourselves without paying the guard.

In the middle of our fourth night, a throbbing trumpet wrenched me from my sleep. A guard seized my belongings in one huge arm and my wrist with his free hand. I only just managed to grab on to my staff before he marched me outside, only letting me go when I stood beside a hairy donkey. Before I could open my mouth to ask a single question, a bearded young man took me by the waist and hoisted me into the saddle.

There I was, sitting on my ass in the moonlight. The beast had no bridle, only a packsaddle and a rope around its neck. Singing a jaunty tune, the young man tied my belongings to the saddle. He offered to carry my staff, but I held fast to it with all my strength.

Each pilgrim was given an ass to ride—for a steep fee. None of us was allowed to walk. Only the Franciscan abbot, the Father Guardian of Mount Zion, who would lead our pilgrimage, was permitted to ride a mule. Our guards, however, rode the finest horses I had ever seen, their dappled coats flashing like silver in the torchlight. Patting my donkey's shaggy neck, I told myself that if riding an ass to Jerusalem was good enough for Jesus, it would have to do for me.

Mindful of the monk's warning never to look a Saracen man in the eye, I glanced obliquely at the bearded young man, who I understood to be assigned to lead my donkey. He smiled, his teeth shining as white as the moon. To my good fortune, he spoke some English.

"You can trust me," he said brightly. "My name is Isa, which means Jesus in my language. We honor him as a prophet."

What could I do but nod my assent?

Off we set down a sandy track, a vast column of pilgrims as big as an army, encircled on all sides by our armed Mamluk guards. I tried to accustom myself to the donkey's gait. Slowly night ebbed away. The sun rose, a fiery red orb. By midday, it would be furnace-hot.

As we moved across the unfamiliar landscape with its olive and lemon groves, I saw a building with snow-white masonry and little round towers like a Venetian monastery.

"How beautiful it is," I said, pointing.

"That is a mosque," Isa told me. "Where we worship Allah."

A man climbed to the very top of one of the turrets and cried out in all directions. He opened his arms as though he were trying to embrace heaven itself.

I blinked as Isa and the other local men looked to the east and bowed their foreheads to the earth while saying their prayers. Even the high and mighty Mamluk knights jumped off their steeds, laid down their weapons, and prayed most humbly in words I couldn't even begin to understand. But when their devotions were finished, the guards mounted back up and looked as ferocious as ever.

We passed some women returning from a well. They were completely veiled in black so neither their eyes nor the slightest glimpse of their faces were revealed, yet they strode along in loose breeches, not skirts. Here it was the men who wore skirts.

Soon we came to a village of whitewashed houses with flat roofs, upon which people gathered to point and stare at our caravan, which was truly a moving spectacle. Our progress caused a great cloud of golden dust to rise in the clear morning air. Some of the children lobbed stones at us.

"Moorish dogs!" Cecily's brother muttered when a small stone grazed his shoulder.

Isa called out to the children to stop and they obeyed, hanging their heads while their mothers scolded them.

"They think you foreigners are barbarians," Isa told me. "Because you worship statues and eat the flesh of pigs."

"*I* don't worship statues, I worship God," I was quick to point out. "And I don't eat pigs, or any meat. Only fish."

Isa seemed to view me with a new respect. "You are a good lady. Not like the other Franks who insult us and call us dogs."

Despite having been told never to look a Saracen man in the eye, I could not help myself from meeting his earnest and admiring gaze. Surely this man, young enough to be my son, would not view a woman of my years as a wanton flirt. Yet I found myself blushing to notice how handsome he was. His dark eyes had the same fathomless depths as Martin's, the boy I had loved so long ago. I chided myself for even thinking such a thing. But from then on, Isa insisted on calling me Lady Margery even though I kept reminding him that I was not of noble birth.

What was I to make of this world? All the rules were different here, this land where my fellow pilgrims and I were regarded as pagans and nonbelievers. But Isa was a good-hearted soul who saw my humanity through my foreignness. I slowly learned to distinguish between ordinary Muslims like him, the Mamluk officials, and Eastern Christians from Syria, Georgia, and Armenia who with their unfamiliar rituals, languages, and manner of dress seemed even more exotic than the Moors themselves.

Behind our column followed another smaller group, likewise herded by their guards. Isa told me they were Jewish pilgrims from all over the world.

"Jerusalem is also their holy city," he said.

I thought back to the Jews I had seen in Constance—the bookbinders, the market women, the midwife, and the goldsmiths. *Were any of them in that band of pilgrims?* I wondered. Had they, like me, witnessed the burning of Jan Hus outside their city walls and was that seared into their memory, as it was into mine, to haunt their nightmares forevermore? How curious that our journey could make us kindred spirits, for surely I bore more in common with these wandering Jews than the folk I had left behind in Lynn.

We spent our first night in Ramla, in an ancient caravansary—a group of large buildings built of brick and clay to accommodate travelers. Bone-weary from the long hours in the saddle, I limped toward the open doorway but was only granted entrance after I had removed my shoes in the Saracen fashion and bathed my sweaty feet in a tub of water strewn with rose petals.

"Expecting us to go barefoot like beggars?" Cecily was aghast. "What if they steal our shoes?"

Upon entering the caravansary, we discovered no chairs or stools, only carpets intricately woven in a pattern of lilies and leaping gazelles upon which we were expected to sit with our legs crossed in the fashion of a tailor at his work. We were given clay bowls of some local grain mixed with onions, dates, apricots, an unfamiliar purple vegetable, and salty sheep cheese. After our meal, a troupe of Saracen minstrels entertained us. One man played the harp, another the tabor, another a kind of bagpipe, while a bare-chested and very well-built young man breathed fire, swallowed swords, and danced with undulating movements. Unable to take my eyes off of him, I'll confess that many an unchaste longing entered my mind—these Saracen men were far too attractive. When I glanced sideways at Cecily, I saw that she was flushed and riveted, her jaw dropping halfway to the floor. Rupert looked so enthralled, I feared his eyes would leap out of their sockets.

Later, when we had picked ourselves up off the floor to head for our sleeping quarters, Cecily walked only a few paces before shrieking to the high heavens.

"What is it?" I cried, as she collapsed in my arms.

She pointed at her bare foot and wailed.

One of the Saracen servants, upon hearing her distress and seeing the red mark on her big toe, struck at the floor with a club. A moment later he straightened and lifted up a brown creature as long as my palm. I recoiled and Cecily screamed all the more loudly at the sight of those pincers and eight legs, and that long curving tail. A scorpion. I had only ever seen pictures of them in illuminated zodiacs. Never once had it occurred to me that I would have to sleep in a place where the infernal creatures dwelled.

To compound Cecily's horror, the man then deftly bound the dead scorpion to her throbbing toe, as if its corpse could heal its sting. I supported her weight against my body and guided her into the women's sleeping quarters where I then removed the scorpion with a shudder and soaked her foot in vinegar and cold water.

"It hurts like the devil, no doubt," the French prioress said, before adding in a more cheerful tone, "but it's unlikely to *kill* you, Madame Cecily."

Cecily's face was as white as the local cheese and her tears fell like rain. "Oh, Margery," she said, as we lay down on the carpeted floor and attempted to sleep. "Such a wretched place! I wish with all my heart I was back in England."

That night her sobbing kept us all awake. But I doubt I could have slept much even if it had been quiet. My senses were overwhelmed by the novelty of everything I had seen and heard and smelled and touched and tasted that day. Nothing here was homely or familiar. Despite my desire to see the sights of the Holy Land, I, too, caught myself yearning to be in some cozy English tavern with a mug of beer and a good fish pie.

The next morning we set off on the road to Jerusalem, passing through sun-scorched hills. Dust blew into my face and seeped into everything. I could feel its grit in my teeth and eyelashes. It coated my hands and covered Zaha, my donkey, with a fine brown film. Our way grew ever steeper as we climbed into the mountains.

"It's good we have many guards," Isa told me. "Robbers hide in the mountains and attack travelers, but they won't dare attack us. They fear the Mamluks."

His words gave me pause and made me view our guards with entirely new eyes. Never before had it occurred to me that those fierce men, with their gleaming armor and swords, were not our captors but our protectors.

We passed through villages with stone-built houses and pastures of donkeys who brayed to ours. Zaha dug in her heels, threw back her head, and hee-hawed with such vigor, I thought the noise would be enough to knock me out of the saddle. She refused to move until Isa bribed her with a small sweet cake.

Local women, not as heavily veiled as those in the lowland, sold us peaches, apricots, and clay pots of some thick, tart, creamy substance.

"Yogurt," Isa said. "It keeps longer in the heat than milk."

We pressed on until we passed through the Gate of the Valley, which Isa informed me was four leagues from Jerusalem. But I saw no sign of any valley — the road seemed only to climb ever upward.

In the searing midday heat, we reached a mountain pass where a crumbling old Crusaders' church stood, barely distinguishable from the surrounding rock. Here our way sloped down only to ascend again until we reached a promontory that overlooked the valley.

"Your people call this Mount Joy," Isa said, his young face blooming into a smile. "Look!"

He pointed into the hazy distance. I almost didn't dare look for fear of being sorely disappointed, as I'd been with my first glimpse of Jaffa. What if, after all this effort, the Holy City was just a jumble of unfamiliar buildings in a foreign land?

Then I caught sight of a city upon a massive hill. The great golden Dome of the Rock. But my gaze would not hold steady. Perhaps it was the fierce heat and desert sun that caused everything to blur and glow with an unearthly radiance. Every rooftop shone like polished alabaster. The air vibrated with infinite filaments of light. With the resonance of an endless chorus of singing ringing bells. A voice inside me said, *Jerusalem, your soul's home, where earth touches heaven.*

A sense of overpowering love suffused me in a glory so blinding that I fell off my ass.

The other pilgrims exclaimed what an embarrassment I was and pretended not to know me. A double vision seized me and I saw myself through their eyes. How comical and ridiculous I appeared, weeping in ecstasy on the desert ground with the shaggy donkey peering down at me. Instead of feeling shame, mirth filled me and I laughed in delight. Love was everywhere, in all things and beings. Everything began and ended in unutterable love.

I saw Mary Magdalene weeping before the empty tomb, that dark gash in the earth where all hope seemed to perish. I, her witness, willed her to turn and behold the shimmering figure standing behind her. I was she and she was I. Falling at his feet, I yearned with all my being to embrace him, but he said, *Touch me not, for I am not yet ascended to my Father.*

Yet his arms enveloped me, the embrace of my Beloved at last, the spirit made flesh. I stared up at his bearded face and wept from the ineffable sweetness he performed in my soul. But as the other pilgrims crowded round, I saw that it was Isa who held me. I flushed and my heart began to palpitate.

A hateful voice, which could have belonged only to Friar Timothy, split the hot air. "The vile whore is besotted with that brown Saracen."

"Do not speak evil of Lady Margery!" Isa told him sharply.

Even Timothy couldn't pierce the golden armor of my vision, which ignited all my senses with bliss. Two German friars came to tend me. They placed spices in my mouth to help bring me back to my waking senses. But my merriment lingered. Zaha bent to nuzzle me, her whiskers tickling me, making me laugh.

When I was able to stand again, Isa handed me my staff.

"At first I thought you were possessed by a djinn," he said. "But now I understand. You are a holy woman."

This young man whom I had mistaken for my Beloved touched his first two fingers to his mouth, then gently touched my sleeve before kissing his fingers.

Even after I mounted up and continued on my way, I felt my Beloved's unmistakable presence, his breath on my cheek as I retraced his journey. We look upon this world as a vale of suffering. All the wars and Crusades we fought—such tragedy and waste. It was we, not God, who manufactured hell. If only we could look past the pain and see the love that was everywhere. Divine radiance saturated every living creature, every tree and clod of earth. When I looked at the stone walls bordering the road, they appeared as though they were made entirely of light. As though I could put my hand right through them.

At dusk, we entered Jerusalem through the Jaffa Gate. Singing hymns of praise, we rode into the Holy City. The Dome of the Rock glittered with a thousand lamps. Candles glowed in the windows and torches illuminated the streets and the fine houses made of white stone. Upon the rooftops, families dined and women danced in circles while making eerie ululations that sent shivers up my spine. The aroma of roasting lamb and rare spices wafted from the cookshops we passed. The market stalls were a dazzle of jewels and damask silk.

We pilgrims were then divided up by nationality. The English were brought to the Mauristan hospice where I said my reluctant goodbyes to Isa before following the others to a large drafty hall without any furniture. Here, rich and poor alike, we were left to eat and sleep on the dusty floor. Yet I was too overawed to notice the discomfort. After spreading out my sleeping mat and sheet, I lay myself down. There in the pitch-black, amid farts and snores, my eyes opened wide. Some folk push away the darkness and curse it, but this was my balm, my refuge, for night after night he came to me, my Bridegroom. His radiance lit up the gloom. I rested deep within my heart.

17

HAT A MIRACLE TO awaken in Jerusalem and see its wonders at last.

First, we visited Gethsemane at the foot of the Mount of Olives, the site of Our Lord's arrest. Next, we followed the Via Crucis that led from the site of the Roman praetorium where Jesus was tried to the Church of the Holy Sepulcher. Following the route of Jesus's crucifixion through the maze of busy streets, we meditated on the Stations of the Cross. As I stood in a peaceful alley outside a sandalmaker's workshop, it seemed impossible to imagine that this was where my Beloved stumbled under the weight of his cross and fell for the first time. My faith allowed me to see my Beloved's Jerusalem that existed eternally and overlay this bustling city crowded with Bedouin traders and Levantine merchants. I endeavored to commit each step to memory so I could relive this journey in my heart each time I prayed.

My sense of anticipation mounted as our procession moved ever closer to the most sacred site of all, the Church of the Holy Sepulcher, which housed the last Stations of the Cross. The ancient basilica, built of marble and stone, might have been magnificent were it not in such poor repair. The belfry had no bells in it but merely stood like a sentinel to lost grandeur. The Saracens guarding the entrance allowed us in for Vespers, then locked us inside for the entire night, which we would spend in vigil and prayer. We Western Christians worshiped alongside Coptic Christians, as black as ebony, from Ethiopia in the land of Prester John.

Our Franciscan guide shouldered a massive wooden cross and led us in procession through the vast dark church cloudy with incense. Barefoot penitents, we each carried a burning candle and meditated while our guide described for us what Our Lord suffered in each place. We came to the Chapel of the Crucifixion. The friar then directed our attention to an outcropping of rock jutting from the chapel wall. This, he told us, was the very bedrock of Golgotha. Upon the moment Our Lord died, an earthquake had rent the solid stone, allowing Christ's spilled blood to pour down to Adam's grave located in the chapel beneath us, and so began the redemption of all humanity.

As the friar spoke these words, the stone floor shuddered beneath my feet. I could no longer stand or kneel. Candle and staff tumbled from my hands as I fell writhing. In the city of my soul, I truly *saw* the crucifixion as though it were unfolding before my eyes. I beheld my Beloved's body on the cross so truly, in all his manhood. His precious body slashed and torn, fuller of holes than any dovecote. His blissful hands and his tender feet nailed to the hard tree. Rivers of blood poured from his every limb. The gash in his side gushed with blood and water. Roaring in anguish, I twisted and tremored, my arms stretched out wide, and I couldn't do a thing to control it. The fire of love, *incendium amoris,* burned so hot and bright within me, a pure gift from my Beloved, allowing me to share his passion. With my soul's eye, I saw the Blessed Mother, Mary Magdalene, and John the Apostle as they lamented in a grief deep enough to shake the church to rubble. Their sorrow became my own and I cried out, over and over, as though my heart would burst. The very boundary between agony and ecstasy dissolved and all I felt was *him.*

My night in the Holy Sepulcher transfixed me. Forever after, when I saw a crucifix, or if I saw a person or even an animal who was wounded, or if a man beat a woman or child in front of me, or struck a horse with a whip, I could only see my Beloved being beaten and scourged, my Beloved who is everywhere and dwells in every living thing, and I would weep as violently as I did in the Holy Sepulcher.

"My goodness, Mistress Margery," our Franciscan guide said diplomatically. "You weep more noisily in your devotions than even the Armenians." But his patience with me rapidly deteriorated as the night progressed.

My companions, grumbling in complaint about what a spectacle I made of myself, hauled me off the floor and dragged me onward. Yet still my tears streamed for I saw my Beloved everywhere. When our guide took us to the stone where Our Lord's body was anointed for burial after he was taken from the cross, I had to clutch my staff with all my strength to keep standing.

We entered the Chapel of Saint Stephen through a small door. Passing through an even smaller opening, we arrived at the Holy Sepulcher itself, the crypt where once my Beloved's crucified body had rested. The empty grave opened before me like a portal into another existence, and I could no longer hear our guide or anyone else. Self-possession deserted me. Once more I fell wailing and shuddering, as though I would die. My candle tumbled from my hand. My staff hit the stone floor with such force that its secret compartment sprang open, spilling the cylinder containing Julian's manuscript for all to see.

When I returned to my waking senses, a welter of accusations assaulted me.

"I always knew there was something suspicious about her."

"She's a Lollard! A heretic! Burn her!"

"Did *she* write this? Why, I never!"

"What if it's of military importance? Why, she could be a spy. The Saracens will behead her!"

"Fancy Margery being a spy!" Master Donald exclaimed. "I just thought she was a loud, annoying woman."

I froze, my hands clapped to my ears. To think I had come to the holiest place on earth only to meet the grisliest death—to be buried without Christian rites! Then a defiant voice rose inside me. *If I am to die on pilgrimage, let it be in Holy Jerusalem.* No one could say I wasn't imitating Christ. But my stomach pitched when I remembered Julian. Could the manuscript be traced back to her—what unspeakable consequences might she suffer for my lack of control? I must act to protect her even if I had already doomed myself.

"Silence, I implore you!" our Franciscan guide called out, his voice tight with panic. "The Mamluks won't care if she's a heretic, but if you go shouting about a spy, they'll have us *all* beheaded. Speak no more of this. My brethren and I will examine these papers among ourselves."

But before he could walk away with Julian's manuscript, I seized my chance to speak.

"Good sir, I am but an ignorant woman," I said, rising shakily to my feet. "Yet I can assure you there is nothing sinister in these pages. It's a little-known work by the late Richard Rolle," I added, naming the first deceased mystic to enter my mind, may God forgive my lie. I thought it best to attribute the manuscript to a dead author who couldn't be tried for heresy — Richard Rolle, who penned my beloved *Incendium Amoris*.

Having nothing left to say for myself, I hung my head as though offering it to the executioner's ax. I would play the meek and powerless woman for all it was worth.

"Don't believe her, sir!" a voice cried out. "The poor deluded creature is lying to protect me!"

My head jerked back to see Rupert, his face as pale as mushrooms in the unsteady candlelight.

"She's an unlettered woman," my friend said, "who can't even *read* these pages, let alone have any ill intent with them. But I am a scholar from Cambridge."

A hush fell over our assembly as everyone turned to stare at him.

"I was too great a coward to carry it myself," he said, his voice gaining conviction and power. "And so I took shameful advantage of this confused, overwrought woman."

My heart broke to witness his loyalty. To think my friend would tell such bald and dangerous lies for my sake!

"No, no, Reverend Father!" I shouted in desperation. "It's mine! Master Rupert had nothing to do with this!"

"Silence, woman!" Master Donald snapped. "We've heard quite enough of your bleating already." Clearing his throat, he addressed our Franciscan guide. "She is indeed addle-brained and ignorant," he declared. "And Master Rupert is certainly the biggest lily-skinned, slack-wristed coward to ever wear breeches. It's all perfectly plausible," he added portentously, as though he were a judge on par with King Solomon.

"Richard Rolle, you say?" The Franciscan friar, reading the first page, seemed to exhale in relief. "We have his *Incendium Amoris* in our library. My abbot shall have to examine this, but I doubt the Mamluk authorities will find anything of strategic importance here to warrant any accusations of espionage. But, Master Rupert, I'd advise you to find a more discreet person to carry your manuscript."

Though all the while I shouted and pleaded that the blame was mine alone, the others seemed only to view my protests as further evidence of my lunacy. They seemed to think it utterly preposterous that any woman should be learned or shrewd enough to deliver a secret manuscript to the Holy Land.

I exchanged frantic glances with Rupert. My throat tightened like a vice to see the Mamluk guards circling around him. Evidently undone by the lies he had told and the peril he faced, Rupert appeared feverish and weak, slumping against a pillar. Never strong or hale for all his youth, he looked so wretched, as though he would never have the strength to set foot outside Jerusalem again. I struggled to beat my way across the crowd to him, but the Mamluks blocked my path. Then the Franciscans led my ailing young friend away for interrogation.

"He's innocent," I told Cecily. "The blame is truly mine."

Through her tears, she stared at me as though I, her steadfast friend and travel companion, were an utter stranger.

"How could you keep such secrets from me?" she asked in a shaken voice. "After all we've been through? What else have you been hiding from us? And what will happen to poor Rupert?"

Her look of betrayal foundered me.

Not only had I failed both of my friends, but I'd also been an unworthy bearer of Julian's writings. To echo our Franciscan guide, she should have chosen someone far subtler and more circumspect than I.

Rupert did not return to the hostel that night, and he remained conspicuously absent when we set off on our donkeys for Bethlehem the next morning.

"How does Master Rupert fare?" I asked our Franciscan guide.

His face hardened at the sight of me. "He's very ill. The Brothers are looking after him in our infirmary."

"I must go to him!" I grasped the man's sleeve. "*Please*, good sir."

"That will not be permitted," he said coldly.

"He lied to protect me," I said. "The manuscript is mine, I swear."

The man's eyes glazed as though he could no more believe my claim than he could take my visions seriously. "Enough of your tittle-tattle! You, Mistress Margery, are the reason why honest men make their wives stay at home."

A short distance from Jerusalem, Bethlehem was a poor little town with a ruined wall and one street. In the Grotto of the Nativity, as we processed with candles and sang hymns, the others edged away from me as though I were a leper. But even my shame couldn't keep the visions at bay. I saw the infant Christ and fell gasping and quaking on the floor. Ecstasy seized me along with the unmistakable and overpowering scent of roses and lilies. In a golden haze, I tumbled back into a heavenly place beyond all ignominy and self-reproach. When my visions faded, I discovered that the others had deserted me. Only Isa stood by to make certain I was safe.

"Christians preach about love," he said in a bewildered tone as he lifted me to my feet. "Why are they so hateful to you, Lady Margery?"

In the dusty twilight, Isa and I traveled our lonely way back to Jerusalem. But when we reached the hostel, the steward forbade me from entering. As it turned out, there had been so many complaints about me that he had decided to evict me. He shoved my bedding and travel bag into my arms.

"But where shall I sleep?" I asked in alarm.

Night had fallen and the other hostels would be bolting their gates.

"No concern of mine," the steward said, slamming the massive door in my face.

My despair soon turned to a blinding sense of resolve. Perhaps this sad turn was a sign from God as to what I must do.

"Isa, please escort me to the Franciscan Monastery of Mount Zion," I said. "They cannot refuse me hospitality."

Rupert languished in the monastery's infirmary. My place was at his side where I might right the wrongs that would otherwise befall him. Perhaps the abbot would believe my story even if no one else did.

The friar who had been our guide in the Church of the Holy Sepulcher was none too happy to see me at the door, but his religious vows forbade him from turning me away. I think if it had been up to him, I would have slept in the byre with the asses. It was fortunate that the porter was a kindlier man who found me a well-appointed room in the guesthouse, but this only compounded my guilt and misgivings. How could I sleep on a featherbed in soft linen sheets while poor Rupert suffered on account of my deeds?

"Good sir, I must urgently speak to the abbot," I told the porter.

He replied that I must wait until morning.

Early the following day, the porter informed me that the abbot was too busy to grant me an audience but that a certain Brother Ambrose of Kent wished to speak to me. He led me into a narrow reception room where a thin monk with ice-blue eyes sat at an olive-wood table. An angry scar ran across the man's razor-sharp cheekbone. He was so savage of aspect, I could only tremble before him.

"So you're the weeping mystic my brethren have told me so much about," Brother Ambrose said, raising one inquisitive eyebrow. "It's an honor to meet a pilgrim of such deep devotion."

He gestured to a stool where I might sit. Though the hour was early, he offered me a cup of wine—somehow the Brothers at the monastery were allowed the fruit of the vine though it was forbidden elsewhere. But I couldn't bring myself to sit, and my hand was shaking too hard to grasp the cup. *Was he truly trying to set me at ease?* I wondered. *What if this was a trap?*

"Every pilgrim prays for visions of the crucifixion and begs to partake in Christ's passion," he said. "But when someone in their midst actually receives the epiphany, they accuse the person of playacting and false piety. Especially we English, who can't tolerate any display of strong emotion. I think you would find a far warmer welcome among the Eastern Christians who weep for God without shame."

As he said this, I broke down sobbing. I was prepared to grovel on my knees like the most wretched beggar. "Reverend Sir, you must not allow Rupert of Cambridge to be punished for my crime. The manuscript is mine. He lied to save me."

Brother Ambrose grinned. "That much I deduced in five minutes."

He reached to a shelf below and placed Julian's manuscript on the table between us. The sight left me so weak that I could only sink to the stool and take a long swallow of wine. Brother Ambrose leafed through the pages and began to read aloud.

Just because I am a woman, must I therefore not tell you of God's goodness, when I saw at the same time both his goodness and his desire that it should be known?

I closed my eyes and saw Julian's wise face. *All manner of things shall be well.*

"Not the work of Richard Rolle, as you and young Rupert claimed," Brother Ambrose said. Something very much like mirth rang out in his voice.

I opened my eyes to see the monk smiling in a way that completely transformed his severe face.

"This is none other than the writings of the holy anchoress, Julian of Norwich," he said in triumph.

"You know of her?" I asked, completely beside myself. Did Julian, in the deep simplicity of her life, have any clue that her reputation had traveled all the way to Holy Jerusalem?

"I never thought to see her work with my own eyes." He gazed down at the pages with reverence. "You'll forgive me for keeping this long enough to copy for our library, won't you? I promise you shall have it back before you leave the Holy Land."

I stared at him in astonishment. "You, sir, are a scribe?"

"Head librarian," he said with some pride. "But I served as a humble scribe for many years. That's how I got this scar—with my pen knife. Who says a clerk's life is without peril?"

We laughed like old friends.

"May I see Rupert?" I asked him. "I've been so worried."

"He's still ailing but improving. Of course you may visit him. He's asked after you and will be happy to see you."

I arose gaily from the stool and prepared to head to the infirmary.

But Brother Ambrose turned grave once more. "Mistress Margery, be ever mindful of the danger you are in."

My skin prickled.

"I counsel far greater caution," he said. "My abbot is tolerant because we exist outside of Christendom. He is far too occupied keeping the peace with our Muslim neighbors to concern himself about possible Christian heresy. But should you be found with this manuscript in Europe, let alone in England, I fear you might not find much mercy."

Holding his ice-blue gaze, I considered how close I had come to losing everything. Even Rupert, my dear friend.

Though still convalescing, Rupert seemed in fine spirits, his eyes bright and cheeks pink.

As grateful as I was to see him so restored, I couldn't help but upbraid him for taking such risks for my sake.

"Why would you do such a thing?" I asked. "You might have been beheaded!"

Rupert remained serene, appearing more contented than I had ever seen him. "Remember when I was ill on the Rhine and feared I would die before we even reached Cologne? You and your medicine saved my life. And you foretold I would indeed reach Jerusalem and there find my heart's desire."

My heart warmed at the memory.

"Your prophecy has come true. The Brothers here are so kind, Margery." Rupert gazed in adoration at the handsome young infirmarer, who seemed particularly taken by him and gave him the most attentive care. "In faith, I have no desire to ever return to England. When I'm well again, I shall ask to take holy orders here and serve as a scribe. But what was that manuscript you carried?" he asked. "And why did you hide it — even from me?"

Sitting at his bedside, I told him how Julian had sent me on this mission to carry her writings across the known world. As he listened, a new respect seemed to dawn in my friend, as though he had never imagined I could be so daring or risk so much for words on parchment.

Later that day, I paid a messenger to seek out Mistress Cecily at the Mauristan hospice and tell her that Rupert was out of harm's way. But whether the messenger boy could actually locate Cecily among all the other pilgrims was anyone's guess.

I stayed on at the monastery guesthouse and continued my daily pilgrimage excursions with only Isa for company.

After much coaxing, Isa managed to get Zaha on the ferry. We crossed the River Jordan, then rode to Jericho. Though we had set off in the cool hours of dawn, by the time we reached our destination, the Mount of Temptation in the Judean Desert, it was afternoon and ferociously hot. The soles of my shoes had worn so thin, I feared the sizzling sand would sear my feet. Yet I was determined to climb this mountain, for this was where my Beloved had fasted for forty days and nights. We were only allowed to walk to the top, so while Zaha dozed in the shade with her nose over the water trough, I struggled up the path, which seemed impossibly steep and barren, not a blade of green grass in sight. But Isa took me under his arm and led me up to the very heights.

There we stood beneath the harsh desert sky while Isa pointed out the sights we could see from the summit. The Jordan Valley. The Dead Sea. The mountains of Moab and Gilead. Heat hammering my head, I sank to my knees on the burning ground. The sweeping vista shimmered like a hallucination. This was where my Beloved, during his long fast, had been tempted by the devil three times. I prayed to be spared from the temptation that flared inside me whenever I looked at young Isa, the handsomest man to ever hold my hand.

We pilgrims were allowed to stay in the Holy Land for only five weeks, which flew past all too quickly. Only a lucky few had the funds and the permission to travel onward to Gaza, Mount Sinai, Cairo, and Alexandria. The rest of us, alas, had no choice but to return to Jaffa and board the galley back to Venice.

Before leaving the Mount Zion monastery, I bade my farewells to dearest Rupert, now restored to health, and to Brother Ambrose, who had repaired my staff and returned Julian's manuscript to its hidden compartment.

His parting words, spoken with both fondness and urgency, still make me shiver at their prescience. "Guard your secrets well, Margery Kempe."

18

WORRIED THAT THE OTHER pilgrims would regard my staff with suspicion and question me about my debacle back in Jerusalem. But our return voyage to Venice was so harrowing, with half the passengers ill from the bloody flux, that it didn't seem to enter their minds.

Poor Cecily was delirious with high fever, diarrhea, and blood gushing out of her rectum. Thrashing on her mat, she clung to my hand and begged me to pray for her, for she was convinced that demons had come to snatch away her soul. I nursed her as best I could. The flatbread and the flasks of almond milk I had bought in Jaffa proved far kinder to her stomach than the stone-hard ship biscuit and sour wine. Seeking to rekindle our friendship, I revealed all that I'd kept hidden from her—my secret mission to carry Julian's manuscript. Cecily begged my forgiveness for shunning me in Jerusalem. If anything, our ordeal made us closer, as tight as sisters.

When we arrived in Venice, Cecily was still so weak that her brother and I took her to the Dominican Sisters of Corpus Domini where she could convalesce. I was loath to continue my pilgrimage without her, but Cecily insisted.

"The Sisters will take good care of me," she said. "Even if I can't make the journey to Rome, you *must*. Do it for me, Margery. Pray for me at all the holy basilicas."

And thus, carrying dear Cecily in my heart, I set off on my pilgrim's way, this time accompanied by a rich Florentine lady and her maid, two Franciscan friars, and an Irish hunchback named Richard.

We reached Rome on Michaelmas in late September. By this time, I had been gone from England slightly more than a year. Now a seasoned traveler, I had never felt so free. The mistress of my own path.

How can I describe the magnificence of that ancient yet ageless city set among the seven hills? After giving thanks for our safe arrival at Saint Peter's, our traveling party dispersed, and we went our separate ways — the friars to their friary, the wealthy Florentine lady to her kinsfolk, and Richard the hunchback and I to the English hospice since the Irish hostel was already full.

My heart gladdened when we entered the Hospital of Saint Thomas of Canterbury in the Via Monserrato, for it looked a very welcoming place with pilgrims gathered at long tables to share wine, bread, and travelers' tales. The steward hailed Richard and me in jolly fashion and was about to show us to our dormitories when a glowering cleric stalked over.

"Do not give hospitality to that creature!" an all-too-familiar voice thundered. "She's possessed by devils and makes enough racket to curl Satan's toenails."

"Friar Timothy?" My blood ran cold at the sight of my old foe. Although I had managed to evade him in the Holy Land with Isa and the Mamluk guards making sure no improprieties could transpire, now I was at his mercy. Without a word of protest, I fled to the darkening streets — far safer in my mind than any hostel where that man was staying.

Out of a bewildered sense of chivalry, Richard fled the hostel in my wake, but he was none too pleased with this turn of events.

"Alas!" he cried. "Must I, too, suffer on your account, Mistress Margery?"

"Have you so little faith?" I reproved. I took a deep breath and attempted to summon Julian's wisdom and resourcefulness. "Follow me. All shall be well."

The Irish hunchback rolled his eyes as I led him off down one of the shabbier lanes sloping down toward the Tiber. Rome, despite its splendid basilicas and marble ruins, was a city of great poverty. Scores of beggars assembled outside the entrance of every church. Even in the gathering darkness, scrawny children darted here and there to see if they could find any edible refuse in the streets. And I feared that I, low on funds after the considerable expenses of my journey, fit right in. My white clothes had grown threadbare and tattered. My shoes were worn so thin, I might as well have been walking barefoot. My only object of value that remained was the golden ring Julian had given me with *Ihesus est amor meus* inscribed on it.

"Oh, this is an evil place," said Richard. "Thieves will slit our throats."

He wanted to bed down for the night on the floor of the nearest church, but that would hardly have been a refuge—we both knew pickpockets prayed on poor pilgrims who slept in such places.

I marched resolutely onward, turning into another street, the preserve of the working poor. We passed a smithy, a shoemaker's workshop, and a metal foundry, all closed for the night, until we came to a dead end right at the river's edge. There I found a crooked little house with a candle glowing in the unshuttered window. I lifted my hand to knock.

"What are you doing?" Richard hissed. "You haven't a clue who lives here! What if they murder us?"

Ignoring him, I rapped on the door, which was finer than the rest of the house, the pine sanded to a silken finish. A blinking young man opened. In the background, I smelled bubbling fish soup. The young man's clothes were patched and thin, his eyes were sad, but his face looked as honest as that solid pine door.

"Signore," I said, addressing him in my best Italian. "My friend and I are poor pilgrims and our hostel is full. Can you offer us shelter for the night? We will gladly pay for your hospitality."

When I opened my palm to show him my coins, I could tell he was tempted, yet he wavered.

"My wife is very ill."

He rubbed his hand over his brow and looked as though he could weep. His despair cut me like a knife.

I touched his arm as though he were my son. "What ails her, my good man? I have willow bark in my satchel for lowering fever and other herbs, too."

The bewildered young man ushered us into his cottage with its beaten-earth floor. His wife, lying in her bed built into a recess in the stone wall, was as beautiful as the Madonna with her golden hair and violet eyes. But her face was pearled in sweat. She shivered, fevered, and gasped in the throes of ague.

"Malaria," her husband said, as he wiped the sweat from her brow.

The intermittent fever I knew well for we suffered enough of it in the fens of Norfolk. But this Roman fever was a particularly virulent form. They called it *malaria* because it was caused by the noxious air coming off the swamps skirting the Tiber. What made it even worse was that this young woman looked at least seven months pregnant. Her malady might cause her to miscarry, which at this late stage in her pregnancy could kill her.

"Don't just stand there," I told Richard, who was frozen like a post in the middle of the room. "Go fetch water from the well up the street."

When Richard returned with the water, I set a kettle to boil and brewed a decoction of willow bark and sweet wormwood. I coaxed the young woman to drink the brew, then swaddled her calves in cool, damp cloth to bring down the fever.

"Who *are* you?" she asked, lifting herself up on her elbows to stare at me.

"Margery Kempe of England," I said helpfully. "What is your name, signora?"

"Rosangela," she said. A name as lovely as she was.

By and by, she stopped shivering and her breathing grew easier. She managed to eat some soup and bread before falling into a peaceful sleep. Marcello, her husband, tenderly kissed her brow and drew the bed curtains closed for her privacy.

Richard and I sat with Marcello at the scrubbed pine table and shared the remaining soup, bread, and watered wine.

"We've never had pilgrims lodge with us before," Marcello said, dividing the last bit of wine between Richard and me.

Our host explained that he and his wife were newly arrived from the countryside and still struggling to make a livelihood here. Marcello was a carpenter and a fine one, I gathered, if the front door and table were any indication of his skill. He received commissions from various churches and wealthy families, but both work and pay were irregular as he struggled to establish himself. To further complicate matters, both he and Rosangela were plague orphans and had no family to help his wife through her illness and first pregnancy.

"I have borne fourteen children," I assured him. "I know a thing or two about helping pregnant women."

Marcello looked at me with shining eyes. "God sent you to our door."

The sincerity of his words flooded me in a warm rush.

When I later spread my sleeping mat on the beaten-earth floor and lay myself down, I reflected that God had indeed guided me to this house. For serving the poor was as much a part of pilgrimage as lighting candles in pretty churches.

The next morning Richard left to try his luck at the Irish hospice while I settled in with Marcello and Rosangela. Marcello refused to take the coins I tried to pay him so instead I attempted to spend them in the market buying food. But owing to my tattered white clothes, a well-dressed lady mistook me for a penitent beggar and gave me two stale loaves of bread, a turnip, an onion, and a river fish that had only just begun to smell. Back at the house, when I cooked the fish, I managed to disguise the odor with judicious use of onion, garlic, and thyme.

And so my days passed, tending Rosangela and the household while Marcello labored in his carpenter's workshop at the back of the house. The cottage walls rang with the rhythms of his sawing and hammering. He taught me to string wooden beads and crosses to make simple rosaries that I could sell in the market. I earned enough to buy fresh milk and a jug of decent wine to put the color back in Rosangela's cheeks. Sure enough, she rallied. After a week or so, she was strong enough to rise from her bed and share the household tasks with me.

"You must stay with us," she said, "for as long as you like. When the baby is born, you shall be the godmother."

Her simple goodness and trust left me tongue-tied, so I just smiled and ducked my head. To lighten the mood, I told her tales of crossing the Alps, of the splendor of Venice, and of the exotic sights I had seen in the Holy Land.

"You're so far from home," Rosangela said, gazing at me with what seemed a mixture of awe and pity. She confessed that she still pined for her native village, poor though it had been. "But *you* still have a mother who lives," she said wistfully. "And your children! Don't you miss them terribly? Oh, it must break your heart."

I lowered my eyes to the bowl of peas I was shelling. My heart indeed ached. I imagined holding baby Juliana in my arms while my young sons gathered round, eager to hear tales of my adventures. Yet my longing for my children was matched in equal measure by my anger and bitterness over the awful servitude I'd fled. All those wasted years I had lived in fear of John, whose pig-selfish lust had made me despise my own flesh. Even now, when I looked back at the life I'd left behind, a sense of giddiness and guilty relief stole over me when I considered that an entire continent separated me from my husband. I'd sacrificed mothering my own children to seize this freedom. What would Rosangela think of me if she only knew the truth?

I arose before dawn. In the patch of moonlight shining through a chink in the shutters, I dressed and gathered my things as silently as I could so as not to wake Rosangela and Marcello. Now that Rosangela was well again, it was high time I continued my pilgrimage, or so I told myself. In truth, this young couple's innocent faith in me made me feel the worst of imposters. They assumed I was a widow. What if they, in their newlywed adoration for each other, discovered that I had willfully left my husband?

I lifted the door latch and was about to steal away when the bed curtains rustled.

Marcello stuck his head out and called after me. "Margherita! Where are you going so early?"

As quick as a fox, the young man leapt to light a candle from the hearth embers as I stood there with my packed bags and staff, as guilty as a thief.

Rosangela emerged from bed, her golden sweep of hair flowing over her nightdress. "Margherita, are you leaving us?" The hurt in her eyes was enough to break me.

"I wish to continue my pilgrimage," I said lamely. "Today I shall visit Saint Bridget's house in the Piazza Farnese. I think there will be room for me in the English hostel," I lied. "I thank you for your hospitality, but I don't want to be a burden."

Rosangela's eyes filled with tears. She threw her arms around me before taking my satchel from my shaking fingers. "How could you imagine you are a burden to us? You're our *friend*. Please stay for as long as you like. Marcello can clear a corner of his workshop for you to sleep in if you would like more privacy."

Marcello rested a gentle hand on her shoulder. "Let's get dressed and go with Margherita to Saint Bridget's house. We shall give thanks for your recovery, *cara*, and ask the saint's blessing for the baby."

After sharing a breakfast of bread and milk, the three of us set off for the Casa di Santa Brigida. Rosangela linked arms with me as if frightened that I would bolt away.

The house where once Bridget of Sweden had dwelled was part of a double monastery shared by Bridgettine nuns and monks, and presided over by a single abbess who wore blue robes in honor of the Virgin Mary.

As I stepped through that arched portal, my face still throbbed in embarrassment for how my cowardly attempt at escape had been met with such kindness and concern. I prayed to Bridget for direction and clarity, Bridget who had always been a guiding inspiration. At age fourteen, she had been offered into a dynastic marriage. Yet even that and the eight children she bore hadn't stopped her from traveling to Jerusalem, Rome, and Santiago de Compostela. After her husband died, she became a nun and later founded her own religious order. She died in this very house in 1373, the year of my birth and the year Julian had received her divine showings.

An aged nun showed us up to Bridget's rooms, which were lovingly preserved.

"I was Holy Bridget's maid," the nun said fondly, in heavily accented Italian. "I followed her all the way from Sweden."

It moved me to the depths of my heart to think that this old woman was a direct connection to the saint — a living, walking relic.

"What was Saint Bridget like?" I asked in a reverent hush while Marcello and Rosangela leaned in to listen.

"She was meek and gentle and so kind to everyone," the nun said with a faraway smile, as if recalling their days together more than forty years ago.

The nun grew solemn when she led us into the adjoining room. "This was where she died. And *this*," she said, beginning to unroll a length of heavenly blue linen, "is the very cloth on which she breathed her last breath. I was there, holding her hand. You may touch it," she added, as if granting us a privilege that was not lightly bestowed.

As I reverently stroked the linen, I meditated on Bridget's life. She had received divine revelations from the time she was ten years old. Certain visions of hers seemed similar to the ones I had been granted through God's grace. Like me, Bridget had been shown that she would travel to Jerusalem. But she had been given another boon that God had thus far not granted me, namely, the knowledge of how and when she would pass from this world. When I tried to plunge into the depths of my heart and glimpse my own demise, all I could see was a dark cloud of unknowing.

Bridget had been privy to the full measure of her life. She had known where the long bowshot of her seventy years would take her — to founding the Bridgettine Order and writing her books. She had made her every hour on this earth count. In contrast, my own wanderings, for all the holy places I had glimpsed and all the good people I had met, seemed haphazard, almost aimless.

Yes, I had carried Julian's writings to the edge of Christendom and back, and shared them with some wise scholars, but after the disaster in Jerusalem, I had come to heed Brother Ambrose's stark warning. Now I was too terrified to consider mentioning those secret pages even to the mild-faced nun who stood before me. What harm and danger might I wreak here in Rome, so close to the prelates keen to hunt down any whiff of heresy? Besides, the manuscript was Julian's lifework, *her* task and purpose. What was my true calling? It seemed I could only continue moving forward, one foot in front of the other, and trust that my Beloved was guiding me. But any hint of an ultimate destination remained a mystery. My gut clenched at the very thought of returning to Bishop's Lynn and picking up the threads of my old life with John. Now that my money was nearly all spent, I wondered if I would even be able to afford the journey home.

My hand still resting on the blue cloth, I swayed in thrall of Bridget's palpable presence. It was as though she stood in the room with me, blessing me in my turmoil. Stunned by the touch of her sweetness, I wept bitterly, roiling in my unworthiness. I fell to my knees, my bones racked by long shuddering sobs. Surely this would disgust my young friends and drive them away just as my weeping had driven so many others away.

When my spell had passed, I found the old Swedish nun on her knees beside me. She was weeping helplessly for her mistress, as though Bridget had died just yesterday. I wrapped my arms around her bony shoulders and gently helped her to her feet while Rosangela and Marcello, also in tears, found a chair for her to sit on.

"Sometimes," Marcello said, "we must all weep. For the saints. For beauty. For love."

The very walls seemed to ripple, as though in a dream. At last I had arrived in a place where ordinary people understood what it was to receive the gift of tears. *Now I am home,* I thought, hugging Rosangela. *Among kindred souls.*

But my conscience wouldn't allow me to let Rosangela and Marcello think me better than I was. That evening as we broke bread, I revealed with savage honesty how I had left my husband, my baby girl, and four sons under the age of thirteen to go on pilgrimage. I even opened the hidden compartment of my staff to show them Julian's manuscript and told them how she had asked me to carry it for her. I poured out my whole unvarnished story, starting from when I had gone stark mad after my first pregnancy and was only cured when I received my first vision of Christ. How he had appeared to me, over and over, ever since. I described how some of my fellow pilgrims had condemned me as the worst hypocrite. This shook me more than any confession I had ever made to a priest. I hardly dared lift my eyes from my clenched hands.

"Now that you know the truth," I told my friends, "I will understand if you want me to leave."

Rosangela reached for my arm. "If you hadn't come to our door that night, I could have died. My baby, too. You saved *our* family, Margherita."

She turned to her husband, who looked solemnly at me.

"The apostles left their families to follow Christ," he said. "Sometimes we are called for something more than an ordinary life."

Rosangela touched the manuscript with timid fingers. I think it was the first time she had ever seen so many written words.

"Will you please tell us what the holy anchoress wrote?" she asked.

So I leafed to my most beloved passages and attempted to translate them, sentence by sentence, into my best Italian.

"Our Lord opened up the wound in his side and told Dame Julian to look within his body. She saw his heart cleft in two for his love for us. And she beheld all creation and all creatures there, all of them bathed in unending love. She could see no hell, no wrath. All our anguish and defeats are the tastes of Christ's passion, but the mystery of his love underlies our deepest suffering. Know this: love was his meaning. All shall be well."

My heart warmed and expanded. Telling my honest story and speaking of Julian's revelations to these poor, unlettered, dearworthy souls was even more important than delivering Julian's manuscript to wise scholars and scribes. Julian, after all, had written her book in plain and homely Norfolk English so common folk might understand it.

Marcello stuffed a pallet with fresh straw for me to sleep on and curtained off a corner of his workshop to create a makeshift room for me. As I tended Rosangela through her pregnancy, I was sometimes seized by visions that I was tending the expectant Virgin Mary and gathering swaddling clothes and clouts in preparation for her divine infant. Every morning I picked raspberry leaves from the riverbank to brew in a tonic to strengthen Rosangela's womb. I sold wooden rosaries in the market to pay for the food I ate.

When Rosangela could spare me, I walked the pilgrims' circuit around the great basilicas of Saint Peter, Saint John Lateran, Saint Paul Outside the Walls, Saint Mary Major, Saint Lawrence Outside the Walls, Saint Sebastian Outside the Walls, and the Holy Cross of Jerusalem. Just as I had promised, I prayed for Cecily, that she might recover from her illness and that one day she might join me in Rome. How I yearned to see her again.

From time to time, I came across Richard, the Irish hunchback. Due to his deformity, he was mistaken for a beggar more often than not and gleaned a full satchel of victuals donated by charitable folk. Apparently still feeling guilty for abandoning me on our first morning at Rosangela and Marcello's, he surrendered his choicest pickings to me.

"Share this with the good people," he said, passing me a loaf of bread, a bunch of grapes that were only slightly bruised, and a hunk of cheese that smelled like a pilgrim's hot and tired feet. "And pray for me, Mistress Margery."

Richard was hoping for a miracle to straighten his spine.

Just before Christmas, Rosangela gave birth to a healthy boy. I fussed over mother and baby every minute, hoping to spare Rosangela from the torpor and melancholy that had possessed me after my first birth. While convalescing, she passed her time teaching me to sing lullabies from her native village.

True to their word, Rosangela and Marcello named me as godmother to their son, Giuseppe, named after Marcello's deceased father. The baby, with his huge wondering eyes and golden ringlets, looked just like Rosangela.

"Our Christ child," I said, rocking him in my arms on Christmas Eve. The very sight of the baby was enough to make we weep. My Juliana would be two by now. Walking and toddling around, getting up to all manner of mischief. Guilt and longing stabbed me like a bodkin.

But then Marcello filled my cup with wine and Rosangela drew me into her songs and laughter.

I was so happy in Rome. For all my foreignness, it seemed the place on earth where I most belonged. In the tiny scrap of land behind Marcello's workshop, an orange tree grew and we ate its sweet fruit through the mild winter. All was well as well could be. In February it grew so warm that the almond trees blossomed. Little Giuseppe thrived.

But the languid weather brought swarms of mosquitoes and the miasma of the swamps. Rosangela suffered a relapse of her ague. Raving and delirious despite my every effort to bring down her fever, she could no longer nurse the baby. Then Marcello fell ill from the malaria as well and could no longer work. All I could do was beg from door to door for food and milk. I carried the screaming baby in my arms so people might take pity on us.

One housewife narrowed her eyes and guffawed. "If you're so poor, why don't you pawn that gold ring you're wearing?"

"A holy anchoress gave it to me," I said, trembling as I tried to comfort the hungry baby. "I could never part from it."

She spat at my feet.

As my last resort, I trudged to the English hostel to plead my case. Surely Friar Timothy would be gone by now, I reasoned. God willing, the steward might take pity on me and at least give me milk for the baby. I made sure to hide my golden ring on a string beneath my gown so no one could try to take it or force me to sell it.

Muzzy with hunger, I wobbled through the open doorway. Everyone turned to stare in silence and shock, for I must have appeared like an apparition. A ghost-white woman with chapped white lips in ragged white clothes who carried a baby wrapped in white swaddling.

Not a soul spoke until the steward came swaggering.

"Get away with you and your bastard!" he snapped, not a shred of mercy on his countenance. "This is no foundling home."

When I stammered that the baby wasn't even mine, he would hear none of it and was about to muscle me out the door when his attention was diverted by a brawl unfolding in one of the upstairs dormitories.

Richard the hunchback, who had been watching this exchange, crept forward and sneaked me into the refectory where the aroma of clam stew and freshly baked bread nearly undid me.

"The steward's as hard as bricks," he said. "But I think you'll find his wife has a soft heart. She's the only reason I stay here instead of the Irish hostel," he added, sounding as though he were besotted with her.

He pointed to a rosy-cheeked young matron of good cheer who was pouring wine for the pilgrims seated at a long table. When men teased her or attempted to flirt, she answered them smartly, losing none of her composure. *There is something so familiar about her*, I thought.

I followed Richard as he approached the young matron to make the introductions. But when she turned and saw me, she shrieked and dropped the wine jug, which crashed to the floor and shattered, splashing red on my white clothes. Likewise, I was so flabbergasted, it was a miracle I didn't drop the baby.

"Nell!" I cried, staring in disbelief at my erstwhile maid, who looked plumper and more buxom than I had ever seen her. "I thought you were a ruined woman."

So well turned out she was, in fine new clothes, albeit ones that were now stained with wine. Round her waist was a leather belt and a chatelaine with her many keys to the cellars and storerooms. Though I had feared the worst for her, it seemed she had landed on her feet and done quite well for herself. Married to the steward of the Hospital of Saint Thomas of Canterbury!

"Me, a ruined woman? Fine talk from you, Margery Kempe," Nell said, her hands on her hips. "God's teeth, did you truly abandon your children back home just to breed a bastard in the Holy Land? Who's the father, pray tell? That milk-faced Rupert? Why, I never!"

The pilgrims at the table swung round to listen, their mouths hanging open like lobster traps.

I hastily explained that the child's parents were poor and desperately ill, and that I was out of money and reduced to begging to feed them. All the while, I gazed deeply into Nell's eyes, willing her to remember that night in the wild German forest when she had clung to me as though I were her mother. Once indeed we had been close if only fleetingly. Friends and allies, not foes.

Though I'd managed to keep Giuseppe relatively quiet thus far, he began to wail in hunger, which made the front of Nell's dress go dark and wet. Grabbing my arm, she hauled me off into a chamber that must have been part of her and her husband's private apartment. Seating herself upon a stool, she took the baby from me, opened her bodice, and began to nurse. I nearly wept in relief to see that poor baby drinking his fill at last.

Nell caught my eye and scowled. "Whatever you do, don't start with your tears," she said crossly. "You'll wake my little girl."

Only then did I notice the cradle, tended by a young maid, where Nell's baby daughter slept peacefully. To think that my former maid lived in plenty with servants of her own while I had to grovel for her charity.

"What a lovely little lass," I said, peering into the cradle. The infant appeared to be about four months old. I began to count the months on my fingers. "She isn't Hugh's?" I whispered in consternation.

Her maid looked askance while Nell threw me a tight-lipped glare. She ordered the girl out of the room.

"I was an honest widow when my good husband married me," she said loudly, as if she expected the girl to be listening at the door.

Then she crooked her finger, beckoning me to come and put my ear to her lips.

"And don't you *dare* say otherwise," she whispered murderously.

I sat down and bided my time until she had finished nursing. Giuseppe burped into her snood, then gazed at her worshipfully as if Nell were the font of all goodness.

"Could you find it in your heart to help the boy's parents," I began.

Nell cut me off. "Now you shall go out into the refectory and eat your fill so you don't drop dead on my clean floor. Next, I shall follow you to that family's house and give them what charity they need. But under one, and only one, condition, Margery Kempe. You must promise to do exactly as I say."

"Anything, Nell," I said. What other choice did I have?

"I will give you money for the passage home," she said. "You will leave Rome tomorrow morning and never show your face in this hostel again."

I buckled on my stool, partly from hunger but mostly from the thought of being wrenched away from Rosangela and Marcello.

"But I'm the little boy's godmother," I said. "I swear I won't breathe a word about your past." I knew she was forcing me away because she was terrified I would betray her and so unravel her good fortune.

Nell regarded me as though I were the most infuriating creature she had ever encountered. "For the love of God, go home to your own children, Margery Kempe."

<h1 style="text-align:center">19</h1>

TRAVELED BACK TO ENGLAND with an especially dour group of herring merchants from Yarmouth. The only other woman in the party was Jennet, thirty and yet unwed, who served as long-suffering nursemaid to her father, who complained constantly of his sore feet and indigestion.

As we sailed down the Rhine, a journey at once swifter and more dangerous than my arduous upriver passage well more than a year ago, Jennet marveled at how long I had been away from Lynn.

"If we return to Yarmouth in good time, we'll have been away nine and a half months, *and* we've seen all the holy sites in Rome and Jerusalem. But *you've* been away for more than a year and a half and all on your own! Aren't you afraid what folk will surmise? Many a woman has lost her reputation for less."

I replied, perhaps too defensively, that it had never entered my mind that traveling to Jerusalem on my departed father's behest and serving the poor of Rome would damage my good name, but if it did, so be it, for good works meant more to me than the vanities of this world. Still, Jennet's words left a chill on me. What *would* people in Lynn think when I returned after such a long absence?

I hoped to pass through Zierikzee on my return voyage and visit Godelieve. But when we reached the River Waal, our boat's captain insisted that he would not be landing in Zierikzee.

"Have you not heard that most of the city burned to ash last year?" he asked. "Someone's thatch caught fire and it spread through the entire town. No, we'll be sailing to Middelburg instead. From there, you can sail back to England."

Rigid with apprehension, I fretted about the fate of Godelieve and her sister beguines—and the copy they had made of Julian's manuscript.

After landing in Yarmouth, I hastened to Norwich where I hoped to spill my every tale to Julian. Oh, to sit with her again and receive her wise counsel, her friendship as comforting as coddled wine. But when I arrived at her anchorage window, the shutters were closed. Her maid sadly informed me that Julian was ill and not receiving visitors. Alas, I had no money to stay on in Norwich while waiting for her recovery, and the Sisters at Carrow Priory accommodated me for only two nights before they packed me off home in a wool wagon. To my deep disappointment, my daughter Anna remained lukewarm to me and seemed relieved to see me depart.

Thus, not a ha'penny left in my purse, I returned to Bishop's Lynn after nearly two years of travel.

When pilgrims first set off on their jubilant and perilous journey to holy places, nobody ever warns them what an ordeal it is to come home. My travels had utterly transformed me. I had witnessed a holy man being burned alive as a supposed heretic. I had conversed with all manner of educated holy women across Europe. Saint Bridget's maidservant had wept in my arms. I had learned to speak Italian. I had crossed the Alps on foot, ridden an ass across the Holy Land, and befriended a Muslim man. I had swooned in thrall of my visions in the Holy Sepulcher.

But what did anyone here in Lynn care? The town was just as money counting and full of snake-tongued gossips as ever. When I crossed the Saturday Market, my pilgrim's staff ringing out against the cobbles, fishwives and cheese mongers pointed and sniggered, as though they were in on some nasty surprise in store for me. I dragged my feet every step down those all-too-familiar streets.

First, I went to my mother's house in Briggate where I hoped to reunite with Juliana who would be two and a half by now. More girl-child than baby. Mother, at least, would welcome me with open arms. She understood the reasons for my wandering.

I knocked on her door, but the shutters were closed and no one answered.

Uneasiness spread through me as I pressed on to the house I had shared with John, the seat of too many unhappy memories. Girding myself, I went round to the back and attempted the kitchen door, but it was bolted. So I knocked, thinking that one of my boys would open. I sought to arrange my face in a suitably loving expression. *They're your children, not terrifying strangers.*

Who should answer but Hester, our hatchet-faced maid. Her enormous pregnant belly filled the doorway. When I stared in shock, she smirked, as if daring me to reproach her.

"A lusty man John Kempe is," she said. "Such a disgrace that a married man is forced to sin to have his needs met."

I'll confess that my first thought was *God be praised, it's her and not me bearing John Kempe's fifteenth child.* So much for his vow of chastity.

I brusquely squeezed past her bulk, strode into my kitchen, and called out to my boys. "Edwin! Lucas! Alan! Peter!"

How I regretted having no gifts for them. But I'd stories in plenty. Tales to last the rest of our lives together. When I heard no answering calls or footfalls, I darted up the stairs and called out again. My voice echoed through the empty rooms.

"They're off helping their father in the brewery," Hester shouted from the bottom of the stairs. "Even little Peter's nine by now. Poor motherless lad."

In my old life, I would have dismissed her on the spot for speaking to me with such impudence. But I felt too dried up and empty to be angry with her.

"Juliana's at Mistress Isabella's," she went on, in that same harping tone. "Your mother, bless her immortal soul, died in December with both you and your brother abroad. Terrible lonely end for the good lady."

At this, I cupped my hands to my face, my pilgrim's staff crashing to the floor.

An hour or so later, when John and the boys returned from the brewery, I hardly recognized my husband. It seemed he had aged a decade during my absence. He'd gone quite bald and his jowls hung loosely. His bunions gave him such trouble that he could only limp along like a knackered old horse. No longer able to move freely, he had grown fat. When I went to greet him, I stopped short. His hostility and resentment flared up like an invisible fortress wall.

As to Hester's condition, John seemed both uneasy and defiant. Most men would have cast out a pregnant servant even if they were the father of her child. *Had John kept Hester on out of Christian charity, or guilt, or because he truly cared for her?* I wondered. In truth, I think he held on to her in order to humiliate me. So all of Lynn would know how I had forced him into a life of perdition by abandoning him.

When we sat down to sup, John avoided my gaze and drank too much beer. Our sons, meanwhile, regarded me across the distance of the table as though I were a stranger of whom they had heard only the most hideous rumors. The air was so heavy with blame, I nearly choked on it. Not to mention Hester's awful stockfish soup, full of brittle little bones that caught at the back of my throat.

While we ate, Hester stationed the bulwark of her body in the chamber doorway. Her arms folded across her belly, she stared at me spitefully, clearly wishing me gone.

"Peter, why won't you smile for your mother?" I asked, reaching across the table in an attempt to take his hand.

The boy gazed down into the sludgy gray soup. "You're sitting in Hester's place," he mumbled, before turning to her with mournful eyes.

The maid smiled and winked at my son before glaring at me again.

The knock on the door came as a blessed reprieve. With a sigh, Hester trundled off to see who was calling so late. A moment later my daughter Isabella entered with little Juliana in her arms. Roger, my son-in-law, trailed in her wake.

With a cry of joy, I leapt to embrace my little girl who appeared as chubby and peachy as an Italian cherub. But when I tried to take her in my arms, the child recoiled and clung to Isabella, calling her mama.

I looked at Isabella in confusion.

"I've been raising her as my own," she said quietly. "It's easier that way." She glanced at her husband. "Roger and I thought it best if you stayed with us, especially if you wish to continue to live chastely."

John stared sullenly into his beer.

I turned to my son-in-law to see what he made of this arrangement. The tall young man appeared goggle-eyed, as though someone had shoved a pine cone up his backside.

The following dawn, I stole through the silent streets to seek out Mother's grave in Saint Margaret's churchyard. Though it was the height of spring with the thorn trees in full blossom, my deep grief at Mother's passing gripped me like a killing frost. It laid waste to my soul. If only I had been there to say goodbye to her. My noisy weeping rent the morning stillness.

I cried the whole day long, my tears jarring the quiet order of Isabella's household. In her last will and testament, Mother had bequeathed her house in Briggate neither to my erstwhile brother in Danzig nor to John Kempe, much to his bitter disappointment. Instead, Isabella and Roger were the new owners.

While I was exceedingly grateful for their hospitality and for the refuge they gave me from John and Hester, how odd it was, at the age of forty-two, to return to my girlhood bedchamber where once I had pined for Martin and dreamt over the pilgrimage map. Being penniless, I was wholly reliant on Isabella and Roger's charity and goodwill—and also beholden to live by their rules. My daughter found my tattered white clothes unseemly and gave me some of Mother's old gowns to wear. Every Sunday my boys dutifully came to visit me, but their stiffness and awkwardness around me never softened. John didn't visit me once. For this, I was secretly relieved.

Isabella was kind yet distant, immersed in her housewifery and in caring for Juliana and her own child, Little Roger. Perhaps on account of my grief and weeping, Juliana remained leery of me no matter how I tried to coax her. When I attempted to help Isabella, she brushed me out of the way, preferring her own manner of doing things. As for Roger, he saw and spoke to me as little as he could. I think he had only agreed to take me in to appease Isabella, whom he adored and doted upon.

One morning I awakened feeling a bit feverish. Nonetheless, I resolved to visit Master Alan at the Carmelite friary. I was convinced that he at least would listen eagerly to my pilgrim's tales. His company would be the very best medicine for what ailed me. He, my dearest friend in all Lynn, would find some mystical text that described precisely the weeping seizures that had overpowered me in the Church of the Holy Sepulcher. Though Isabella disapproved, I changed back into my white clothes, bedraggled though they were, before rushing off to the friary.

For the first time in many weeks, my heart lifted as I hastened up the church nave to his anchorage window. Dropping down on the bench, I peered through the bars to see the holy man seated at his desk and immersed in one of his weighty tomes.

"Master Alan!" I called out. "I'm back from Jerusalem!"

His head snapped up. "Indeed you are, Margery Kempe," he said in a chilly voice. "I've heard the talk about you."

I faltered. "The talk that I'm back in Lynn, you mean?"

"Don't be coy." His face was as hard as an iron spade. "What did you do with that brown Saracen bastard you bred in the Holy Land? Did you just abandon it—like your children here in Lynn?"

I froze, too flabbergasted to speak. Had the vile gossip from the English hostel in Rome followed me all the way back to Lynn but now so embellished as to have me pregnant by blameless Isa? I flinched to recall the slurs Friar Timothy had hurled my way when Isa lifted me from my swoon on the road to Jerusalem.

"False rumors," I said. "God knows that since I went away I never did anything that could *get* me with child."

Master Alan shook his head in disdain. The wicked talk had poisoned him and turned him against me. He slammed his shutters in my face.

Had my sons heard those rumors, too? I wondered, as I trudged out of the friary gates. Is that why they couldn't forgive me for going away on pilgrimage? For a moment, I almost wished I *had* sinned in the Holy Land. Fallen into Isa's arms on the Mount of Temptation. At least then

I might have had some pleasure from this whole sordid story. Never mind that my desire for Isa had been completely one-sided and that he, in all his dealings, had treated me with the utmost honor and respect.

As I plodded back to Briggate, the beggars laughed at me, a woman in white rags. Friendless and outcast. For the rest of my days, I would be the fool of Lynn, the butt of every joke. I told myself to pray and rise above this, to abide in holy serenity, but Master Alan's condemnation lacerated me.

Cornering Isabella in the kitchen, I appealed to her with frantic urgency. "Those rumors you may have heard about me aren't true. Surely *you* wouldn't believe such horrible things of me!"

Isabella's pale brow rumpled. "Mother, you don't look well. You'd best lie down."

My head was pounding, my skin scorching. Though I had remained hale and hearty during my long pilgrimage even when those around me had suffered all manner of disease, only now, in the comfort of my daughter's well-appointed home, I fell deathly ill with the bloody flux.

I thought I was done for. At last I would return to my Beloved. My sufferings would finally be over.

Isabella called out Father Spryngegold to give me the last rites. My sons and little Juliana peered at me solemnly from the opposite end of that dim room. When the priest held the crucifix over my face, my silent prayer was *Please let this be the end.*

Yet however much I willed myself to depart from the agonies of this existence, my stubborn old body clung to life, though it took me all the long winter to regain my strength. As I lay convalescing, I wrestled with my despair. If I was to go on living, I needed a purpose. Before it had always been Jerusalem, but now that I had returned from the Holy Land, what else was there?

Still, the pilgrim's path kept calling me. I imagined myself following Ignatius's footsteps, embracing the open road as my true and eternal home, devoting my life to that never-ending journey to the sacred places. Once a wanderer, always a wanderer. Even in my sickbed, I was too restless for this town, this sedentary existence. I meditated upon the life of Saint Bridget who had traversed the world to visit the three holiest shrines—Jerusalem, Rome, and Santiago de Compostela, the resting place of Saint James the Apostle. The following year, 1417, was a jubilee year, when the Feast of Saint James, July 25, fell upon a Sunday. The apostle's relics, normally concealed in the sacristy, would be on display in the cathedral. Anyone who visited Santiago that year would be granted a plenary indulgence, the full remission of all punishment due for one's sins. Making this pilgrimage would wipe the slate of my soul clean and give me a brand-new purpose. The next jubilee year would not come for another fourteen years.

Slowly, in the depths of my heart, a seed was planted. A new calling that gave me the fortitude to claw my way out of the living grave that Lynn had become.

In March 1416 I was finally well enough to attend church again. It being the middle of Lent, all the holy images and even the giant crucifix above the rood screen were obscured in white cloth. The church seemed as bleak as nature in this cold, late spring when the branches remained bare and frost glittered on the ground.

After Sunday High Mass, with all the townsfolk of Lynn milling around me, I made my announcement, my voice amplified beneath that vaulted stone ceiling.

"Ever since my return from the Holy Land, false rumors have plagued me and unjustly besmirched my reputation," I said, holding my head high to meet the gaze of those who gawped at me. "But God knows my innocence even if some of my fellow burghers are prey to gossip and lies. God has called me to go on pilgrimage again, this time to Santiago de Compostela, when I have sufficient funds. If anyone wishes to donate a few coins, I promise to pray for you at the Shrine of Saint James."

My declaration was met with mockery. As the never-ending refrain went, who did I think I was? Isabella and Roger looked mortified that they couldn't even accompany me to Mass without my making a spectacle of myself. John rolled his eyes and my sons looked as though they wanted to pretend they didn't know me.

But none of this mattered anymore. For once, I remained unruffled, for I had nothing left to lose. Their ridicule only served to drive the point home that I didn't belong here. Had never belonged here. The far-flung holy places beckoned me to a whole other life of service far beyond the stifling walls of Lynn.

None dared approach me in the crowded church that morning, but in the following weeks and months, women discreetly walked up to me in the streets or the market. The midwife slipped me a few coins. The candlemaker's wife offered me all she could spare along with the request that I pray for her to finally conceive a child. The butcher's wife gave me a golden noble coin and asked that I pray for her husband to leave her in peace so she wouldn't have any more children — the poor woman had already endured nearly as many pregnancies as I had. An old friend of my father's gave me forty pence and a distant cousin of Mother's gave me seven marks.

Master Alan sent a messenger to fetch me to his anchorage where he awaited me, his eyes blinking and sad.

"After much prayer and contemplation, I realize that I have wronged you, my friend," he said. "I should have known better than to believe gossip. I hear you wish to make the journey to Santiago. May I offer you this along with my most humble apologies?"

Through his barred window, he attempted to pass me a heavy sack of coins. But I refused to take it.

"This is a sudden turn of face," I said tepidly, for I could still not get over the sting of his betrayal. "How could you have believed, even for a second, that I would abandon a helpless baby in a foreign land? To think *you*, of all people, could be so fickle."

With a defeated air, he rubbed his brow with his ink-stained hands.

"Forgive me, Margery. I'm just an old man bricked within these walls while you wander the wide world. Perhaps my years of confinement have made me easy prey to the sin of envy and, thus, to believing idle rumors. But please listen to me."

He gripped the window bars and leaned in to face me.

"Last night I dreamt about you," he said. "You were in grave danger and crying out to me for help. I yearned with all my heart to come to your aid, but I remained trapped within these walls. You were surrounded by strangers." He shuddered as if a scorpion had skittered down his spine. "High-ranking church men accused you of far worse crimes than bearing a bastard child. If you're set on leaving Lynn, I beg you to take care, Margery. There are more evil things in this world than wagging tongues and gossips."

Looking into his eyes, I saw how frightened he was for me. Yet I remained calm. Undeterred.

"You know why I can't stay in Lynn," I said. "When God calls us to adventure, how can we refuse? It would be the death of my soul."

Master Alan regarded me with what appeared to be the most solemn respect. "You're more courageous than I could ever hope to be, Margery Kempe. I implore you to at least let me give you this."

He passed his heavy bag of coins to me. This time I accepted it.

But the most astonishing twist was still to come. When I returned to Isabella's house, my daughter called me into the parlor, sat me in Mother's old chair, and served me wine in a silver-rimmed cup.

Roger entered the chamber, his face shining with resolve. A merchant with a shrewd head for business, he had done very well for himself of late. Now he handed me a purse heavy with gold.

"A pilgrimage to Santiago is a most holy endeavor," he said. "This should pay your way."

I thought my son-in-law would dance a jig, he looked so pleased with himself to get me out of his house with a clear conscience. I wonder if he kicked himself for not thinking of this sooner.

Isabella sparkled in good cheer. "I shall sew new white clothes for you, Mother."

My daughter was so generous, she made two white gowns for me, so I would have a spare if the first wore out.

20

HUS, ALMOST TWO FULL years after I had returned to Lynn, I left once more, setting out for Santiago in April 1417. The instant I stepped free of those city walls, exhilaration coursed through me. I felt as though I could leap over the moon and kick up my heels to graze the stars.

First I headed to Norwich where, at long last, I was reunited with Julian. When she saw me at her anchorage window, her smile was as wide as the sky.

"Dearest Margery, what a joy to see you looking so well. Every single day since we parted, I've prayed for your safety and happiness."

Oh, the wonder of seeing her again, she whose counsel and visions had been my refuge. Yet I felt a tug in my heart to see how she had aged and wizened and shrunk into herself since our last meeting almost four years ago. She appeared more birdlike than human, so thin she was, her cheekbones standing proud of her mild and loving face. She was short of breath and it taxed her to speak for too long. But her blue eyes were as luminous as ever, and she marveled as I told her of my travels and about the learned women and men who had copied her manuscript. Murmuring in her ear, I confessed how close I had come to betraying us both in Jerusalem. But that, thanks to Brother Ambrose's discretion and God's grace, all had been well. I then confided how miserable I had been in Lynn. How I'd finally gathered the courage and funds to make a new pilgrimage to Santiago de Compostela.

"*Campo stella,* Saint James's field of stars!" she exclaimed, clapping her hands in glee. "How I wish I could go with you." Something caught in her voice that made me reach for her hand. "I will be with you in spirit," she said firmly. "Every step you take."

"Julian," I said. "In God's name, I never want to go home again. Is that a sin? I want to dedicate the rest of my life as a pilgrimage even when I return from Santiago by God's grace. All the years that remain to me I shall wander from one holy place to the next. Like my friend Ignatius who guided me across the Alps."

She listened so patiently, this woman who had more faith in me than any other human being.

"Your words are bold," she said. "But your voice is full of doubt. It's not me you must persuade if you yourself lack conviction."

"If I were a man, I wouldn't have the slightest hesitation," I said, speaking more forcefully. "But I've never yet met a woman who wandered her whole life long as some men do."

"I don't know of any wandering holy women either," Julian said, after a long and thoughtful pause. "Except for Saint Ursula, but she didn't walk alone. She had her eleven thousand virgins as companions. I've read of lone female hermits, such as Mary of Egypt, but she didn't wander to the ends of the earth like you, dear Margery. Perhaps you shall be the first. Perhaps you will forge a path that others might follow."

She spoke with such warmth and encouragement, as if she wanted with every fiber of her being for me to set off on that journey so she might live vicariously through my adventures.

After a week in Julian's company, it was an agony to tear myself away, especially considering how old and frail she was. Would I even see her again? But I could tell how our long conversations had begun to tax her. She needed more and more rest to keep up her remaining strength, and she also had other visitors who sought her counsel.

On the day we parted, I asked her if she wanted me to return her manuscript or continue carrying it in the hidden compartment of my staff.

"I want you to keep it," Julian said, her blue eyes shining, "for as long as you live and wherever you wander, my friend. I hold you in my prayers. Now go in grace."

In the Carrow Priory guesthouse, I had the good fortune to meet Mistress Lucy, a fellow pilgrim. She and her husband, a wealthy wool merchant, were also making the pilgrimage to Santiago and they invited me to join their small band of fellow travelers. Julian's old friend Master Thomas, the tailor who had sewn my original set of white clothing, found a horse for me at a good price, a stalwart black gelding.

On the morning of my departure, I bade farewell to Anna. Ever in the thrall of her prioress who thought the worst of me, Anna embraced me hesitantly.

"I'll bring you a cockle shell from Santiago," I told her. "Even if you can't travel with me, you'll have a keepsake."

Her eyes softened and suddenly she was my daughter again, squeezing me tightly. "Mind how you go, Mother."

She waved from the priory gates when I rode off with my fellow travelers. We headed down the King's highway toward Bristol, England's great western port, where the pilgrim ships to Spain embarked. On that mild spring day we made excellent progress, reaching Thetford before nightfall and finding good accommodation in Thetford Priory.

Though our journey to Bristol was long, stretching over two hundred miles, and though Lucy's husband fretted about rumors of thieves lurking along the King's highway, all was well.

I counted myself blessed to ride through parts of England hitherto unknown to me. We passed through Cambridge with its venerable colleges rising from the banks of the placid River Cam, and I thought of Rupert who had studied in those halls and shared so much of his knowledge with me. I hoped he fared well in his new life in Jerusalem. Some days later, we reached the West Country, which beguiled me with its rolling hills, blossoming orchards, and ancient churches.

We arrived in Bristol in high spirits. A vast city of more than ten thousand souls, Bristol was almost as big as York. Its walls were massive and its castle was one of the grandest in the land. But what impressed me most was the High Cross, as lofty and ornate as a cathedral spire, that took pride of place at the crossroads of the four main streets. On our way to the pier, we passed ropemakers' and sailcloth weavers' workshops. Bristol Harbor was the biggest I had seen in all England, with ships from distant corners of the world. Yet, though my companions and I spent all the remaining daylight hours making inquiries, we could not find a single ship bound for Spain. As it transpired, our King Henry, intent on invading France, had requisitioned shipping and ordered all English vessels to assemble in Southampton.

This most unwelcome news pitched my companions and me into despair, leaving us to wonder if we would ever reach Santiago. The notion of returning to Lynn in defeat filled me with dread. That sleepless night in the hostel, I prayed for some sign of how to proceed.

The next morning, Lucy and her husband and the others decided to ride from port to port in search of a ship to Spain. Like me, they were determined to persevere, not wanting to miss this jubilee year pilgrimage.

It made absolute sense to journey onward with them. But a quiet voice inside my heart urged me to stay in Bristol. So I waved goodbye to my friends, then went to the horse fair to sell the black gelding to help pay for my bed and board. I didn't know how long I would have to wait in Bristol, and the many other stranded travelers were driving up the price of accommodation. I could only bide my time and pray.

Yet I felt so curiously lighthearted and free, for I had escaped Lynn and I felt Julian's blessing as sure as my own breath. Every morning in that crowded hostel where we slept three to a bed, I awakened to the cries of gulls and I reminded myself, *You are just as free and untethered.* My fellow travelers were far too perturbed about the dearth of ships to bother much about my quirks and eccentricities. Perhaps this *was* my true home, I thought. Not Bristol, not this pilgrims' hospice, but the pilgrims' path itself with all its unexpected obstacles and detours. It helped that it was spring and so clement in the West Country, everything gilded in dazzling sunlight that made it hard to believe that across the Channel English armies were waging war on France. Many an hour I spent in prayer and sweet contemplation in Saint Peter's Church in the shadow of Bristol Castle.

On Palm Sunday, I joined the great and solemn procession that reenacted Christ's triumphant entry into Jerusalem. Since no palms grew on these shores, we carried yew branches to symbolize Christ's victory over death. Singing hymns, we surged through the streets and laid down our greenery in the path of the wheeled platform bearing the wooden figure of Christ astride the donkey. I reflected on how the joy and welcome of his arrival in Jerusalem was so cruelly overshadowed by his coming betrayal and passion. Following the image of Christ came a priest bearing the holy sacrament in its jeweled monstrance. How I trembled before this mystery of mysteries.

Here in such a big city, I'd little chance of creating a scandal with my weeping, or so I told myself. In such a busy port, with visitors from as far away as Africa and Iceland, the good people of Bristol had seen it all before and would not find me remarkable in any way. And so I allowed my guard to drop. I dared to gaze at the host in its monstrance. Before I could blink, the host became the body of my Beloved, slain for us all. He opened the gash in his side to show me his heart where we all dwelled in Mother God's eternal love. Pilgrims in paradise. As the ecstasies shook me to pieces, I wept so violently that I collapsed in the middle of Corn Street, as if I would die there.

When I came to, I found myself upon a bed in an unfamiliar room. Sitting bolt upright, I exhaled in relief to find my staff propped in the corner, my purse still attached to my girdle, and my gold ring still on my finger. But the back of my head throbbed from where I had crashed on the cobbles. Sliding off the embroidered counterpane, I made my way to the door, but it was bolted from the outside. I went to the dormer window and looked out on a garden many stories below. Too high to jump. Judging from the sun's position in the west, it was early evening. I had lain there for hours, utterly insensible.

A decently appointed room, this was, with fresh rushes on the floor and a pewter jug of water for washing. No doubt this was some wealthy merchant's house. Perhaps they had taken me here out of charity after I'd collapsed. But why was I locked up like a prisoner? My first thought, may God forgive me, was that my inner voice had betrayed me. I should have followed my companions when they rode off to other ports. Perhaps they had already arrived in Spain and were walking the Camino Inglés toward Santiago. What would happen to me now—had I created such a disturbance that the Bristol authorities would send me back to Lynn in disgrace?

I banged on the door and called out until I heard footsteps and the bolt sliding free. A finely appareled lady entered, followed by her maid who brought me a tray of bread and milk.

"Thank heavens you're finally awake," the lady said. "You must forgive me for leaving you alone, but my maid and I were attending the Bishop of Worcester's men, who have come to deliver you to their master."

Panic washed through me. "What have I done to warrant such attention?"

The lady, about my age and clad in the sort of fine brocade I had once so coveted, smiled archly, one ash-blonde eyebrow curving up her white forehead. "You were crying out over and over to Mother God."

Her words made me sink weakly on the edge of the bed, my hands clenched in my lap. The maid stared at me with wide-open eyes as though wondering whether I was a saint or a heretic. Then she lowered her gaze and set down the tray of bread and milk. The very thought of food made my stomach turn.

"Some people said you must be drunk, but we could smell no drink on your breath," the lady continued. "Others thought you were mad, but the steward of the pilgrims' hospice swore you were as sane as the day. Perhaps you're a Lollard. One of Oldcastle's instigators." Her eyes were as hard and brittle as glass. "Their women are preachers, are they not? I heard it rumored they even serve communion." Her voice shook at the blasphemy of it.

I thought the roof would come crashing down on me.

The lady, all business, ordered her maid to pour washing water in the ewer so I could make myself presentable.

"You haven't far to go," the girl murmured, as she laid out my shoes and handed me my staff. "The bishop's palace is only three miles away."

Many a tale I'd heard concerning Thomas Peverell, the Bishop of Worcester. Some years ago, he had condemned to death one John Badby of Evesham as a heretic. But just as chilling to me was the fact that this bishop hailed from Lynn, where he had begun his vocation as a monk in the same Carmelite friary where Master Alan dwelled. The man had been well acquainted with my father, one of the friary's main benefactors. He had known of me since I was a child and had no doubt heard the rumors concerning my spotted reputation.

All these thoughts galloped through my head as I followed the maid down steep stairs while the lady followed behind me. They kept me between them as though to discourage any hope of escape, the maid taking the lead in case I was mad enough to attempt to push her down the stairs in my attempt to flee.

The bishop's men, assembled at the foot of the stairs, were arrayed like princes, their doublets modishly striped and slashed to reveal the richly dyed and embroidered silk they wore beneath. Their boots were polished to such a shine as to rival that of a communion chalice. The very sight of these men made my bones knock together with such force, I feared I might collapse.

Sparing not a second, they marched me toward their wagon.

At the bishop's palace at Henbury, they delivered me to the private chapel where I shivered and wrung my hands before a fresco of sinners and heretics tumbling into the hellmouth.

When the door opened and a servant announced the bishop, I knelt on the frigid stone floor and braced myself. The man who hobbled in was as bent and shriveled with age as Julian but with none of her peace. His pale gray eyes looked haunted. He could only shuffle along by grasping a hazelwood cane in his bony hand.

His servant did him the mercy of bringing him a chair to sit on. But none for me. A supplicant, I remained on my knees.

"I hear you hail from Lynn," the bishop said in an overly familiar tone that set my nerves on edge. "John Brunham's only daughter. Meg, is it not?"

"Margery," I said thinly. "Margery Kempe."

"I remember seeing you in the Corpus Christi procession when you were only a slip of a girl," he said with strained nostalgia, as though wishing to turn back the years. "Dressed like a princess in all that silk." He chuckled, which irked me beyond reason.

"Just like your men who dragged me here from Bristol," I said, more tartly than was prudent.

My retort made him wince.

"Reverend Sir," I said, taking advantage of his momentary loss for words. "Would you do me the honor of explaining why you summoned me? I am but an honest pilgrim on my way to Santiago, by God's grace."

"You caused much consternation," he said, "with your cries to Mother God. The canons of Bristol raised the alarm and all but ordered me to examine you for heresy, such a terror they have of Oldcastle and his Lollard plots." He sounded weary, as though he wanted no part of this but his hands were tied.

I had always been able to elude such accusations before, but what defense could I offer after so many witnesses had heard my utterances? My only hope was to defiantly bluster through.

"I'm no Lollard," I declared. "I've nothing in common with poor John Badby."

Badby, I knew, had been sentenced to burn because he had denied the sacrament of the Eucharist and proclaimed that the host was simply a wafer made of flour and water, not the body of Christ.

"All Bristol saw me falling in reverence before the true host," I said. "As for calling out to Mother God, Bernard of Clairvaux and his Cistercian Brothers did exactly the same three centuries ago. You yourself know me to be a good man's daughter."

I hoped to hide my terror under my boldness. But what if the bishop or his henchmen discovered Julian's manuscript?

If anything, my tirade seemed to relieve the bishop. His hunched shoulders eased.

"I forget my hospitality," he said.

What astonished me most was how he bent with great humility to draw me to my feet even though he was so frail that I feared he might fall.

"You must stay here as my guest, Margery Kempe, until a ship arrives to take you to Spain." At that, he smiled, as though in gratitude that we could put this ugly talk of heresy behind us.

I dined with the bishop in his parlor. Though the night was sultry, his windows were closed and he wore a fur cape around his bony shoulders. Famished from my ordeal, I devoured the plaice and turbot as though I were a plowman who had labored twelve hours in the field. The bishop, however, only ate and drank sparingly.

"You mustn't think me a heartless man," he said, his face spectral in the unsteady candlelight. "I will never forgive myself for the burning of John Badby. I had no desire to persecute him—he was an honest man. A tailor with a great brood of children. I turned a blind eye on his preaching against the sacrament for as long as I could. But when he made his proclamations in the very shadow of Bristol Cathedral, the canons and prelates would give me no peace and threatened to accuse *me* of Lollardy unless I examined him."

He set down his silver cup and covered his face in his thin, ropy hands.

"I spent many an hour with him in earnest entreaty, thinking I could bring him back into the grace of the Church. Send him home to his wife and children. But he would not recant."

His shoulders shook—the man was weeping. I bowed my head as his grief filled the air.

"A year later, they took him to Smithfield to be burned. Prince Henry, now our king, begged him to back down and repent. Still the man refused. Such unshakeable principles."

The bishop's voice trailed off. Despite the heat of the evening, I shivered, at a loss for words. I remembered Jan Hus burning alive in Constance, how Christlike he had been in his courage and forbearance. Like Jan Hus, John Badby had been only one dissenter. But they had made him a martyr, and now he would never die.

"Seven years ago, he burned," the Bishop of Worcester said, his eyes glittering with tears. "His ghost will give me no rest. Night after night I awaken to the nightmares. His ghost told me I've only two more years left to live. I fear I'm bound for hell."

"Wisht," I said, reaching to take the bishop's hand as though he were my child. "God forgives all sin."

He uttered a hollow laugh. "What confessor will absolve me for regretting with all my heart that I performed the duties of my office in upholding the doctrine?" He pushed away his goblet and turned to me, as if I were the only soul who could understand his anguish. "All my days I have loved and served the Church. But I fear a new age of terror has dawned. The Church is becoming more and more intolerant."

A premonition gripped me, for hadn't I heard Julian say just the same almost four years ago when I first sought her blessing before leaving on pilgrimage?

The bishop's head sank so heavily, I feared his neck might snap.

"Margery," he said. "By all that is holy, I can never forgive myself for being a part of that terror."

During my fortnight at Henbury Palace as the Bishop of Worcester's guest, I sought to comfort him as best I could. I nearly read to him from Julian's manuscript, but that would have been a risk too far for the poor conflicted man.

Then came the news that a ship from Brittany had sailed into Bristol Harbor and was bound for Spain. Only the bishop's intercession managed to secure me a berth on that vessel with all the other Santiago-bound pilgrims clamoring for passage. The bishop gave me ten marks to help pay for my journey.

"If only I were younger and stronger, I would go with you," he said when we parted at his palace gates. "Pray for me, dear Margery." He embraced me as though I were his daughter. "I wish to die in charity."

21

LESSED BY FINE WEATHER and favorable winds, our voyage from Bristol to Ferrol in Galicia lasted a mere six days. Then I was walking down the Camino Inglés, a cockleshell pilgrim with a scallop shell sewn to my wide-brimmed hat that protected me from the strong southern sun. I joined the ranks of countless others, mainly English and Irish. The hordes of us crowding the Camino were enough to make the bandits throw up their hands in despair, for there were too many of us to attack.

In the churches on our way, we pressed in so tightly that all I could do was stand as stiffly as a marble statue with my staff clutched against my side lest I accidently poke out someone's eye. The hostels heaved with pilgrims. More often than not, I had to spread my ship mat on the floor since the beds were full. Yet despite the crowded conditions, everyone was jubilant, for it was a miracle we were here at all. King Henry's wars be damned, we were walking the Camino in this jubilee year. Oh, the fellowship we shared along with the potent red wine and octopus stew each evening after a long day's march.

How can I describe the beauty of those Galician hills, as green and lush as anything in England but far warmer, with apricots and peaches ripening on the trees and sweet melons growing in every garden? Just as it seemed to become *too* hot, the rains came to cool us and make the honey-colored stone buildings in the towns and villages glitter like gold, with crystal waterfalls gushing from the mouth of every gargoyle. Soon enough, the weather lifted again, leaving only a few fluffy sheeplike clouds in an endless field of blue. How could I not be merry?

My closest companion for the journey was a fifteen-year-old Cornish girl named Derwa with red-gold curls, a face like a lily, and failing eyesight. Though she was proud and independent, and sought to make her own way using only her staff to guide her, I persuaded her to let me take her arm and help her navigate the obstacles in our way — the streams we had to ford, the many ruts in the road, the razor-sharp brambles, and the countless cowpats. It was my deepest honor to serve her, for I was so in awe of this girl and the perilous journey she had made, a blacksmith's daughter who had set off on her own with only her faith and her staff to protect her.

Yet a deep air of melancholy shrouded the girl like a thick and impenetrable fog. She suffered crying jags that rivaled mine but with no hint of the ecstasies I experienced. She was prey to nightmares that sent her screaming and raving until some of our fellow pilgrims worried that she must be mad. But as one who had spent a fair amount of time raving and screaming myself, I sensed that Derwa was no lunatic. *No,* I thought, *she suffered from a deep wounding of the soul.*

One afternoon, when the fierce sun drove us to seek shelter under a chestnut tree near a rushing brook, Derwa remarked, in what sounded like forced cheer, that she hoped that this jubilee year pilgrimage would save her from hell. My thoughts turned to Julian's manuscript and how Julian would shake her head at the very idea of young Derwa burning in eternal damnation. But what use was the manuscript to this girl who couldn't even see the words on the page?

Derwa seemed to be slipping into despair. Seeking to lighten her mood, I asked her to tell me the legend of Saint James — when she was spinning her tales, her worries seemed to fall away. At once her weak eyes lit up, as though she saw Saint James standing before us, his cloak and hat covered in scallop shells.

"James," she said in her young, warm voice, "was a simple fisherman on the shores of the Sea of Galilee when Our Lord called him from his nets and summoned him to become a disciple."

My thoughts traveled back to the Holy Land and my own visit to Galilee. I could almost feel the desert sun burning my skin.

"Later, after Our Lord's death and resurrection, the apostles dispersed to spread the Gospels," Derwa went on. "And where did James go but Spain?" Her voice lilted like an angel's. I wanted to place a harp in her hands and hear her sing her tale.

"Much later, Saint James returned to Jerusalem, only to be beheaded by Herod." She spat out the tyrant's name like a curse. "But James's followers carried his corpse to Jaffa where a boat made of stone without crew or sails appeared, and it bore the dead apostle in just seven days to Padrón on the Atlantic coast of Galicia." Her voice rang with the wonder of it all. "Lupa, the queen, buried Saint James in a marble tomb some distance inland. But soon thereafter, his tomb was forgotten." Her voice grew somber. "Meanwhile, the Moors laid waste to Spain."

While she paused for dramatic effect, I passed her my wineskin filled with water so she could soothe her parched throat.

"*Then*," she said, waving her hands in excitement, "many, many, *many* years later, a hermit was led to a hill by a vision. When he climbed to the very top, he discovered that the grass was covered in stars!" Her voice caught in awe at this ineffable marriage of heaven and earth. "So he called the hill Compostela, the field of stars. And what did he find there but Saint James's tomb, forgotten for centuries?"

I smiled to hear the joy in her voice.

"By and by, they built a chapel over his grave. And then a church. And then a great cathedral! With Saint James's intercession, the Spanish won many a battle against the Moorish heathens," she added with savage glee.

"They're not heathens," I said sharply. I remembered how Isa had blessed himself with water from Mary's Well in Nazareth. "They, too, believe in God." On the Camino, I had been troubled to see the countless statues that depicted Saint James as the Moor-slayer—a knight astride a warhorse trampling a turbaned man.

Derwa seemed too shocked by my outburst to reply. In a gentler tone, I told her about Isa's kindness and the beauty of the mosques I had seen in the Holy Land. This gave her pause for thought.

"To be sure, you know far more of the world than I," she said. "I've never met a woman like you, Margery Kempe."

"Nor have I met anyone as brave as you," I replied. For all my intrepid bravado, I had never dared to travel alone as she had done. And I could see the road before me.

But my words, far from emboldening her, only made her draw into herself, her hands clenched before her breast.

"You keep calling me brave," she said bitterly. "I'm only brave because the worst has already happened and I've nothing left to lose."

"Tell me what troubles you," I pleaded. "Let me help carry your burdens."

Because she still couldn't bring herself to speak of her past, I told her about mine, sparing no shameful detail. How insufferably vain I had been at her age, caring for nothing but beautiful gowns and headdresses. How I had gone stark mad after the birth of my first child and bit my own flesh—I showed her the scar that still marked my left hand. How I had then begun to see visions of Christ. How I'd left my husband and children to go on pilgrimage. How my family had not been able to forgive me. How I had ruined my reputation, been the subject of cruel slander, and yet I still managed to walk this Camino, for what other path was there but this pilgrimage through our earthly existence, our painstaking journey back to the One who had created us?

"If you go to my hometown of Lynn," I confided, "nearly every person you meet in the street will swear I'm wicked. Look at those pilgrims walking down the Camino. Every one of them, even those who appear the most holy, have committed deeds they deeply regret."

Lowering my voice, I told her about the Bishop of Worcester who had condemned a man to burn and thus believed that he, too, might be damned despite all my attempts to convince him otherwise.

"What could you have possibly done, as young as you are, that's so terrible you can't tell me, as flawed as I am?" I asked her.

Derwa found her voice and told me her story. Her own father had taken to ravaging her and so she found herself pregnant at the age of fourteen. In a panic, she ran to the midwife and begged for a potion to loosen the child from her womb. The midwife helped her as best she could, but Derwa became so ill that she nearly perished and was left so damaged, she would never be able to have children. In the aftermath of Derwa's near death, it was impossible to keep her crime a secret. Both she and the midwife were locked in a dank underground dungeon for two and a half months before their trial. Derwa's eyesight had always been poor, but being imprisoned in darkness with no natural light made it far worse. When they dragged her out for the trial, the glare of sunlight after ten weeks of blackness was enough to blind her. She could hardly see the judge, jury, or jeering crowd.

The midwife—the only one in thirty miles—was sentenced to hang. But both the magistrate and the parish priest took pity on Derwa on account of her youth and the injustice done to her by her father. Instead of hanging her, they sent her on pilgrimage to Santiago as her penance, and they ordered her father to give her all his silver to pay her way.

"I can never go home again," she said in dull resignation. "My father will murder me. No one will even hire me as a servant with my eyes so poor."

She feared that after she ran out of money she would have no other choice but to join the beggars who congregated in places like Santiago, many of them blind or crippled. But what frightened her more than anything was the fate of her soul.

"Even if I walk to Santiago on my knees," she declared, "I fear I'm damned. The midwife was a good woman. I lost my mother and the midwife was like an aunt to me. She didn't want to do what she did —she was so afraid of damaging me—but I begged and pleaded until she gave in. On account of me, she was hanged. Not even God can forgive that."

Then she uttered the words I had so often told myself when in the grip of deepest turmoil.

"I belong nowhere."

How could I give this girl hope? I remembered my first glimpse of Julian at her anchorage window almost four years ago when she had reached out both arms to comfort the weeping young prostitute. When I opened my mouth, it was as though Julian spoke through me.

"Derwa, don't tremble before God as though he were a wrathful father." My voice shook as I thought of her earthly father and the evils he had inflicted upon her. "God is also our Mother. Think of the most tender mother's love for her only child. Even greater than this is God's love for you."

Taking a deep breath, I told her of Julian. Of Julian's message of the all-powerful divine love that cannot damn a single soul.

As we drew closer to Santiago, the Camino Inglés converged with the Camino Francés and the Camino Portugués. Before long, I heard the unwelcome racket of English and French pilgrims insulting one another. Fearing they might come to blows and fight their unholy war on the Camino, I took Derwa's arm and rushed ahead, finding refuge amid a group of stout and stalwart Portuguese nuns who cheerfully chattered like sparrows. We had no common language, but the Sisters communicated their goodwill by beaming at me and pinching Derwa's cheeks to give her courage.

Derwa and I clung to each other lest we be separated as the crowd swept through the Porta do Camiño into Santiago. We marched up the Rúa das Ánimas, the street of souls. Flowing along in that sea of bodies, we reached the Praza do Obradoiro where the western face of the cathedral rose before us, magnificent sun-gold granite touching the sky. Saint James gazed down in benediction from his niche in the central tower. Since Derwa trusted me to be her eyes, I described it to her in as much detail as I could. She threw her arms around me and exclaimed in triumph.

Arm in arm, we joined the vast queue to enter the cathedral. When our turn came to pass through the Door of Glory, I guided my friend's right hand to the carved stone roots of the Jesse Tree, the central column in the portico, while we offered prayers of gratitude for our safe travels. Once inside the cathedral, we processed to the high altar where we ascended the steps to embrace the most holy statue of Saint James and kiss his bejeweled cape. My heart caught in my throat to see Derwa lay her hands on his broad shoulders and weep. Afterward, I carefully led her down the slippery stone stairs on the other side, then into the crypt where we took our turn kneeling before the stone casket containing the saint's earthly remains.

Next, we wandered through the great echoing nave where scores of priests, each of them fluent in two or more languages, waited to receive our confessions. One steely-eyed priest, hearing us speak English, beckoned to us, but he was so severe of countenance that I babbled inanely to him in Italian before steering Derwa quickly away. I would not have an unkind priest destroying my young friend's fragile peace. Instead, we walked on until I found a young English-speaking confessor with such a benevolent face, he could have been Julian's grandson.

While Derwa knelt and sobbed at the shriving bench, I prayed that she would find solace. After her confession, she hugged me fiercely as if a great weight had been lifted from her.

"What penance did he give you?" I whispered.

Her eyes widened. "To walk from here to Finisterre, where the land ends and the sea begins, and to burn my old clothes."

Then it was my turn to kneel at the shriving bench and confess how I had turned my own children against me with my eccentric ways even as I sought to embrace a holy life. How I had never been able to reconcile my spiritual quest with my earthly lot of being a wife and mother. How I was only at peace when faring forth to holy places even if that made me a hypocrite.

My confessor did not lecture or upbraid me. "There is no false reason to go on pilgrimage," he said in his Galician-inflected English. "Are we not all searching for something? We must answer the call we have been given. But one day, perhaps when your children are older and can better understand why you left to walk this path, you can reconcile with them. Keep your heart open."

I bowed my head and nodded, thinking of the day when I could talk freely of my journeys to Juliana. To all my children.

"What is my penance, Father?"

He regarded me with both warmth and urgency. "To accompany your young friend to Finisterre and keep her out of harm's way. Doña Pilar, who runs the hostelry there, will make you both very welcome."

"Father, I would have done this even if you hadn't told me," I said solemnly.

"Perhaps you're a much better mother than you think." He smiled. "A mother to the motherless who have no one else. Perhaps God called you to be there for that poor girl."

With a lightened heart, I rose from the shriving bench and joined Derwa. Her smile was enough to melt iron. I had never seen her looking so serene. She embraced me as though I were her lost mother. I had failed my children in so many ways, yet God gave me the grace to comfort Derwa. *Perhaps this girl is my redemption.*

Shriven of our sins, we joined the hundreds of other pilgrims for High Mass amid the swinging of the Botafumeiro, the giant incense burner big enough to crack a titan's skull. It swooped a few feet above our heads, filling the nave with frankincense to purify the air and fumigate us sweaty and none-too-sweet-smelling pilgrims.

The way to Finisterre, some fifty-odd miles west of Santiago, was far less traveled than the main pilgrimage routes. After being hemmed in by crowds for more than a week, what a change it was to bask in birdsong. Clutching my pilgrim's staff as though it were a spear, I kept a stern lookout for thieves on our lonely way, but no one troubled us. We hiked up pine-and-heather-clad hills. Past carved stone crosses and farms with stone grain stores on stilts. Past round stone cottages with conical thatched rooves that brought to mind the refuges of ancient hermits.

Later, our path met the coast where we wandered down white sand beaches and gathered scallop shells as a remembrance of our pilgrimage—I would give the most beautiful shell to Anna as the keepsake I had promised. Derwa carried one in her hand—the curve of it in her palm seemed to give her comfort. To judge from the softness of her face, her worries about her future had dropped away.

Nor did I dwell on what lay in store for me when I returned to England. There was only this beach, the silky sand seeping into my worn shoes. This moment in time, as we placed one foot in front of the other, that seemed to stretch into an eternity of peace and purpose. Every step a prayer.

Our path climbed upward as the coastline grew rocky and treacherous with sheer cliffs plunging into the savage Atlantic. Little wonder the local people called this the Costa da Morte, the Coast of Death. When the sky clouded over and the mists descended, I shivered at the bleakness.

But this rugged outpost had quite the opposite effect on Derwa. Cheeks flushed, she stood with her palms outstretched as if to embrace the misty air that tasted of salt.

"It smells just like Cornwall," she said, as though swept off her feet with a wistful sense of homecoming.

That night we slept in a farmhouse for a few coins. I communicated with hand and foot, not knowing a word of the strong Galician dialect, but Derwa sparked with attention when she listened to the farmwife speak.

"A few of their words sound almost like Cornish," she said in amazement.

She could not seem to get over her sense of the miraculous. It was as though she had entered some enchanted fairy realm that mirrored the world she had left behind but that held none of its dangers. A world where her father could have no more power over her.

"Some people back home," she said, as we set off the next morning, cutting through a pasture of inquisitive heifers, "said my blindness was God's punishment for my sins." Her voice caught and I thought she might weep, yet she soldiered on. "But the priest in Santiago said my suffering makes me closer to God. That I'm not damned—I was never damned. Just like your Julian said, is it not?"

She turned to me, one red-gold tress escaping her snood, her eyes shining with yearning. "Tell me more of what Julian told you."

It was as if the priest in Santiago had sent us to Finisterre to give us the solitude to contemplate all we had experienced on our pilgrimage. Walking with Derwa, I tried to convey everything Julian had taught me.

On the fourth day, we arrived at Finisterre, or Finis Terrae, the end of the earth, which was at the very tip of the long cape. In the shadow of the lighthouse, we hid in the bushes to change into our spare set of clothing. Then we gathered firewood, Derwa deftly seeking out dry, dead branches by touch with a dexterity that astonished me, but I was vigilant lest she wander too close to the cliff edge.

When we had heaped the wood in a pile, I struck flint to kindle a spark as Ignatius had taught me on our journey across the Alps. Once the fire caught and began to dance high, Derwa and I burned the garments we had walked in, my white gown and veil gone grimy from the miles of dust and mud. Leaping flames burned our old clothes to ash, which the wind whipped away while the sun set in crimson glory over the western ocean.

"Our slate is wiped clean," I told Derwa, hugging her close. "We can start anew."

I felt as though our feet would leave this earth. We would soar with the gulls over that endless ocean. I caught Derwa's hands to lead her in a merry dance, thinking that surely she must be as elated as I. But her face was set in brooding lines as if she were wondering what lay in store for her now that our pilgrimage had reached its end.

We retired to the small hostelry run by Doña Pilar, a widowed farm-wife who had hosted pilgrims for decades and even spoke some English. She was every bit as warm and hospitable as the priest in Santiago had promised she would be, serving us huge bowls of lobster stew. Back home this would have been considered pauper's food, but after our hours of walking in the fresh sea air, it tasted like the finest meal to ever pass my lips.

As we supped, I commented on the harp hanging on the white-washed wall.

"That belonged to my late husband," Doña Pilar said. "No one has played it for many years."

"A harp?" Derwa sat bolt upright. "May I play it?"

Doña Pilar brightened. "But of course."

After the meal, Derwa spent some time plucking the dusty strings and tuning the instrument before playing a Cornish tune of haunting beauty. Her music filled the farmhouse like a blessing.

"I'm so glad of your company," Doña Pilar said. "You must stay here as long as you like. After walking for many days, you must rest, no? Aye-yay, it can be so lonely out here."

She described what a struggle it was to run the farm and hostel on her own. None of her seven children had survived into adulthood.

"I even have trouble keeping servants — it is so far away from the rest of the world."

Derwa insisted on washing up. Once Doña Pilar had directed her to the tub of water, Derwa scrubbed out the crockery by touch and even scoured the cast-iron cooking pot with sand.

"What a lovely girl," Doña Pilar told me when Derwa excused herself to go outside for her ablutions. "You must be so proud of your daughter."

My eyes pricked. "I'm proud of her indeed, but we are no blood relations."

I quietly informed Doña Pilar of the girl's tragic history. Her eyes moistened in compassion.

Later, when we climbed up to our straw pallets in the room above the kitchen, Doña Pilar made sure Derwa slept in her finest linens with her warmest woolen blanket to keep off the chill sea air.

Derwa was clearly in no hurry to move on. Instead, she baked bread for Doña Pilar. I offered to help, but she waved me aside and I watched as she measured the heft of flour in her hands, then mixed it with water and yeast. Leaving the dough to rise, she went out to call in the cows and milked them by touch, placing the wooden bucket firmly between her feet so it wouldn't tip. All the while she sang her Cornish songs, lulling the cows into placid tranquility. She churned their milk into butter. Returning to her bread dough, she kneaded and pummeled it into shape before placing it in the heavy cast-iron baking pan, which we placed in the hearth. These were the very chores Derwa had done in her old life, but now she could work in peace and dignity while listening to Doña Pilar praise her to the high heavens as though she were a living saint sent to her by God.

Julian had written that God is homely. How homespun and simple miracles could be, like this wonder unfolding before my eyes. Derwa coming back to herself, finding hope again. Doña Pilar opening her arms and home to this girl who had banished the widow's loneliness and filled her house with song. In the week I stayed at Doña Pilar's, I even heard Derwa learning the Galician dialect with all the speed one might expect from the young and quick-witted.

A gregarious band of Irish pilgrims arrived at Doña Pilar's and I joined them on their journey back to Santiago and Ferrol but not before bidding my fondest farewells to Derwa and Doña Pilar.

Seeing Derwa claim her place in the world again helped me find my own. Derwa taught me that it was not enough to be a perpetual wanderer, a pilgrim without rest or home. Not enough to share Julian's writings with scholars and scribes. Julian hadn't intended for her words to remain hidden inside scrolled parchment and only studied by a handful of high-learned folk. No, she had intended for her revelations to bring comfort and hope to all who would receive them, including those simple folk who could not read. Her message of ineffable love and grace was meant to be lived. I elected to be her messenger, speaking of her revelations of divine love wherever I went to all who would listen. To spread her tidings of consolation like seeds so they might take root and flourish in people's hearts.

With this summons ringing in my head, I boarded a ship in Ferrol. After five days of fair sailing, I disembarked in Bristol but didn't dare tarry there long. Too well I remembered my close call in this city —were it not for the Bishop of Worcester's clemency, I might have been burned.

Instead, I traveled onward with some pilgrims I had met on the ship. Venturing north, I arrived in York in the middle of June, just in time for the Corpus Christi mystery plays. But now the mysteries played in the depths of my heart, and these were the revelations I imparted to the women gathered in the shadow of York Minster—the burghers' wives, servant girls, pie sellers, and baker women. *Every living creature shall be saved,* I told them as they circled close to imbibe my every word. This was the path that led to my arrest.

III

The Cloud of Unknowing

22

 FTER SLAPPING THE SHACKLES on my wrists, the mayor's men dragged me out of the minster and all the long way across York. The women I'd spoken to in the cathedral yard clasped their hands to their hearts and wept to see me being hauled off to prison.

"Good mistress, we'll pray for you!" the pregnant young fishmonger shouted.

Beggars dove to touch the hem of my white gown, but the mayor's men kicked them away. When my captors marched me past my lodgings in Petergate, Master Thwaite, my innkeeper, ran out and threw himself in our path.

"My Lord Mayor, I'll vouch she's a godly woman. Send her home to her husband." Master Thwaite looked at me, his eyes wide in entreaty. "Mistress Margery, go back to Lynn and spin and card like the other goodwives. This life of yours will only bring you shame. I promise to keep your belongings safe until you're released." But his voice trembled in uncertainty that I would ever be freed.

"Send word to my husband, I beg you!" I cried out. "John Kempe of Bishop's Lynn." Never before had I resorted to such a measure — summoning John to come to my rescue. For all I knew, he was still bitter and would never forgive me. Even if he rushed to York with all speed, I might well be dead by the time he arrived. "If they don't release me, give my satchel and belongings to the poor. Only my pilgrim's staff

—promise me you'll save that for my husband, that he might have a token from his faithful wife."

The mayor laughed in derision and shoved me on my way past the timber houses in Haymongergate, where housewives darted out to shake their distaffs at me.

"Burn the false heretic!" they shouted.

Cries of "Lollard" followed me as we passed the Guildhall and then the Franciscan Friary. The castle keep loomed before me, rising from its high grassy mound. I staggered all the way up that hill, staining my white skirts with the sheep manure we trod upon. My innards clenched at the very thought of prison. Already I could smell the filthy straw, human excrement, reeking flesh.

But before we reached the massive door, Master Fenwick, the prison keeper, stepped out and blocked our entrance.

"My Lord Mayor, I've no room for a woman," he said. "Unless I put her in with the men."

White-hot panic seized me. My legs buckled and I collapsed in a heap at the mayor's calfskin boots. Clasping my shackled hands, I wept and pleaded. "I beg you, sir, don't put me with the men. In the name of almighty God, spare me. I'm a good man's wife."

All I had left to protect me from the worst imaginable degradations was my reputation, as tattered as it was. If I lost that, they would treat me no better than a street harlot and throw me in among the murderers.

The mayor remained unmoved, but through my tears, I saw something like pity in the prison keeper's eyes.

"I'll take her home and lock her in my attic," Master Fenwick said. "My wife shall look after her until she comes to trial."

"Bless you, sir," I said. *Please God, let him be a good man and keep his word. Let him not misuse me.*

Then Master Fenwick led me off by the chain attached to my shackles, as though I were an ass he'd won in a bet. As I hobbled through the maze of twisting streets, a few bold children lobbed clumps of horse dung at me. But my back prickled with the sense that my well-wishers were trailing me at a discreet distance.

To my great relief, Mistress Fenwick met us at the door of their tall narrow house. Sober in her starched linen snood, she led the way up the steep stairs into a clean-swept attic smelling only faintly of mice. The sharply pitched oak beams and thatched roof gave me just enough room to stand without stooping. Master Fenwick took my gold and silver from me, along with the golden ring Dame Julian had given me. I sagged, bereft to lose this token of my recently departed friend. But my eyes teared in gratitude when Master Fenwick removed my shackles. Then the prison master and his wife departed, bolting the door behind them.

Rubbing the red marks on my wrists where the cold iron had bitten into my skin, I paced the creaking elm floorboards. In the corner was a straw pallet with canvas sheets and a woolen blanket. There was a three-legged stool, a clay chamber pot. All of this was far greater comfort than I had ever hoped to find. But what heartened me most was the unglassed window on the gable end. Of course, it was too small to squeeze out of even if I had been witless enough to try to leap to my death. But it was big enough for me to stick my head out, feel the sunlight on my face, and breathe the fresh air. I heard the cries of a dozen or so women gathered in the street below.

"Mistress Margery!" the pregnant fishmonger called out. With her flushed cheeks, she looked no older than twenty, so fresh with youth and good health. "May Our Lady and all the saints protect you!"

"I have faith in God and I'm not afraid to die," I told them, even as my heart lurched in dread at what lay in store.

The women exchanged wide-eyed glances before a stout brewer with a broad, kind face stepped forward. Even from the attic window, I could smell the odor of hops and yeast coming off her kirtle and coif. "Mistress, can you tell us any more of what Dame Julian told you?"

"Hush!" a merchant's wife cried. "You'll get poor Mistress Margery into even deeper trouble."

"Peace," I said. "As long as I have a tongue, I'll speak. Dame Julian said Our Lord showed her a little thing as round and small as a hazelnut in her palm. She looked at it and asked herself what it could be."

The women clustered tightly, their faces raised as they listened.

"God told her, 'It is all that's made.' Yet she wondered how it could last, being so small—it looked as though it could simply disappear."

Despite my every resolve to remain strong and steadfast, my voice broke. "The answer appeared in Julian's mind. 'It lasts forever and will last forever because God loves it.'"

At the word *love,* I lost all power to hold back my tears at the loss of her. How could I go on without her, my friend who knew my soul better than any confessor? Not only that, I feared I had failed her. Failed to keep the oath I'd sworn to her almost four years ago—that I, unworthy though I was, would keep her book safe so it couldn't be destroyed. Her precious pages, hidden inside my pilgrim's staff, now lay at the mercy of Master Thwaite. Could he be trusted to keep his word and give it to my husband if I never saw freedom again? If so, what would John do if he discovered the manuscript?

Seeing my tears, the women, too, were moved. The oldest among them cried out to me as though I were her daughter. "Alas, Mistress Margery! Why should you be burned?"

"They might burn me," I called down. "But they can never burn the truth."

Master Fenwick had confiscated my purse and golden ring. But he had overlooked my Ave beads, which I'd hidden beneath my gown. After the women had departed, I reached for that rosary of Baltic amber my parents had given me when I was a girl. What a comfort it was. Some beads bore the delicate tracery of insect wings in the smooth honey-gold stone. As I prayed my rosary, I reflected how my life was like this circle of beads, each day like precious amber sliding through my fingers until at last I reached the cross. The very specter of suffering and death and what lay beyond.

Many hours later, as the long June twilight ebbed into darkness, a sharp knock on the door below awakened me from fitful sleep. Who could be calling at this late hour? Had they come to interrogate me? I'd heard inquisitors had all manner of tricks to unnerve and intimidate suspected heretics, such as depriving prisoners of sleep so they might trip up under examination and so condemn themselves.

Cautiously, I stuck my head out of the window, but I could scarcely make out the two cloaked figures standing in the shadows. I strained my ears to hear Mistress Fenwick as she answered the door.

"My husband won't return until tomorrow," she said sternly. In truth, she sounded as suspicious as I was of these mysterious callers. "You must return at a more civil hour."

Then, to my horror, one of the two figures spoke to her insistently in a hushed voice and somehow convinced her to let them in. They clattered up the creaking wooden stairs. Barefoot in my shift, I didn't even have time to dress properly, could only throw on my cloak and hug it tightly around me. The sound of their feet on the attic landing was accompanied by the twist of the key in the lock.

"My husband will be furious if he ever finds out," I heard Mistress Fenwick say in a shaking voice.

This was followed by the clink of coins. I closed my eyes and covered my face. My unwelcome visitors, whoever they were, had bribed Mistress Fenwick to get at me. What mischief could this be? Having neither candle nor lamp, I swayed in the dark attic, my breath sour with fear. The door opened with an unearthly squeak that raised my flesh. Two lanterns shone in my eyes, blinding me.

"I shall return when the bells ring midnight," Mistress Fenwick said. "Then you must be gone."

At that, she hung one lantern on a wall hook, took the other with her, and locked the door behind her. Her retreating footsteps sounded furtive, as though she were a thief fleeing in the night.

I quaked at the sight of the two black-cloaked figures, their faces concealed by deep hoods. *No*, I wanted to scream.

"Mistress Kempe, we understand you're a holy woman," the shorter of the two figures said.

A woman's voice.

I nearly wept in relief. She lowered her hood so I could see her face. She looked to be about five years younger than I was. Her companion, who also tugged down her hood, appeared to be around twenty, with fearful eyes that rested on me as though I were her salvation.

"Please forgive us for the late hour," the older woman said. "We seek your urgent counsel."

I blinked. "Who *are* you?"

"It's safer for us all if we remain anonymous," the older woman said. "I must beg you to keep this meeting secret. Let no one know we ever spoke to you."

I was utterly mystified. Their black cloaks and veils were conspicuously plain, as if to hide their identity, yet the older woman's refined accent revealed her noble birth. She certainly had gold to spare, judging from how she had bribed her way in. She was so regal in her bearing, she might have hailed from the highest aristocracy.

"My lady," I said, indicating that I had deduced her station if nothing else. "God has given me visions, it is true. But I'm no seeress. No fortune-teller."

What, I wondered, would bring a woman like her to this attic in the dead of night?

"But you are a godly woman," she said, "who understands the travails of our sex. I hear you have borne fourteen children. I bore sixteen over two marriages. I was married off for the first time when I was only thirteen."

I winced at the very thought of such a young girl being given in wedlock, though child brides were ubiquitous enough among the nobility—the younger, the better to insure the girl's virginity and fertility.

"Likewise," she said, "I was obliged to marry off my own children at a tender age despite my better judgment. To serve the dynasty."

I nodded. In elite families, every marriage was strategic, a power play that could change the course of an entire kingdom.

"My good lady," I replied. "What counsel could I possibly give one as elevated as you?"

"It concerns my daughter." She nudged the young woman forward.

The girl's eyes spilled with tears. She looked so miserable that I wanted to put my arms around her and rub her hair despite whatever distance in rank divided us.

"She's my firstborn," the lady said. "But she—"

"I want to leave my husband," the young woman said with such vehemence that I thought she might harm herself. Bash her head against the sloping eaves.

Before her mother could stop her, the girl shoved up her sleeves and held out her forearms, which were dappled in fresh bruises. I even saw a mark that looked like a brand. Her eyes were wild and her breathing was unsteady, as though the cruelty she had endured had tipped her to the edge of madness. This made me recall how I, too, had gone stark mad when I was her age.

"Calm yourself, Lizzie," her mother said, holding the girl's shoulders. "Mistress Kempe can't help you unless you listen to her with a clear mind."

Lizzie yanked down her sleeves and swung round to face me, her hands clasped before her heart. "I did my duty by him. I gave him a healthy son and heir, but he still won't leave me alone. He doesn't take pleasure unless he can hurt me."

Her torment filled the room like a black cloud.

I gathered my thoughts. "Can the marriage be annulled?"

The mother shook her head gravely. "Neither her husband nor mine will hear of it."

My heart tore for both of them. "What can I do but offer my prayers?"

"*You* left your husband," the mother said with an edge of desperation. "You left your *children* and traveled to Jerusalem. How did you get away with *that?*"

My neck prickled that these strangers would know the intimate details of my life.

"My lady, as you can see for yourself, I got away with nothing," I said, my patience at an end. "I'm a prisoner."

With a sigh, I sank down on the stool, leaving the noblewomen to stand. At this ungodly hour, any sense of politesse deserted me. Surely the mother must recognize that her daughter's tragedy was down to her own machinations — why hadn't she arranged a more worthy match for the girl? Why put the dynasty over her daughter's happiness? I would never have done such a thing to my Isabella or little Juliana. I wanted to order these women to leave so I could finally get some sleep — who only knew what lay in store for me in the morning.

But then something else took hold of me. I spoke about my visions. How God had called me to be chaste, to wear white, to walk the pilgrim's path. Putting aside my weariness and annoyance, I rose from my stool and took Lizzie's chilly hands in my own.

"God is our master, not our husbands," I told her firmly, peering into her troubled gray eyes. "You owe fealty to God alone. If your husband is destroying your soul, then you must leave him."

"But how?" mother and daughter asked me, as if their two voices had become one.

How indeed! A brewer's wife from Lynn might—with difficulty —leave her husband to go on pilgrimage, but the wife of a powerful lord? These aristocratic women might be wealthy but their lives were so constrained. They had far less liberty than the washerwomen of York who could go to the alehouse whenever they pleased and swim naked in the Ouse on hot summer days.

Suddenly the answer crystalized on my tongue. "Seek refuge in a cloister," I said. "The most powerful and established one you can find —say the Franciscan Sisters at Denny near Cambridge." My friend Rupert had praised this abbey to the high heavens. "Even the most powerful lord in the land would find it hard to drag you out of the cloister. As a married woman, you can't become a nun, but you could live there as a vowess if you swear an oath of chastity." Despite the late hour, my voice took on a new authority, as if my words could truly save this young woman. "The only way to escape one master is by seeking refuge in a higher master. You have given your husband his heir. Now you wish to serve God."

Scores of church bells across York rang the hour of midnight, signaling the end of our time together. We heard Mistress Fenwick's footsteps rushing up the stairs. It occurred to me that I could beg these women to help me escape. To take me along to Denny Abbey. But if I did that, I might place myself in even deeper peril if the young woman's husband came after us and blamed his wife's exodus on me.

"May all the saints protect you," the mother said. "I would like to pay you for your trouble, but Mistress Fenwick said that prisoners can accept no money."

"I don't want your gold," I said. "But I'll pray for your daughter's peace."

"And I shall pray," the lady said, "for your release and long life."

The key turned in the lock. Lizzie pressed my hand before Mistress Fenwick herded them out and bolted the door.

It seemed I had only just nodded off to sleep when I was awakened again by the key in the lock and the prison master's heavy footsteps striding across the attic floor. The faint light of dawn trickled through the window. I pushed myself up from the straw pallet. Hovering beside her husband, Mistress Fenwick's eyes were as red from lack of slumber as mine must have been.

"Get her ready and presentable," her husband told her. "The Steward of York wants to examine her at seven bells."

Mistress Fenwick carried a ewer of water for washing and a basket with my breakfast of bread and milk. To my astonishment, she had taken the trouble to butter the bread, an extravagance indeed for a prisoner.

When I had washed, dressed, and eaten, Master Fenwick returned to slap the shackles back on my wrists. We set off early, perhaps to evade the crowd of women that had gathered under my window the day before. At this hour, the streets were eerily deserted, but I was grateful to move my body again, so stiff and cramped from the confines of the attic.

Summoning my courage, I asked Master Fenwick the purpose of the day's proceedings.

"The Lord Steward will question you to decide if there's a case against you worth pursuing," he replied, his eyes fixed straight ahead.

A fragile hope beat inside me: if I could somehow prove my innocence, they might let me go.

I expected Master Fenwick to take me to a courtroom or a church for questioning. Instead, he marched me to the Steward of York's lordly mansion in Stonegate. Walking through those rooms with their tapestries and tiled floors filled me with the most painful nostalgia for my childhood home. I nearly expected my mother to appear, restored to life and twenty years younger, to bring me a cup of elderflower posset.

We entered an oak-paneled parlor with large mullioned windows lit golden in the morning sun. Many men had assembled here, both secular authorities and clerics. Of all the bodies crammed into that room, I was the only woman. I didn't even see a maidservant lurking in the shadows.

"Will you stay with me during the proceedings, good sir?" I asked Master Fenwick, my anxiety prickling. I fought the urge to grab his hand and not let him go. Though I was his captive, he had been decent to me. I had no idea what to expect from these other men.

"I shall wait until they've finished examining you, then take you back to the attic," he said, speaking impartially as a man of duty, but I detected a hint of sympathy in his voice. At the very least, he did not seem eager to see me burn.

The Steward of York sauntered into the room. He was young and modishly attired in a knee-length black houppelande with dagged sleeves over a crimson doublet. Likewise, his hat was in the latest fashion, shaped like an upended sack and adorned with a ruby set in silver. Despite his foppish appearance, he reeked of menace. When he first laid his flinty eyes on me, it was enough to make my throat constrict, as though I had swallowed poison.

The steward slid into a finely carved thronelike chair while the prison master released me from my shackles, then positioned himself in front of the parlor door to insure I did not escape.

Before I could even collect my wits, the steward leapt to his feet and circled me like a wolf eyeing his prey. He began interrogating me in the most aggressive manner, speaking not in English but in Latin, while the clerics and lay officials looked on, their faces impassive. I cast a helpless glance at Master Fenwick, but he only dropped his gaze to the floor.

I knew this much—the steward was setting a trap for me. The barrage of Latin was all a ruse to tempt me into revealing any hidden knowledge or education forbidden to a woman such as I. If I showed any sign of comprehension, he would brand me as a woman who read the Scriptures for herself. A Lollard and heretic. Or else a runaway nun who must be whipped and returned to her cloister.

"Speak English, if you please, sir," I said, when the steward, now red in the face, at last stopped for breath. "I don't understand a word you're saying."

"Why are you in York?" He jutted his face so close to mine that I could smell the pickled egg he'd eaten for breakfast.

I replied without hesitation. "I come as a pilgrim to see the Corpus Christi Mysteries and to make an offering at the shrine of William of York." Both points proved I was no Lollard, for they viewed mystery plays and saints' shrines as base idolatry.

He then questioned me on the Articles of Faith, beginning with my views on the Eucharist. I knew well enough that this was the typical procedure in heresy trials. The Bishop of Worcester, the poor haunted man, would have interrogated John Badby in much the same fashion. At least I knew what to say and what *not* to say to avoid damning myself.

I answered loudly and clearly so everyone in that parlor could hear. Even the old clerk snoring in the far corner woke up with a startled cry.

"Good sirs, I believe that if an ordained priest, no matter how wicked a man he might be, duly speaks the words over the bread that Our Lord spoke when he celebrated his Last Supper with his apostles, the bread becomes Our Lord's true flesh. Once it is said, it cannot be unsaid."

Clearly impressed by my erudition, the clerics nodded to themselves in approval while all the breath seemed to hiss out of the steward's lungs. I had spoken as a model of orthodoxy. But I then made the unfortunate mistake of allowing myself a little smile, thinking that this might be the end of it. They would declare me innocent and let me go. Master Fenwick would return my purse and ring. Then I'd rush back to the inn in Petergate, claim my pilgrim's staff with Julian's manuscript, and be gone.

The steward had other ideas.

"Let me have a private word with the accused," he said, seizing my wrist and yanking me through a small side door and down a narrow corridor away from any witness.

"What's the meaning of this?" I cried in alarm.

He grabbed hold of my nape and shoved me into a bedchamber hung with tapestries that served to muffle the noise of my screams. He struck me across the face, threw me on the bed, then pinned me down. One hand across my mouth, he yanked up my skirts and shoved my thighs apart. My head exploded in terror.

"Tell me whether you get your speech from God or the devil," he hissed, lifting his hand from my mouth only to clutch at my throat.

"For the love of God, spare me!" I shouted as loudly as I could in hope that someone might hear. "I'm a good man's wife!"

He laughed, tightening his hold on my throat so that I struggled to breathe. "If you don't answer my question, I'll throw you in prison among the men and they won't care whose wife you are."

I had never been so frightened in all my life. Yet somehow I found my voice.

"My speech comes from the Holy Ghost." I tried to embody the dignity and courage I'd witnessed in Jan Hus as his enemies had led him to the pyre.

The steward reached to open his breeches, but fortunately for me, his many layers of voluminous clothing slowed his progress. Meanwhile, one of my hands wriggled down to reach my Ave beads hidden under my skirts. I seized the large crucifix carved from hard black obsidian.

"Jesus, save me!" I roared, jabbing the sharp end of the crucifix into the steward's ballocks, which caused him to scream and writhe.

I shoved him off of me, jumped from the bed, and threw down my skirts.

He raised his fist and lunged, but I ducked, and before he could do anything more, the door flew open. Master Fenwick looked on in shock at my disheveled state and the steward with his breeches open.

"Lord Steward, for shame! She comes from worthy kindred. What will folk say of you if you misuse the poor woman?"

"Get that witch away from me," the steward squeaked, clutching his sore groin.

I flew to Master Fenwick's side and gladly offered my wrists to his shackles. He marched me through the parlor where the men murmured in consternation, as if wondering what had gone on in the other room. I made my face a mask, trying to conceal my horror of what had almost happened. We stepped out the door into the street to find my women well-wishers waiting for me.

"Margery, why is your veil askew?" the washerwoman asked.

"What are those red marks around your throat?" The pregnant fishmonger's eyes filled with tears. "Did they mistreat you?"

The stout brewer woman rounded on Master Fenwick. "Can you not do a better job of protecting her honor?"

Their sympathy broke through my armor and I let loose my tears, sobbing in the middle of Stonegate. I felt filthy and unclean, and longed to flee all the way to Finisterre and fly into the arms of Derwa and Doña Pilar.

Master Fenwick allowed the women to neaten me and press damp cloths to my face before he walked me onward. The women surrounded us in a tight knot, shielding me from the ridicule of onlookers.

"Why was the Lord Steward so hateful to me?" I asked Master Fenwick, when we had returned to the attic. "I proved before all the priests that I'm no Lollard, but the steward still tried to force me . . ."

My voice broke. I was shaking from crown to toe, a shattered wreck of a woman. Exactly what the steward had intended.

Master Fenwick's broad shoulders sagged. "It's the ugly business with John Oldcastle. Folk live in fear of a Lollard uprising, so men like the steward are out for blood. If he can prove you're some Lollard instigator, the King will reward him with a title and estate."

So they thought I was in league with Oldcastle. It seemed my doom was well and truly nigh. Though Oldcastle's plot to kidnap the King had gone nowhere, the renegade was still on the loose and his supporters were on the move, spreading tracts for the Lollard cause. Some said Oldcastle was conspiring with the Scots to bring down our kingdom.

"A woman like you appears in York out of nowhere," Master Fenwick said. "Then you preach to the women in front of the minster! How could they not arrest you?"

"But I'm no Lollard," I insisted. "You heard me today. The clergy were pleased with my answers about the Eucharist."

Master Fenwick regarded me as though I were the most naïve creature he had met in all his days. "It's not so simple. Under interrogation, even Oldcastle upheld the Eucharist—at least in the beginning. Many Lollards can speak of the Articles of Faith as convincingly as any learned clerk. But they're false and cunning and hide their true beliefs."

"Then what am I to do?" I asked, the knife-edge of despair cutting into me. "I answer well from the heart and they still think I'm guilty."

The look he gave me was level and stern. "When they question you tomorrow, stick to your catechism. Don't be tempted to show off or say anything too clever. Just play the simple woman."

My heart raced in panic. "They'll question me again tomorrow? Will it be the steward?" *Where will this end?*

"No," he said, with a gruffness that bordered on kindness. "Tomorrow you face the clergy. Fear not. I won't let any man take you out of my sight."

"Thank you," I said. "You saved me today, Master Fenwick."

When Master Fenwick left me alone in the attic once more, so many thoughts churned inside me. If Oldcastle did seize power, England as I knew it would no longer exist. He would dissolve the abbeys. Destroy the saints' shrines.

I felt hollow inside, as if one strong gust of wind could blow me away. Just as the King was waging his wars across France, an invisible war was tearing England apart. And it seemed that I was stranded in the middle of that battlefield.

Where would I fit in a Lollard commonwealth? Would there be a place for women like me, women who refused to be obedient wives or cloistered nuns but chose to wander freely in the world? What if it was true that their women were preachers? That women in their order even served communion? The shock of such a possibility left me giddy.

If the Lollards won, would women stand shoulder to shoulder with men? Or would they resign themselves to being wives and mothers with no other path available to them? A deep well of loss opened inside me when I imagined a world without beguines, or wise anchoresses who wrote books of their visions, or Holy Sisters who copied priceless texts for their libraries. No nunneries where oppressed wives could seek refuge. No pilgrim's path to lead women like me away from an existence of endless wifely servitude.

I went to the window and stuck out my head. The day had grown humid, dark clouds crowding the sky. But the gathered women below cheered at the sight of me.

"Mistress Margery, have you eaten today?" the pregnant fishmonger asked.

I nodded and smiled, trying to appear braver than when they had seen me roiling in shame that morning.

"I am no Lollard," I called down to them.

If no one else believed me, at least these women would.

"But you question everything," the stout brewer woman called back. "So I, too, must question everything."

You question everything—the refrain I'd heard all my life, particularly from my parents or from John when they complained how unbiddable I was. Never had I imagined that my questioning would be something other women would find commendable and wish to emulate. That it would inspire them to ask hard questions of their own.

Before I could say anything in response, the wind picked up, taking my breath away. The first drops of rain needled my face. I looked up to the bruised heavens and told the women, "You'd best go home, my friends. A storm is coming."

That night Our Lord sent such weather, of thunder and torrential rain, that I feared the roof would come crashing down. I closed the shutters, but the wind was so violent, it wrenched the old shutters clean off their hinges. Rain poured through the window and soaked my straw pallet. I wrapped myself in the blanket and spent the rest of that turbulent night on my stool staring into the darkness until lightning, one bolt after another, illuminated my hands clenched in prayer.

I begged my Beloved to blaze forth in my heart. To show himself to me. My divine husband had come to me in visions during the most wretched moments of my life. Never had I yearned for him more than I did now. Just a glimpse of him, to know that he had not forsaken me. But though I called out to him with my entire soul, there was only the storm. The night. That dark cloud of unknowing.

By morning, the storm had passed and the sky glimmered watery blue. But the tempest had wreaked its havoc. The attic floorboards beneath my bare feet were sodden. The excess water had flowed under the door and down the stairs. I heard the Fenwicks' voices arise from below, lamenting the damage.

"What if God sent the storm to punish us for keeping her in our attic?" Mistress Fenwick asked.

I stiffened, not knowing whether she intended to eject me and throw me into prison among the men.

"God's punished all of York," her husband replied, sounding every bit as shaken as she.

I grasped hold of the damp windowsill and looked down at the street inundated in debris and filth. Yet still the women had gathered, as loyal as ever. I tried to smile for them, but I felt like an imposter. Would they truly place their trust in me if they knew how barren I felt inside? My night of prayer had left me no solace, not even the faintest gleam of hope. I was bereft of proper sleep for two nights in a row, and the darkest thoughts raced through my mind. What if my visions weren't real, had never been real? What if I was as mad as the folk of Lynn had said all along? A wicked, selfish woman deluded by demons. I had abandoned my children. How could God be responsible for that?

What a fragile thing faith was. How easily it could all unravel.

23

TORM OR NO STORM, Master Fenwick came to fetch me to my trial at York Minster.

This time he allowed me to walk unshackled so I might lift my skirts above the filth as we waded through the stinking streets awash in human turds and drowned rats. The women thronged round us. I was more grateful to them than ever —the crowd had turned rank. Though I held my head high and stared straight ahead, I could not ignore the catcalls.

"Oldcastle's whore!" a man hissed. "God sent the storm to punish the heretic!"

He gripped a block of wood. If the women hadn't been shielding me, I think he would have lobbed it at me.

"Hold your false tongue," the stout brewer woman shot back. "The storm is God's wrath upon the City of York for holding a good woman captive."

The minster, built on higher ground, was dry at least. My trial took place in the chapter house. The women were forced to wait outside in the nave.

As Master Fenwick led me into the vast chapter house with its soaring stained glass windows, the magnificence transported me beyond my misery if only for a moment. My eyes rested on the window that depicted Saint Anne teaching the young Virgin Mary to read. Mother and daughter bent reverently over their book.

This time I faced a Church court for an official examination as to whether I was a heretic. The Abbot of York, an esteemed doctor of divinity, would be the judge of today's proceedings. The octagonal room was ringed with low stalls where the abbot and his canons and deans were seated, each according to his rank. From the carved limestone canopies above their seats, gargoyles and grotesque human heads leered down at me. Many laymen had also joined the assembly. I saw the fat mayor with his golden chain and medallion. My stomach filled with acid at the sight of the steward skulking beside him.

As I stood there shaking like a palsied wretch, the abbot bade me to place my hand on a Bible so massive that two clerks had to carry it.

"Margery Kempe," the abbot said sonorously. "We bid you to answer in truth and honesty to the Articles of Faith."

First, they questioned me about the Eucharist, just as the steward had done only a day ago. I answered in the same words I had used previously, then went on to answer other questions, as many as they would ask me, about Church doctrine. Even after two sleepless nights, my tongue had a will of its own as I affirmed, over and over again, my belief in the sacraments. In the veneration of Our Lady and all the saints. In the sanctity of pilgrimage and shrines, holy orders and monastic communities. Surely it must be clear to every man in that room that I was no Lollard.

Then the mayor had to butt in. "Reverend Father, truly this creature doesn't mean with her heart what she says with her mouth."

I faltered, remembering how Master Fenwick said that the most hardened heretics gave eloquent testimony about the Articles of Faith while keeping their real beliefs hidden.

"My Lord Mayor," the abbot said. "As far as I can see, she's sincere in her faith. What complaint do you have with this woman?"

I warmed to hear the abbot's kind words. For all my being a reputed heretic, the Church authorities appeared eager to exonerate me. It was their secular counterparts who had the most to gain from seeing me burn.

"She's luring the women of York into her band of disciples," the mayor said. "At least a dozen of them are outside in the nave as we speak! They sit under her window in thrall of her every word. I fear if we let her loose, they'll abandon their husbands and follow her Christ only knows where."

"My Lord Mayor," I interjected. "It offends me when you take Our Lord's name in vain."

The mayor turned puce. "She's a woman of loose virtue, Reverend Father. The Steward of York very nearly had his way with her yesterday."

"You mean he tried to ravish me!" I said, blunt and bold. "Probably under your orders, Lord Mayor."

Steeling myself, I looked the steward in the eye. He glared back, as balefully as ever, but I noticed he held his hands protectively over his groin.

"Reverend Father, my prisoner speaks the truth." Master Fenwick stepped forward. "The Lord Steward tried to misuse her yesterday and probably would have succeeded had I not come to her rescue."

The clerics exchanged frowns and mutters while the steward sullenly stared down at his shoes with their stylishly pointed toes.

The mayor, undeterred, began to insult me in earnest, calling me a Lollard. A whore. John Oldcastle's handmaiden.

"Margery Kempe," he said bitterly. "I will not allow for your release unless the Archbishop of York himself declares your innocence. Then and only then can I be rid of you with a clear conscience."

His words felled my hope like an ax.

"Ill tidings, this is," Master Fenwick muttered, as he escorted me back through the flooded streets. "The Abbot of York's as mild a man as you'll ever meet in a Church court, but the archbishop's as fierce as any bloodhound if there's so much as a whiff of Lollardy in the air."

I knew this well enough without Master Fenwick telling me. Henry Bowet, Archbishop of York, was not only notorious as a stern prosecutor of heresy but was also one of the most powerful men in England, having served in the Papal Court and in the King's innermost circle. Thanks to Oldcastle, Lollardy wasn't just a threat to the Church but to the royal family and the governance of the realm itself.

The mob in the streets had grown more brutal than ever, with missiles of horse dung flying my way. All the while they chanted their litany of hate: *Burn the Lollard whore! Wolf in the white gown! Oldcastle's witch!*

But the women walking around me in formation shielded me from their wrath. I had learned their names. Lucy, Peg, Emlyn, Tess, Moll, Joan, Mildred, Anne, Lorna, Sally, Alice, Mathilda. I could not help but witness the stark fear in their faces. How long before the crowd turned on them for their loyalty to me? How long before they stood accused of heresy and sedition?

When Master Fenwick delivered me back into the attic, I was astounded to discover that Mistress Fenwick and her servant had not only cleaned up the worst of the storm damage but had also replaced my sodden bedding. A pallet of fresh, fragrant straw lay made up with real linens instead of canvas sheets. A fine woolen blanket lay folded at the foot of the mattress.

"Where did this come from?" Master Fenwick asked suspiciously.

In faith, I was just as flummoxed as he. Mistress Fenwick would hardly go to the market to purchase such lavish bedding for a prisoner.

"One of her well-wishers had it delivered," Mistress Fenwick said. "Anonymously. Along with *this*."

The maidservant carried up a hamper full of cheeses, fresh wheaten bread, spice cakes, havercakes, a punnet of red currants, and a flask of French claret.

Before unshackling me, Master Fenwick painstakingly searched the pallet, linens, and hamper for any hidden weapons or missives. He even broke the bread and cake apart to see if anything had been concealed inside. Finding nothing, he allowed me to keep these inexplicable gifts.

"It seems you have friends in high places, Margery Kempe," he said, finally unlocking my shackles.

Mistress Fenwick and I exchanged the most fleeting of glances and I thought of the noblewomen who had visited me in the dead of night.

"And by God," said Master Fenwick, "you'll need them once Bowet gets his teeth into you."

As soft as my new linens were, they did little to ease my paralyzing fear.

What could I do but pray? Except every prayer turned to dust in my mouth. My most fervent devotion could not pierce that darkness, that terror that was choking me. Not only was I on trial for my life, at the mercy of men who would stoop to every trick and treachery to see me burn, but my Beloved had abandoned me and left me in silence.

<h1 style="text-align: center;">24</h1>

 HREE DAYS LATER I was summoned to appear at the archbishop's palace in Cawood, ten miles south of York. To my unending relief, Master Fenwick escorted me to insure I wouldn't be mistreated. Mistress Fenwick insisted on coming along, both for propriety's sake and because this might be her one chance to see Cawood Castle.

"A right glorious place, they say it is," she said, as we set off that midsummer dawn. "The Windsor of the North, they call it!"

"Wisht," her husband said irritably. "This isn't some lark."

My spirits dragged, glum and flat. All the long way I rode shackled in the back of a wagon, jostled about like a sack of onions, while the birds offered up their dawn chorus, as if in mockery of my distress. My friends followed in our wake and shouted out their encouragement. It tore my heart that they still had faith in me when I lived in mortal fear of losing my faith altogether.

"Courage, Mistress Margery!" Mathilda the brewer shouted. "God is with you."

I twisted my head to smile at her. How I longed to believe her.

Some men joined my band of well-wishers, the brothers and husbands of my friends. They walked tall and resolute, as though prepared to accompany my wagon all the way to Cawood. Alas, my foes were out in force even after we left the city walls. Crowding on both sides of the lane, seething folk shook their fists and bellowed that I must burn. Some looked fit to drag me down from the wagon and set me alight then and there, sparing the archbishop the bother of hearing my trial. Mistress Fenwick cried out to the Holy Blessed Mother for protection while her husband sent the horses into a swift, ground-covering trot. I shouted my farewells to my friends before we left them behind in a cloud of dust.

Two hours later, we came into view of Cawood Castle, near the meeting of the rivers Ouse and Wharfe. Mistress Fenwick brightened at once.

"How splendid!" she cried, though we could see nothing but its double moat and fortified walls. "I've heard it said that the grounds have *five* fishponds!"

Our wagon traversed the wooden drawbridge and passed through the gatehouse. Then the gates closed behind us, blocking all view of the outside world.

Mistress Fenwick was not mistaken. This was as magnificent a palace as I had seen anywhere in the world, little joy though that gave me. I duly observed the orchards, the gardens, the sparkling fountains and ponds, and the vast banqueting hall, which was separate from the main residence.

When Master Fenwick helped me down from the wagon, my legs, numb and rattled from the journey, foundered and I collapsed face-first in the gravel. My bladder was fit to explode. If I didn't get to a privy soon, the archbishop would have a brand-new pond on his property.

Mistress Fenwick helped me up and brushed the dust from my gown and veil.

"Dearie me," she flustered. "You can't face the archbishop looking like you've been dragged through a hedge." She turned to her husband. "There must be some private chamber where I can help her wash and get her in decent fettle."

A gangling servant boy who looked no older than fourteen showed us in through a rear door and up the stairs into a small chamber on the uppermost floor of the palace, its windows tiny to discourage any hope of escape. Still, it was a handsome chamber.

Mistress Fenwick was beside herself. "Margery, you shall sleep like a gentlewoman tonight!"

Master Fenwick unshackled me before standing guard outside the door. With a long sigh of relief, I made use of the chamber pot while

Mistress Fenwick marveled over the embroidered bed hangings and the painting of Saint Lucy, the virgin martyr, serenely holding her severed eyeballs on a golden plate.

Pouring fresh water into the basin, I cleaned my face and hands. Mistress Fenwick dampened a sponge and did her best to scrub the stains from my white gown. She even pinched my cheeks to give them color.

"May God protect you from all harm," she said.

I pressed her hand before Master Fenwick took me down to the chapel for my trial. This time he made do without the shackles, seeing as it was nigh on impossible to escape from this walled and moated palace.

The chapel was exquisite, its ceiling painted deep blue with golden stars, reminding me of the churches I'd seen in fair Italy—which now seemed so long ago.

The place heaved with men and boys, servants in the archbishop's household come to have a gander at me.

"A bit long in the tooth to be Oldcastle's whore, is she not?"

"The older they get, the more lascivious. I hear she couldn't keep her filthy hands off the Steward of York."

"Enough of that now!" Master Fenwick thundered.

But the lads wouldn't allow a mere prison master to spoil their amusement.

"Blood of Christ!" a pimpled oaf cried out. "Burn the ugly old whore!"

I could take no more. "Young lad," I said sternly, shaking my finger at him. "Shame on you for swearing such unholy oaths. You've broken the Third Commandment."

At that precise moment, the archbishop glided into the chapel with a swish of silks. He was stooped with age but as formidable as an eagle with his hooded, penetrating eyes.

"It's heartening to hear that the heretic knows her Ten Commandments," he said, his voice like acid.

The servants roared in laughter while Master Fenwick winced, as though sharing my humiliation.

"Why is this creature unshackled?" the archbishop demanded, rounding on Master Fenwick. "Put the shackles on her at once! The faithless heretic must be fettered." He spoke with scathing contempt, as though he had already condemned me.

His eyes sorrowful, Master Fenwick shackled my wrists behind my back as gently as he could. Still the iron bit into my already chafed and broken skin.

"Forgive me," he whispered.

Alas, his mercy did not go unnoticed.

"Fenwick, why are you even here?" the archbishop demanded. "She's no longer in your jurisdiction. I order you to return to York immediately. And take your noisy wife with you."

Master Fenwick's throat wobbled. His eyes were suddenly wet, though he blinked hard to hide the fact. "God go with you, Margery Kempe," he said, lifting his hand in salutation before trudging out the chapel door never to return.

My eyes filled to see him go, my only well-wisher in this hostile crowd. I had lost everything. Lost the Fenwicks. Was even losing my faith.

The archbishop then swept out of the chapel, leaving me chained like a circus bear before all those smirking men and boys. Sinking to my knees, I attempted to pray. My body trembled and shook so hard, I could no longer mask my terror.

In his own sweet time, the archbishop returned, accompanied by his court. He mounted his throne and his clerics took their seats in the intricately carved wooden stalls on either side of the high altar. Lay officials and scribes squeezed into the nave. The mayor was there, but his steward, blessedly, had remained in York. I was thankful that they saw fit to remove my shackles so I could place my hand upon the Bible and swear to tell the truth.

The clerics' questions flew at me like missiles.

"Are you a wife or a virgin?"

"Are you a Jew?"

"What know you of Oldcastle's whereabouts?"

"Did you attempt to seduce the Steward of York so he would release you?"

Faced with their wall of malevolence, I didn't even attempt to reply but only sank to my knees and gazed up at the archbishop, who craned his neck to peer down at me.

"The Abbot of York has told me he's found no evidence of heresy on your part," the archbishop said. "Yet others have told me very evil things about you, Margery Kempe. I've heard tell that you're an utterly wicked woman."

I answered in a clear voice. "Likewise, Your Reverence, I've heard tell that you're a wicked man. If you're as cruel as people say, you must repent and mend your ways here on earth before entering the Kingdom of Heaven."

The room echoed with the clerics' fury that a mere woman would dress down an archbishop in his own court.

"Why, you wretch!" The archbishop's face empurpled in rage. "What have people been saying about me?"

"Other people, Your Reverence, can tell you well enough," I replied. "No need to take my word for it."

"Hold your tongue, woman!" a canon in a furred hood interjected. "You're here to talk about yourself, not slander the archbishop."

The archbishop summoned one of his men to bring forth a massive Bible.

"Place your hand on the Holy Writ," he commanded me. "And swear you'll leave my diocese as soon as you can and return to your husband's house."

Hope flickered inside me. Would they truly let me go?

"She's too dangerous to release," the mayor said. "The common folk put great faith in her chatter. What if she leads them astray? As for her husband, word was sent to him on the day of her arrest and he's not stirred from Lynn nor sent a single word in reply. In faith, I think he's as eager to see the end of her as I am."

His words chilled me to the bone. So John hated me enough to let me burn?

"Silence," the archbishop said. He looked as though his patience had reached its end and that he just wanted to be rid of me. "Before I release you," he said, causing my heart to trumpet in hope, "you must make a solemn oath that you shall neither teach nor scold people. Now swear that you will go back to Lynn where you belong. Then and only then will I let you go."

All I had to do was agree to his terms and I would walk free, the mayor and his plotting be damned. Yet to obey him was to be silenced. To return meekly to Lynn to never wander again. Only sit by my husband's hearth and spin and possibly bleed to death bearing a fifteenth child.

My voice, quavering and strange, sounded like it belonged to another woman. A woman bold and brave enough to lay down her life for her principles. A woman as courageous and as true to her vision as Marguerite Porete.

"No, Your Reverence," I said. "My conscience will not allow me to swear to this. Good sir, the Gospels themselves give me leave to speak of God's goodness."

If Master Fenwick had been present, he would have clapped both hands over his face in despair. These words, uttered from the depths of my heart, condemned me.

The clerics wasted no time in making a meal of this.

"Your Reverence," said the canon in the furred hood. "By this, we have our proof. How could she claim such knowledge of the Gospels unless she's a Lollard?"

The mayor stepped up, his eyes gleaming. "She was preaching in front of York Minster."

"*Any* unlicensed preaching is forbidden," the canon said. "But coming from a woman, it's doubly sinful."

Another prelate hefted the massive Bible onto the lectern, turned to the First Epistle of Paul the Apostle to the Corinthians, and read the verses first in Latin and then in English. "Let your women keep silent in the churches, for they are not permitted to speak; but they are also to be submissive, as the law also says."

"Lollard women presume to preach the Gospels," the canon said. "They seduce both sexes with their insidious teachings. Such is the madness of their heresy that some housewife from Lynn can expound on evangelical doctrine as though she were a doctor of divinity."

"By way of Wycliffe's Bible," a prelate said.

"Good sirs, I can't read!" I cried, repeating the half-truth as if it were whole. I wasn't literate in Latin. Let them think me unlettered in English as well.

"If you're truly the late Mayor of Lynn's daughter, it's most unlikely," the archbishop replied. "The Mayor of York's daughter can read in English, can she not?"

The mayor nodded smugly. "How can she run a household if she can't communicate with tradesmen? I told you this woman is a liar and dissembler."

"Behold, we see a great perversion of the Gospels," the canon proclaimed, "when an ignorant woman makes free to teach and scatter the word of God."

"She's one of those Lollard women," another cleric said, "who make themselves so wise by their English Bible that they presume to preach and argue and dispute with holy and learned clerks."

"Woman, what say you to this?" the archbishop asked.

They turned to scrutinize me as I knelt there shaking like a curtain in a storm.

My voice was small but steady. "I don't preach, Your Reverence. I only use good words to praise God's goodness."

"Don't listen to her," the mayor said. "Like every Lollard preacher, she speaks ill of the ordained clergy. I eavesdropped as she was preaching before York Minster, and she told the women of our city the worst tale of a priest I'd ever heard."

My mind flew back to that Corpus Christi afternoon and the story of the wicked priest I had told my friends before telling them of Julian's writings of love and salvation.

The archbishop's spine was rigid. "Let her tell it then."

I rose unsteadily to my feet. Since I'd knelt for so long, the pain in my knees was excruciating.

"Your Reverence, this is but a parable of a priest who lost his way in the forest when night was falling. Lacking any shelter, he found a beautiful blossoming pear tree, lit silver in the moonlight. He lay down to rest beneath those sweet-smelling branches, which he found so delectable to look upon."

The archbishop sighed. "Enough of the pretty details. Get to the point."

"As he slept beneath the blooming pear tree, Your Reverence, a huge vicious bear lumbered out of the forest. The priest could only look on in terror. The beast came straight up to the tree and shook it, causing the blossoms to fall. Then the bear greedily devoured those sweet blooms. When he had eaten every last one of them, he turned his enormous rump to the priest and voided the pear blossoms from his bowels."

"Your Reverence, you'll allow her to waste our time by telling some yarn about a shitting bear?" a canon asked.

"Silence!" the archbishop said sternly, raising one palm. "Let her finish."

He spoke as though, in spite of himself, he was anxious to find out how the story ended.

"The next morning the priest awoke to discover it hadn't been a dream," I continued. "There in front of him was the bear's huge stinking pile of droppings. The priest became quite miserable, wondering how to interpret these events. So he wandered on through the forest in utter dejection until he met a wise old pilgrim who asked him why he was so downcast. The priest explained that he felt great dread when he'd seen the horrible beast defile such fair flowers, then void them so crudely, and he couldn't understand what this meant.

"The wise old pilgrim, revealing himself to be a messenger of God, answered him thusly."

As I paused for breath, I noted that all the men in the room, save for the mayor, were leaning forward in eagerness to hear the moral of the tale. These men, who had accused me of illegal preaching, were so keen to hear me finish my homily. My inquisitors, at least for a moment, had become my congregation. Indeed, the only thing distinguishing me from them was the pulpit and the priestly office.

"'Priest,' the old man said. 'You are the pear tree, partly flourishing and flowering through your serving the holy sacraments. Though you do so irreverently, as you pay little attention to what you say in your Matins—you're just babbling till you reach the end. You go to Mass without devotion and are barely contrite for your sins. You receive the Eucharist—the fruit of everlasting life—in a very base frame of mind. You fritter away your days haggling in the market, stuffing your belly with gluttonous feasts, and indulging in all manner of lechery just like a man of the world. You swear, lie, and slander. By your wrongdoings, you are the ugly bear, causing untold damage to your own soul and that of others unless you receive the grace of repentance.'"

My tale left the men stunned and silent for quite some time, trading covert glances.

"A finely told fable," the archbishop said grudgingly. "I imagine you caused quite a stir telling that to the common folk."

We all turned at the sound of a young cleric sobbing. "Your Reverence," he said brokenly. "This tale cuts to the heart."

"I've heard enough for one day," the archbishop said, leaving me in utter suspense, not knowing if I had saved my skin or condemned myself to the pyre. "The examination of this creature shall continue tomorrow."

The long midsummer day had waned. My mouth was dry from so much talking, and having eaten nothing since breakfast, I was hungry enough to faint.

"Who among you will conduct this woman out of my sight?" the archbishop asked his clerics.

To my astonishment, many handsome young men leapt to their feet.

"I will escort her, Your Reverence."

"No, pray, let me escort her!"

The archbishop raised his eyebrows at the ensuing cacophony. "Enough! You are all too young and impressionable to be left alone with such a creature."

He then called upon his oldest and creakiest prelate, a toothless and wizened man, and bade him guide me back to my room.

But before the old man could stir from his seat, the door flew open and two messengers stormed in. It looked as if they had ridden a long distance at great speed. Their faces were speckled in mud. Their hair, slick with sweat, was plastered to their skulls. One messenger hung back by the door while the other strode down the nave toward the archbishop and dropped on one knee before him.

"Your Reverence," he said hoarsely. "The Duke of Bedford has ordered us to deliver Margery Kempe of Bishop's Lynn for trial in Beverley. Our lord holds her to be the greatest Lollard in England."

The Duke of Bedford. It was enough to make my heart stop. John of

Lancaster, the King's brother who ruled as Lieutenant of the Kingdom while the King waged war in France.

"Well, well," the archbishop said, as if my case would never stop confounding him. "You shall have her. I certainly don't wish the Duke of Bedford to be vexed with me on her account." More than anything, he sounded relieved to wash his hands of me.

But before the messenger could lay hold of me, I took a step back and raised my chin. "On what evidence does your lord make such extraordinary accusations?"

The other messenger, who had waited near the entrance, now marched down the nave. In his right hand, he brandished my pilgrim's staff.

"Is this yours, Margery Kempe?" he asked menacingly.

I thought I would shatter like glass. Struck mute, I nodded.

With a flourish, the man opened the secret compartment, removed the hidden manuscript, and then waved Julian's pages for all to see.

"This creature is so false," he proclaimed in a voice loud enough to be heard in Leicester. "Pretending to be a pilgrim while carrying Lollard writings in her staff! Such treachery as I've never seen."

The room grew dim before my eyes, those men staring at me as though I were the very apparition of Lilith.

"Good sirs!" I cried. "That's no Lollard tract but the writings of the holy anchoress Julian of Norwich."

Commotion broke out, an ugly jumble of mockery and outrage.

"Nonsense!" The canon in the furred hood slammed his fist against the palm of his other hand. "Now you truly blaspheme! To besmirch the name of the holy anchoress who is dead and can't defend herself against your slander."

Since the canon was too livid to say anything more, the archbishop picked up the thread, his every word cold and measured. "The late Dame Julian of Norwich, God preserve her immortal soul, was a Benedictine anchoress who served the Church in perfect obedience. Why would so saintly a woman entrust the likes of you to carry anything of hers, much less a manuscript hidden away in your staff? A creature such as *you*, who abandoned your lawful husband to wander the world like some camp follower while presuming to preach." His nose had gone pinched and white in his barely contained fury.

"I speak the truth," I said, tears falling down my face. "She was my friend, Your Reverence. She gave me counsel. I can explain—"

"It will take more than some fable of a defecating bear to talk your way out of this," he said.

"Carrying a manuscript while claiming she can't read," the mayor said. "What other lies has she been telling?"

"Your Reverence, I pray that you read Dame Julian's writings!" I cried out. "You will find nothing heretical there."

"A trained inquisitor shall read these pages," the archbishop said.

"After your trial, the manuscript shall burn," the mayor said portentously. "Along with *you*."

I opened my mouth but there were no words.

The archbishop abruptly pushed himself up from his throne. "The court is dismissed!" He nodded to the two messengers. "Make yourselves welcome to rest here for the night and take that cursed creature to Beverley in the morning."

The archbishop strode out of the chapel, followed by his court, while I stood and swayed.

"Mistress Margery?" A bony finger tapped my shoulder.

I yelped in shock and whirled round to face the elderly prelate the archbishop had assigned to take me to my room. The man's wrinkled face creased into a smile. With a twinkle, he held up the shackles.

"I don't think these are necessary, do you?" he asked in grandfatherly good humor. "Surely you don't intend to flee tonight."

I shook my head.

The man was so tottering and frail, he had to lean on my arm.

"I believe you," he whispered. "I visited Dame Julian at her anchorage many years ago. She told me she was writing a book about her showings."

An unexpected warmth filled me. I began to cry, undone by his sympathy. By the bond we shared in having Julian as our confidante.

He took my hand and patted it. "Little good my testimony will do you. The archbishop doesn't take a thing I say seriously. Half the time my memory is in tatters. But I remember the day I spoke with Julian. I was in such a muddle, you see. Doubting my vocation. But she told me that all would be well."

He smiled beatifically.

"I haven't many days left in this world," he told me as he struggled up the many stairs to my room. "But whenever I find myself afraid of dying, I tell myself all will be well. Julian is waiting for me on the other side."

Those words made me weep all the more, but my tears didn't seem to disturb him. He was as patient as a steady horse.

"Thank you for your faith in me, good sir," I said, when we reached my door.

"I will pray for your release," he said before locking me in. "God speed, good mistress."

I discovered that a basket of barley bread and a jug of buttermilk had been left in my chamber. I devoured it in a matter of minutes—my ordeal had left me ravenous.

Afterward, I recited every prayer I had ever learned. *O my Beloved, please give me a sign, however small.* But I heard only my own wheedling voice. I saw only Saint Lucy's severed eyeballs staring from the painting on the wall. The more I prayed, the deeper the silence grew.

25

N THE PITCH-BLACK, I awakened to a voice calling my name.

I jerked upright, my hands folded to my pounding heart. Was this the voice of my Beloved at last? Not daring to breathe, I strained to hear more. Strained my eyes to see him. But there was only the darkness pressing all around. The noise of my breath. The sick taste of fear on my tongue.

The clank of the key in the lock sent me rigid. Boots stamped across the floor. A shriek ripped out of my mouth when leather-gloved hands yanked back the bed curtains. Lantern light revealed Bedford's grim-faced messengers.

"Get dressed, Margery Kempe," the taller of the two men barked. "Now we ride to Beverley."

They gave me no privacy as I laced my gown over my nightshift, secured my veil over my hair, or even when I squatted over the chamber pot. The most I could do was arrange my skirts in such a way as to preserve my modesty.

As soon as I stood upright, they threw my cloak at me, shackled me, and marched me down to the stables.

Thirty long miles to Beverley and Bedford's men had no time to waste. Transporting me by wagon would have taken days. Instead, they lashed me to the saddle of a tall gray courser. One of the men led my horse from his own mount. The other rode behind, his sword at the ready should I somehow contrive to leap off this mountain of a horse and burst free of my fetters.

What chilled me even more than his sword was the sight of my pilgrim's staff tied to his saddle. They would use Julian's manuscript as evidence against me. I remembered Jan Hus's trial in Constance. Before burning the man, they had burned his writings. This would be the likely fate of Julian's work. *Oh, Julian, how I've failed you.*

We rode at breakneck speed, alternating between canter, gallop, and a tooth-jarring trot. If they hadn't taken such care to pinion me to the saddle, I would have tumbled off and met my death beneath those trampling hooves. My seat bones kept slamming against the saddle until I thought I'd never be able to sit down again. The stirrup leathers rubbed my calves raw. When we stopped to allow the horses to drink or rest, horseflies feasted upon my exposed skin. With my hands shackled, I couldn't swat them away.

As we rode through each hamlet, the messengers shouted out their herald. "Behold Margery Kempe, the Lollard, who shall be tried in Beverley at the Duke of Bedford's pleasure."

Plowmen and dairywomen gawped to see me pass. A bleary-eyed woman slumped in the saddle, my face coated in dirt, I was a living example of what might happen to any of them if they strayed from the narrow path of obedience to King and Church. I would become the subject of countless sermons and cautionary tales. My thoughts roved back to poor Hawisia Moone all those years ago, sentenced to trudge barefoot in the freezing graveyard while bearing her heavy penitent's candle. Had I only known that one day I would share her shame.

After the agonies of that fast and furious ride, I felt only a dull ache of dread when Beverley emerged on the horizon, its minster tower rising in the clear summer sky where larks soared and sang. To think I had always wanted to come here on pilgrimage to pray at Saint John of Beverley's shrine. Prosperous and ancient, the town was situated at the eastern edge of the wolds above the River Humber's marshy floodplain. No stone walls girded Beverley, only an earthwork ditch. We rode through the North Bar, the gate where ordinary folk were obliged to pay their tolls for the privilege of entering the town. But the guards let Bedford's men pass with much bowing and ceremony and not a single coin passing hands.

We proceeded down the cobbled streets past guild houses and the parish church of Saint Mary. Past the Saturday Market and up Butcher Row where men and boys in bloody aprons goggled at me. I had thought the journey here had been quite hellish enough, but my progress through Beverley soon became a waking nightmare. Though I had been ridiculed and mocked all my days and even openly despised and threatened, never had I faced such pure hate.

"Behold Margery Kempe, the Lollard!" Bedford's men kept bellowing to that roaring crowd of cloth merchants, weavers, hatters, candlemakers, pilgrims, blacksmiths, and goose girls. The townsfolk spat on me and cursed me as though I were the Whore of Babylon. Bedford's men did nothing to stop the crowd from pelting me with dung and stones. A rock struck my temple, drawing a hot trickle of blood. Only when a broken brick slammed into the flank of my horse and it nearly bolted free of its lead rein did Bedford's men draw sword and order the crowd to desist.

By this time, we had arrived beneath the shadow of Beverley Minster, where I faced a rabble of folk so murderous that I thought I would die of fright right there in the saddle.

A red-faced man screamed and pointed to a cartful of firewood and thorns. "The fuel for your pyre, Lollard whore!"

Two other men, the town's executioners, bandied about the wooden barrel they intended to burn me in. Any notion of a trial seemed an afterthought. As far as this lot was concerned, I was damned.

My rising panic blindsided me. There was no way out—this torture would end only with my death. Everything I had endured in my life of wandering and weeping for God had led me to this moment of truth. The shock of clarity made my eyes snap wide open. All my days I had yearned to imitate Christ and walk in his footsteps. Far from forsaking me, he had answered my prayer. This was my via crucis, the price I had to pay for following the call of my Beloved deep in my heart instead of slavishly obeying the men who wanted me to be silent, docile, and cowed. This ordeal was my true inner pilgrimage. Everything had been stripped away from me. Even Julian. All that remained was my tongue. My passion. My love.

As these thoughts careened through my head, one of Bedford's men, in a single deft sword stroke, sliced through the cords that bound me to the saddle. He dragged me down off that poor lathered beast and I fell for the first time, banging my knees against the cobblestones. I cried out, feeling my skin break, blood welling up beneath my white gown.

He hauled me up by the scruff of my neck and maneuvered me through the sea of bodies to the minster's Highgate Porch while the other guard held back the crowd with his sword. Thus I staggered up the porch stairs into the minster, which was so cool and quiet after the heat and din of the streets outside. This beautiful cathedral was meant to be a sanctuary, the Peace of Saint John, where even criminals might find refuge.

Bedford's men could not keep me from gazing in awe at the minstrels and angels sculpted above the north aisle. My soul leapt to see their chiseled hands playing lute, lyre, tabor, bagpipes, zither, fiddle, accordion, harp, and hunting horn, each performing a unique part of the symphony that wedded the longings of earth to heaven's bliss. Though the musicians were carved in mute stone, their divine harmonies resounded within my heart as my tears washed the grit from my eyes. *He never abandoned me. He was always right here. Abiding in silence. All is well, and all shall be well, and all manner of things shall be well.*

Bedford's men marched me into the chapter house. The stalls bristled with high-ranking clerics discussing their business, but they fell silent when my guards delivered me to the Abbot of Beverley. The man peered at me in alarm, as if I were some ghoul. What a sight I must have been, my veil half torn away from my hair after the long ride, my white clothes spattered from the dung folk had hurled at me, my grimy face smeared with blood and tears.

"At my lord, the Duke of Bedford's orders, we bring you the Lollard, Margery Kempe of Bishop's Lynn," the shorter of my two guards announced.

The taller guard, meanwhile, sprinted out again, presumably to deliver word to his lord that I had arrived in Beverley.

The clerics stirred in their stalls and much murmuring arose. I noticed a manuscript on a table. *The Confessions of John Oldcastle*. I quickly tore my eyes away, reminding myself to feign ignorance of the written word, little good it would do me now.

"Are you neither heretic nor Lollard, Margery Kempe?" the abbot asked me.

My head whirled. He had phrased the question in such a way that I didn't know whether to answer yes or no.

"I am a pilgrim, Reverend Sir," I said, choosing my words with care. "I've journeyed to Jerusalem, Rome, and Santiago de Compostela, something no Lollard would ever do."

My guard cut me short. "Though she calls herself a pilgrim, Reverend Father, she is, in fact, a Lollard preacher who gathers disciples wherever she goes. She dares to usurp the very role of an ordained priest."

Bedford's messenger displayed my staff to the abbot. "She concealed Lollard tracts in her pilgrim's staff." He opened the secret compartment while the clerics stared in shock. But it was empty. I could not stop myself from gasping aloud. What in the name of all the saints had happened to Julian's manuscript?

"I see no tracts," the abbot said.

"The Archbishop of York has taken the pages for examination," the messenger said, looking somewhat less puffed up than he had a moment ago. "He shall appear in Beverley to deliver his verdict in the coming week."

So my fate wouldn't be decided today—that hard ride had been nothing but my guards' demonstration of obedience to their lord. My lungs expanded and I felt a small opening of hope. Perhaps the elderly canon who had known Julian could convince the archbishop that the manuscript was indeed Julian's work, thus sparing both her book and my life.

"Why did you not say so sooner?" the abbot asked irritably. "In that case, it's pointless questioning this woman further until the archbishop arrives. Take her away and give her something to eat. The creature looks like she's about to drop dead."

The words had only just left his mouth when Bedford's other messenger returned, followed by a flurry of richly attired noblemen.

"I announce the presence of His Grace, John of Lancaster, the Duke of Bedford, Lord High Constable of England," the winded messenger panted.

A jolt shot through me as I dropped in a low curtsy.

"So there she is," a pitiless voice said. "The Lollard witch."

From my vantage point, I could see only his calfskin riding boots with their enormous silver spurs—pity the man's poor horse.

"Tell me the whereabouts of John Oldcastle," he said. "Or I shall have you whipped."

Pulling myself upright, I attempted to gather my wits. "Your Grace, with all these holy men to bear witness, I swear I've never had anything to do with Oldcastle. I've no more knowledge of his hiding place than anyone in this room."

My mind then lifted from gloomy contemplation of my fate to marvel at how extraordinarily ugly the Duke of Bedford was—the most hideous person I had seen in all my days. By Our Lady, I had encountered toads who were better looking. Though he was still in his twenties, he'd a round lumpen face as white as fresh cheese, thin pale lips, and beady eyes. He wore his hair in the French style, in a sort of reverse tonsure, with a mop of brown hair atop his skull, but the sides and back of his scalp were shaved clean. Thus, he resembled a bald man wearing the pelt of a large brown rat upon his pate. His nose was grotesquely huge—you could crack a walnut on that beak of his. Beneath all that gold brocade, sable, and ermine, he sweated and reeked like a tanner. I thanked all the saints I was not his wife.

"How dare you dissemble?" The duke glowered at me as though I were a piece of excrement he had discovered on the bottom of his boot. "You told my Lady Greystoke, the King's cousin and mine, to leave her husband! Meddling in the royal family with your Lollard intrigues. For that alone you could burn."

My head reeled in confusion. "I can recall no such meeting with the woman in question, Your Grace."

"How feeble your memory must be," he said scornfully, "if you cannot recall what transpired a week ago. My informant tells me that my Lady Westmorland and Lady Greystoke, her daughter, visited you in the attic in York where you were kept under lock and key."

A shock rippled through me to recall the two noblewomen who had appeared in the dead of night. Had I only known their true identity. Lady Westmorland was none other than Countess Joan Beaufort, daughter of John of Gaunt. The King's aunt. What a web I was tangled in.

"If this creature was locked in an attic, how would your kinswomen come to converse with her, Your Grace?" the abbot inquired, while his scribe scribbled furiously to record all that was said.

"The prison master's wife foolishly let them bribe their way in," Bedford said. "Rest assured, she will pay for this indiscretion."

I shuddered to think that poor Mistress Fenwick and her husband would have to suffer on my account after their many kindnesses to me.

"Margery Kempe," the abbot said. "Did my Lady Westmorland and my Lady Greystroke come to speak to you?"

The women had sworn me to secrecy. I decided to prevaricate.

"Reverend Father," I said. "Why should the King's own kindred seek out one as wretched as I?"

"Why indeed?" Bedford spat. "Because you spread insubordination among women with your Lollard homilies. Thanks to you, my cousin fled her husband and sought refuge with the nuns at Denny Abbey. *And* she took her son with her."

Despite the danger I was in, a trill of vindication shot through me. It took all my self-control to hide my pleasure at this news.

The abbot remained skeptical. "Your Grace, it might be true that your informant saw your kinswomen enter the prison master's house or even that he observed them speaking with this creature through the attic window, but surely your informant was not in the room with them. How can you prove what was discussed in any such clandestine meeting?"

Bedford flared at the abbot. "When questioned, my cousin said that she acted upon the counsel of a holy woman in York."

"Did she mention any name?" the abbot asked, rapidly losing patience.

"What other self-purported holy woman would tell a wife to take her son and flee her lord husband but a woman such as her, who deserted her own husband and used God as her excuse."

"And what do you say to all this?" the abbot asked me. "You never answered my question, by the way. Did the duke's kinswomen visit you a week ago? Yes or no."

I bowed my head. "Two ladies came to the attic that night, Reverend Father, but they were veiled and very plainly dressed. I had no clue who they were."

"Liar," Bedford hissed.

"Let the woman speak, Your Grace," the abbot said. "Margery Kempe, did you tell my Lady Greystoke to leave her husband?"

What could I possibly say that wouldn't condemn either me or the young woman? "She was deep in turmoil, Reverend Father. She said that her husband treated her brutally. I told her God was a higher master than her husband and that the Franciscan Sisters could offer her refuge if she embraced a life of chastity and devotion." I paused, my mouth as dry as chalk, and gazed slowly around at the assembled clerics. "If there is any clerk among you who can say that I said any word other than I should have, I'm willing to amend it with good will."

The abbot inclined his head. "As far as I can tell, Margery Kempe, you've committed no crime."

His verdict sent Bedford into spasms of outrage. "How can you sit there, as mild as a girl, while this creature spreads her heresy? You *know* there's an underground army of Lollards seeking to overthrow the King. This creature is one of their agitators. Oldcastle has been forced into hiding so instead he sends her, his Trojan horse, to do his bidding. Don't be so foolish to think she's harmless because she's a woman. That's precisely why Oldcastle chose her. She infects other women to wreak acts of chaos and disorder. Even my cousin!"

For all his temper, Bedford never went red in the face. He only turned paler and paler, as though he were reptile, not human. As he unleashed his venom, I knew that this man wouldn't rest until he saw me burn.

My soul flew out of my body and hovered high beneath the vaulted ceiling where I gazed in pity upon that doomed woman below. From this height, I could see so far and wide. See into the future. Looking down upon the duke, the entire tableau of his life unfurled like a vast tapestry. I saw that despite his two marriages to young, healthy women he would never father a legitimate child. A man of strife who lived to persecute others, he would die on the battlefield. But before that day came, he would wreak much malice. He was still young, still green. He had yet to grow into his full powers. But I saw him, fourteen years from now, in his terrifying prime. Sly, calculating, and despicable. He was in France, scheming against a maid called Jehanne. One like me, haunted by visions and guided by voices. Only a slip of a girl, but one bold enough to lead armies. I saw her burning on her pyre before Bedford's cold lizard eyes. Burned not only as a heretic but a witch. All my hairs stood on end as my soul crashed back into my body. I fell a second time. Collapsed in a heap of bones.

"Satan's daughter," Bedford spat. "Get back on your feet or I'll pull you up by the hair."

Dazed, I began to shake uncontrollably. Outside in the crowd, I had encountered hatred, but Bedford's wrath went far beyond hate. Never had I looked into the eyes of such evil.

"She's not fit to be questioned further until she's fed and rested," the abbot said. "As for your concerns about subversive plots, Your Grace, surely if this creature was a Lollard instigator, she would not have advised your cousin to flee to a *nunnery* of all places. I'm afraid we cannot proceed until the archbishop joins us. This hearing is adjourned."

I regarded the abbot in awe. What staggering courage he possessed to defy the Duke of Bedford, a man even the archbishop feared.

The abbot then summoned the prison master to take me away. A fearsome-looking man, he was, with one eye missing and a neck as thick as a bull's.

"Throw her in among the murderers," the duke commanded. "Perhaps that will bring contrition to her lips."

"According to canon law, she's to be held in a church prison" was all the abbot ventured to say.

The prison master himself was utterly expressionless as he shackled me and led me off. So great was my fear of what lay in store that I could only shuffle along like a crone as he took me out a hidden rear door and through a warren of ginnels and alleyways to avoid the mob outside the minster.

"Master Fenwick of York sent word," the prison master whispered, when he judged us to be out of earshot of any eavesdroppers. "Says you're a good woman and to treat you well. You're in luck." He smiled to reveal the many gaps between his yellow teeth. "Female church prisoners are kept in the Dominican nunnery. My sister Judith will be your guard. She'll look after you, she will."

"Bless you, good sir," I whispered.

He knocked on the back gate of the nunnery, then we waited in the anteroom until his sister came to take me to my cell.

Sister Judith was as big as a warhorse, and she didn't have many more teeth than her brother, but her cheeks were pink and her big brown eyes had a kindly spark in them.

"We don't get many prisoners—most are men and kept elsewhere, of course." She seemed beside herself with purpose and excitement. "Are you truly a Lollard plotter?" she asked, looking me up and down. She sounded both scandalized and deeply intrigued.

"No," I said hotly. "I wish to remain in the good grace of the Holy Mother Church, but wicked men slander me at every turn."

"Oh," Judith said, looking vaguely disappointed.

With a shrug of her enormous shoulders, she led me down a corridor and up a stairway to an upper room with a barred window that looked out into a narrow inner courtyard surrounded by high stone walls. Even if my friends from York had the nerve to follow me all the way to Beverley, they'd not be able to reach me here.

"It's an Ember Day, so you get eels," Judith said cheerfully as she unshackled me. "I love eels, me. My brother Dougie, your gaoler, can eat a whole pot of eels—they're his favorite!"

She left me in my cell only to return in a trice with a great tureen of eels simmered in greens, a loaf of fresh wheaten bread, and a jug of wine—more than I could possibly eat or drink. But she joined me and supped with relish, sharing the small table in the corner.

"Put some meat on your bones," she said between mouthfuls. "You have to keep up your strength for the trial."

The eels were delicately prepared, their flesh tender, but the duke had struck such terror in me that I could hardly taste the food.

"Well, I'd better lock you in and leave you to it," Judith said after our meal as she collected the crockery. "Otherwise I'll be late for Vespers."

"Thank you, Sister," I said, which was about as much speech as I could manage, being paralyzed by my fear of what lay ahead.

The archbishop kept me waiting seven days. First, he and his counselors had to pore over every page of Julian's manuscript, then they had to make the journey to Beverley. Owing to his advanced age, the archbishop was obliged to travel at a statelier pace than my breakneck ride. Forced to bide my time and reflect upon my fate, I could only pace my small chamber and pray. And still I heard no voice of guidance. Saw no glimmer of my Beloved's face. My every prayer opened up into that unending emptiness.

So great was my desolation that I no longer resisted that impenetrable silence. Instead, I surrendered at last, offering up both my yearning and my terror to that dark infinity where God dwells, incomprehensibly vast and inscrutable.

Falling into that void, I relinquished everything I had ever believed or thought to be true. I embraced the dark mystery of God, beyond images or words. O, to know without knowing the glory and love too immense to grasp. Seeing without eyes, hearing without ears, walking without feet into the terrifying vastness of God. Walking without any light but the fragile flickering flame in my heart. I offered up my one-word prayer: *Beloved*. Touched by him who has no hands. He who has no voice but who speaks in all that is. Flying without wings into the silent embrace of Mother God.

26

MY DAY OF RECKONING had come, the trial that would determine whether I lived or burned.

To fortify me, Judith served a gargantuan breakfast of warm bread, coddled ale, gooseberry fritters, and hard-boiled eggs stuffed with fresh farmer's cheese, mashed yolk, and grated nutmeg.

I tried to smile to show my gratitude. Judith had been so good to me, feeding me twice a day and sleeping in the antechamber outside my locked door to guard not only me but also my honor. She had even ordered the lay Sisters to launder my clothes. Indeed, she seemed reluctant to let me go. Over our meals together all that long week, I'd told her tales of my pilgrimages, and she drank down my every word, thirsting for, more than anything, news of the great world beyond her cloistered walls.

When the time came for her to reluctantly clap the shackles on my wrists, she turned somber.

"I hear they accused you of preaching," she said.

I lowered my eyes.

"I've heard rumors that Lollard women don't just preach — they serve the Eucharist." Her voice caught in awe. "Is this true, Margery?"

I met her eager gaze. How she longed, despite her shock, for this to be so. I, her prisoner, was the only soul to whom she could reveal her forbidden yearning.

"I don't know," I told her softly. "I've never seen such a thing, though I've met many learned nuns and beguines."

How I had disappointed her. She flushed, ducked her head, and quickly looked away.

Before she could lead me out to her brother who waited below, I caught her hand and squeezed.

"Pray for me, good Sister. Please."

When the minster bells rang the hour of Prime, my one-eyed gaoler came to fetch me. Judith's words haunted me as I retraced my steps through the maze of alleyways to the chapter house.

My throat constricted at the thought of facing the Duke of Bedford again. But at least this time I had a full belly, clean clothes, and the peace of my Beloved in my heart, which allowed me to walk in dignity despite my clanking shackles. *If I die, I die into you.* I raised my eyes to the slender strip of azure heaven visible between the jutting rooftops. A seagull, as white as a cloud, glided overhead.

A congress of elite men awaited me in the chapter house. The Archbishop of York sat upon his throne, surrounded by his prelates. The Abbot of Beverley and his counselors sat in their seats of honor. Cushioned chairs had been brought in for the Duke of Bedford, his advisors, and the Mayor and the Steward of York—my stomach pitched at the very sight of the wretch. There were more monks and friars than I could count. Some stood on stools to marvel at me, the she-devil heretic who masqueraded as a holy woman. So many bodies crammed into that room and all on account of me, one woman in her middle years. Though the hour was still early and the breeze outside had been fresh, the chapter house was airless and torpid.

My gaoler brought me to stand before the archbishop and unshackled me only long enough to allow me to make my obeisance before him and the abbot, and to swear my oath upon the Bible.

Above all, I needed to keep a clear head. But all self-possession was wrenched away when the abbot called my attention to the stack of pages lying on the oak table. Julian's manuscript. Laid beside it was my staff. My knees shook so hard, I nearly foundered.

"Was this the text you concealed in your pilgrim's staff, Margery Kempe?" the abbot asked me.

"Yes, Reverend Father."

During the last trial, he had seemed like a reasonable man. I searched his eyes for any hint of mercy, but I saw only his exasperation.

"Do you not know, you ignorant creature, that it's heretical to own a single Bible verse translated into English without diocesan permission?" His chilly voice echoed beneath that vaulted ceiling. "Yet you wandered across England—and who only knows where else—with an entire theological book in English."

"A book of Lollard propaganda," the Duke of Bedford interjected.

"It's nothing of the sort, Reverend Father." I kept my eyes on the abbot to spare myself the horror of facing the duke. "These are the writings of Dame Julian of Norwich, the late anchoress, now a saint in heaven."

I imagined my dear friend gazing down at me. I could almost hear her wise, patient voice whispering in my ear. *Courage, Margery. All shall be well.*

"Yet another of her many lies," Bedford said, rising from his chair to loom before me so I'd no other choice than to meet his pitiless lizard eyes. To smell his particular stink of rancid sweat and flowery perfume. "I'll wager *you* wrote that book."

His bejeweled finger with its bitten yellow nail jabbed at my breastbone. I flinched.

"Me? Write a book?" Despite my fear, I laughed incredulously. Laughed in the Duke of Bedford's face. An icy misgiving seized me—perhaps I had just sealed my doom.

My eyes came to rest on the court scribe recording my words on parchment for posterity. *What would it be like*, I wondered, *to write my own story? Or to dictate it to some learned soul like Master Alan who could write it down in his elegant hand?*

The duke, meanwhile, his face only inches from mine, launched into a blistering diatribe regarding my alleged crimes and sins, but I no longer heard his voice. *Beloved, hear my vow*, I prayed. *If I survive this ordeal, I shall tell my own story in my own words. My book to atone for Julian's book these men threaten to destroy.*

"Your Reverence," the abbot said, turning to the archbishop. "What is your verdict on the manuscript. Is it a heretical text?"

A pained expression settled on the archbishop's face, as though he were suffering from indigestion. "My most learned theologians and I have examined the manuscript minutely. Although we could find nothing directly unorthodox, it's still a troubling text. One too dangerous to fall into the hands of simple layfolk. It's far too easily misinterpreted. One could almost infer from this — and I say *almost*, for its author took great care not to step over the line into heresy — that hell and divine wrath only exist inside the minds of men! And this is written in English simple enough for any farmer or housewife to understand."

"It smacks of Lollardy," the duke said, moving away from me to address the archbishop.

"In short," the abbot said. "Although the text itself is not heretical, it could give rise to heretical interpretation and therefore to sedition. Is that correct, Your Reverence?"

The archbishop nodded.

My fettered hands fisted in outrage. Would they truly condemn Julian's book?

"Is it possible that Margery Kempe could have written it?" the abbot asked.

"That's highly unlikely, Reverend Father," the archbishop replied. "I doubt that this creature has such subtlety of understanding. For though it's written in plain English, its meaning is sublime in places."

A canon nodded in agreement. "This text is altogether different from the witterings of Margery Kempe who inflicted some bizarre parable of a shitting bear upon the archbishop's court."

"Shitting bear?" For the first time, the duke appeared confounded.

"Your Reverence," the abbot asked. "Is it possible that this creature told the truth when she said it was the work of Dame Julian of Norwich?"

The archbishop seemed to squirm. Instead of speaking, he nodded to one of his clerks, who rose and approached the table where the manuscript lay. Turning to the relevant page, the clerk began to read in a clear, ringing voice.

"'These revelations were shown to a simple, uneducated creature in the year of Our Lord 1373.'" He then addressed the abbot. "If this date is true and not falsified, Margery Kempe could not have written it. She's not old enough. Later, the text reveals the author to be a woman who claimed to have received these showings at the age of thirty."

The abbot nodded and stroked his chin. "Given those dates, it's possible that it *was* Dame Julian. She would have been about thirty in 1373."

"In theory, it's possible," the archbishop said tepidly. "One of my most elderly prelates claimed as much, saying that he met Dame Julian many years ago and she told him about her book. But he's a doddering old man whose testimony can't be entirely trusted. In faith, I hold Dame Julian in the highest esteem and don't want her reputation tainted by any whiff of Lollardy. And why," he asked pointedly, leveling his hooded eyes at me, "would the sainted anchoress entrust her life's work to *that* ridiculous creature?"

I lifted my eyes to the stained glass window depicting Saint Margaret holding her cross in victory over the dragon she had slain. "Dame Julian gave it to me for safekeeping."

The room exploded with contemptuous laughter. Those men were so eager to believe I was John Oldcastle's whore, but none of them could countenance the fact that I was Julian's friend.

The abbot rang his handbell to call the court back to order.

"So we have established that Margery Kempe is not the author," he said. "Nor is the text in itself heretical, though in the hands of the ignorant, it might give rise to heretical interpretation. Now we must determine whether we have evidence that this creature used the text to spread Lollardy and sedition."

The duke stepped forward with an air of invincible authority, as if his judgment alone could damn me to hell. "My informant heard her preaching to the women in front of York Minster. Telling them that every living creature would be saved."

The silence that followed his statement was more frightening than their derision had been. I quailed to think that the duke's informer had been spying on my every deed in York. Would the duke also persecute the women who had befriended me? I wish I could say I stood strong and fearless in my conviction. But even a glance from the duke was enough to make my skin crawl.

"Is this true?" the abbot asked me.

I took a deep breath. "I will speak of God's love and mercy until I die."

The abbot sighed, then looked to the archbishop. "Your Reverence, in your previous examination of this creature were you able to find evidence of unorthodoxy?"

"No, Reverend Father." The archbishop spoke reluctantly, as if the abbot had to pull every word from his mouth with pliers. "She knows her religion well, but I still don't trust her."

"She stirs up subversion," the Mayor of York said. "She preaches among the women and incites them to rebel."

I remembered Mathilda, the brewer on the street outside my attic in York. *You question everything, so I, too, must question everything.*

"Reverend Father," the duke said. "My informer told me that this wretched woman claims she can weep and have contrition directly from Our Lord whenever she wishes without a priest having to grant her absolution." He folded his arms across his chest and stood with his feet wide apart, occupying the space of three lesser men. "That, Your Reverence, is your evidence of heresy."

The archbishop leaned forward in his seat. Everyone in that room seemed to hold his breath.

"What do you say to this, Margery Kempe?" the abbot asked.

"I receive absolution from a priest at least once a year," I answered honestly. It would have been prudent to stop there, but my tongue would not be still. "Yet above all, I believe in the power of divine love and redemption."

Now I understood why these men feared and hated me so much. If I could live in union with my Beloved and seek his grace and goodness in my heart, what need had I for any of them? Unlike Julian and the other Holy Sisters I'd met on my travels, I hadn't renounced the world but was living in it. An ordinary wife of Lynn could touch the divine. And so usurp these men's power.

I recalled Judith's disappointment that I wasn't the Lollard priest she wanted me to be. But what if I actually was, only I'd refused to admit it even to myself? Perhaps I was a Lollard because I refused to be silenced even by the threat of burning. I was indeed guilty of un-authorized preaching. Speaking of God's love and of Julian's and my own revelations was my calling. Never could I return to being an obedient housewife, silent and meek. I would live and die by my hard-won truths. I had a ministry, a message, a vocation.

The silence in that chapter house seemed to stretch into eternity, and from that silence, my Beloved's voice emerged at last. *No man shall slay you, nor fire burn you, nor water drown you, nor wind harm you, because I cannot forget you and how you are written in my hands and feet.* With my physical eyes, I saw his precious flesh pierced by nails. My story, my love, inscribed on his very body. My wounds were his. His wounds were mine. I crashed to the floor in weeping ecstasy.

"Holy saints above!" The archbishop clapped cushions against his ears.

The abbot appeared completely flummoxed while the duke seemed as though he would die in agony from his bursting eardrums. The Steward of York fled in terror. A few of the clerks fainted and had to be carried away.

When my spell had passed, the men looked quite dazed.

"What shall we do with her?" the abbot asked, shaking his head. "The evidence against her is inconclusive. Either she's a well-meaning woman, if misguided and hysterical. Or else she's the most convincing liar." He looked to the archbishop. "What do you say, Your Reverence?"

The archbishop regarded me for a moment before throwing up his hands. "I'm not of one mind. On the one hand, she knows her catechism. On the other, wherever she goes, she agitates and upsets people. And that *weeping.*" He shuddered.

"Burn her and be done with it," the duke said. "Her sort are not to be suffered."

My chest was so tight, I could hardly breathe for my terror. How could there be any way out of this intricate snare the men had woven? Weak in the knees, I bowed before the archbishop and regarded him through my tears.

"Your Reverence," I said. "You worry that I have attracted a small following. But imagine how that following will multiply if you burn me. You will make me a martyr." I remembered Jan Hus on his pyre, surrounded by a multitude of enemies and sympathizers. "You might kill me, but in doing so, you'll make me immortal in my fame. My reputation will never die."

His Adam's apple quavered, as if he were swallowing the bitter truth of my words.

"But if you release me," I said, "people will regard me as they always have done — as a feeble woman who weeps too much."

The archbishop cast furtive glances at his prelates, who discreetly nodded. The last thing these men wanted was an execution that would trigger a full-blown Lollard uprising.

"Your Reverence," one of the canons said. "If we burn her, we play straight into the Lollards' hands. It would be far more prudent to let this pitiful figure of a woman fade back into the obscurity from whence she came."

It was as if I hadn't spoken and the idea was all his own. I began to tremble in hope.

"You can't just let the creature go!" The duke was incensed.

"Your Reverence," the Mayor of York said. "I beg you to banish her from our shire. If she returns to York, I swear I'll burn her myself."

"Yes, we must banish her from Yorkshire," the archbishop said.

"At least return my purse, my golden ring, and my pilgrim's staff before you expel me," I said, standing taller now. "And the manuscript —"

"Shall be quietly destroyed," the archbishop said. "Lest it cause more mischief than it already has."

The most wretched grief washed through me. It was as though part of my own flesh had been ripped away. *Julian, I failed you miserably.*

"Take this creature out of my sight," the archbishop said. "Before I change my mind and burn her after all."

His words were hanging in the air like smoke when the door opened and a radiantly handsome young man entered. The sun pierced the stained glass to dazzle upon his long waving brown hair. He was so fair to look upon, so graceful in his stride, that I assumed him to be a vision, an angel of light, except all the others also turned to gaze upon him. The archbishop's mouth hung slack as though beholding a marvel.

"Who are you to intrude upon a Church court without my leave?" the abbot asked. But even he seemed so affected by the beauty and mystery of this stranger that his voice lost its edge.

I trembled from head to toe, faint with joy, for the young man's eyes were riveted on mine as he made his resolute way toward me.

"I have come to take Margery Kempe home," he said.

My heart overflowed. Was this the very apparition of my Beloved come to deliver me? A wonder I didn't swoon.

"And your name, sir?" the abbot asked.

"John Kempe."

I shook my head, utterly bewildered until the young man stood before me and held me by my shoulders while I stared at him, transfixed.

"Mother," he said. "Do you not know me?" He spoke with a German accent.

I blinked and saw him as an infant swaddled in my arms. My first-born, named John after his father, except we called him Jack. The rebellious youth I'd sent to live with my brother in Danzig because, like me, he had so longed to see the world. I reached out one shackled hand to grasp his arm. To prove that he was truly flesh and blood.

"Jack," I murmured. "How did you find me here?"

"Your gaoler in York and then the one in Beverley sent word to Father, but he lies ill and bedridden. I returned to Lynn to visit, so Isabella sent me to fetch you home. Are you well, Mother? Did they mistreat you?" His eyes, hazel like mine, were large and worried.

Before I could answer him, my one-eyed gaoler came to unlock my shackles and set me free.

"Take your mother home to Lynn as quickly as you can," the archbishop said, having recovered his composure. "I cannot promise any lenience should she ever show her face in Yorkshire again."

Before they could hound me out of the chapter house, I marched boldly forward and seized my pilgrim's staff before sauntering off, my arm entwined with Jack's.

Stepping out onto the minster porch, I whooped in jubilation to see the women who had followed me from York, along with Master Fenwick. All of them cheered to see me again, alive and at liberty. One by one, the women embraced me.

"Justice at last," Mathilda said. "We knew you'd prevail, Margery."

Master Fenwick clapped my shoulder fondly before returning my purse, satchel, and the golden ring Julian had given me.

"Go in grace, Margery Kempe," he said.

I kissed Julian's ring before returning it to my finger.

My women friends, Master Fenwick, and Dougie, my one-eyed gaoler, escorted Jack and me, shielding us from the hostile crowd. They accompanied us all the way down to Hessle on the Humber where Jack and I boarded the ferry to take us across to the safety of Lincolnshire. Though I yearned to linger with these dearworthy souls who had stood by me in my most perilous hour, I'd no time to drop my guard lest the duke's men come after me. So after paying the ferryman and ordering him to embark, I clung to the rail and waved farewell to my friends.

"Give my love to Sister Judith!" I shouted to Dougie. "Tell her I'll never forget what she told me."

Dougie blinked his one eye and looked somewhat baffled, but he raised his hand in salutation.

"All the saints protect you, Margery Kempe."

What a marvel it was to be suddenly free. I threw back my head to let the warm wind caress my face. Each roll of the waves lifted me closer to heaven.

Once we landed in Lincolnshire, my son and I wasted no time in finding passage on a boat bound for the fishing port of Grimsby. From there, we hoped to find another vessel to take us to Lynn.

As we sailed down the Humber, I could not get over my amazement of seeing Jack again after six long years. Prodigal son reunited with his even more prodigal mother. Jack told me of his life in Danzig, of the lovely young woman he intended to marry upon his return. I was proud to discover that he had become a prosperous merchant like my brother who had mentored him and like my father before us.

"Can you forgive me?" I asked. "For packing you off to foreign parts when you were only young?"

Now that I had this chance to live again, I wanted more than anything to reconcile with my children.

"*Forgive* you?" Jack shook his head and laughed. "Sending me away was the greatest gift you could give me. Lynn's a suffocating backwater compared to Danzig."

My heart brimmed in sweet relief. Jack, bless him, had inherited every drop of my restless, questing blood.

"Tell me of your travels," he said, and he listened with rapt attention while I described how I had crossed the Alps on foot, seen the wonders of Venice and Rome, and ridden an ass across the Judean Desert. I told him of my ecstasies inside the Church of the Holy Sepulcher and how I had nearly stood trial for heresy there as well.

"I've sailed to Hamburg and Stockholm and most of the Hanseatic ports," my son said with pride. "One day I dream of journeying to Constantinople," he added, a faraway gleam in his eyes. "And from there to Jerusalem."

"Don't stop in Jerusalem," I said, enthusiasm stirring inside me. "A young man like you must press on to Mount Sinai and Alexandria!"

Despite my deep joy, I could not keep from dwelling on how I had failed to preserve Julian's book. By the grace of God, copies still existed in Europe and Jerusalem. But not in England. And for that, I was to blame.

"Mother, why do you look so sad?" Jack asked, studying my face.

"I've been banished from Yorkshire." A heaviness settled in my heart to have been severed so abruptly from the friends I'd made there.

My son just grinned, opened a bottle of beer he had bought off the boat's captain, and passed it to me. "Do you not think the rest of the world is big enough for you, Mother? One day you must sail to Danzig to meet Katharina, my betrothed."

We shared the bottle of beer and gazed off toward the watery horizon, the open sea that glistened before us. Then my son grew somber as well.

"Father is in a very bad way," he said, as the wind ruffled his light brown hair. "He fell down the cellar stairs, cracked his skull, and hasn't been the same since. I don't think he's long for this world."

"Poor man," I murmured, a catch in my throat. So John hadn't been silent during my imprisonment but gravely injured.

My son blinked back tears. "He's not right in the head anymore. Some say the fall made him senile. That woman abandoned him. Isabella took in the boys, but her hands are full with raising them and she can't even keep a servant willing to nurse Father." Jack turned to me and touched my hand. "In the rare moment his mind is clear, he only asks for you."

"I'll look after him," I said. "For as long as it takes."

So many emotions fought their fierce battle inside my heart. Reluctance, shame, regret. My old anger and so much grief for all those wasted years. All the blame that others had heaped upon me and all the blame I had heaped upon myself. But John and I had truly loved each other once. As a young bride, I had desired him as much as he had desired me.

Back in Rome, I had nursed Rosangela and Marcello when they were bedridden with malaria. How could I refuse to nurse John Kempe? I vowed to make amends with him and my children. To try once more to be a mother to them now that I had seen the world and knew what I was made of and wasn't just some suffering wife. If I could endure the Duke of Bedford's wrath and live to tell the tale, then I could also rejoin my family and face down the gossips of Lynn. Yet even so, my adventures would continue. One day I would fare forth to Danzig and see my brother again. And by and by, I would find a scribe to help me write my story.

When we landed in Grimsby in the long summer twilight, an unearthly mist arose from the surrounding marshes. The homely little port almost seemed enchanted, a place between the worlds where all normal rules were suspended. Where anything might happen.

We found lodgings for the night in the guesthouse of the Augustinian canonesses. After my son retired to his room, I found I could not sleep. Instead, I wandered in the cloister garden and stared at the full moon that shone through a parting in the mist. All I could think of was Julian.

Julian would not have called herself a Lollard, yet she had dared to defy the men in the Church who demanded her silence. She dared to preach—yes, preach, through her book!—of Mother God's absolute love and mercy. She had dared to listen to the voice of God inside herself and follow it no matter what her superiors might say. She had opened up a middle way between the absolute dominion of the prelates and their demand for submission and Oldcastle's men who would dissolve the holy orders so women like Julian would have no place or refuge at all. Now I walked this same middle way in Julian's footsteps. God willing, I could help open that path for other women. But I could not get over my inconsolable grief for the loss of her book.

What a fragile thing a manuscript is. Her words could simply disappear, her entire legacy erased. The copies of her work abroad could be purged. Or lost in a fire or flood.

Shivering in the misty air, I noticed an open doorway, golden with lantern light, off the cloister walk. A door that should have been kept closed and bolted for it led into the part of the nunnery that was out of bounds for lay guests such as myself. But like a moth drawn to the flame, I ventured through that doorway as though in trance. Down a corridor that led into the library, its door also open. One of the canonesses was reading, utterly immersed and oblivious to my presence. It was as though I had become a ghost. I could have crept away and she would never have noticed me at all.

Instead, I said, "Forgive me, Sister. I can't sleep."

She glanced up in surprise but didn't seem flustered by my presence. Perhaps because of my white gown and veil, she took me for a visiting nun from another order. The canoness was young, her face smooth and open to all the treasures the library—and the world—might offer.

"I couldn't sleep either," she said. "I should be in bed, but I can't stop reading. This book arrived some weeks ago. From the beguines in Zierikzee. Our abbess is a dear friend of the mother of their house."

The beguinage in Zierikzee, Holland. The first station of my pilgrimage to Jerusalem almost four years ago. I froze, then pinched myself. On my voyage back from Rome, I'd heard that most of Zierikzee had burned to the ground and I had feared the worst for the beguines. But it seemed that they and their house had been spared. An irrepressible wonder and mirth bubbled up inside me. God is homely. Miracles are homely. An open door and a young canoness poring over a book in Grimsby on a misty June night.

"May I?" I asked, timidly approaching her and peering over her shoulder.

She smiled and turned to the first page. There, in red ink, was a rubric written in Godelieve's graceful italic script.

This is a vision, shown through God's goodness, to a devout woman, and her name is Julian, and she is a recluse at Norwich and is still alive in the year of Our Lord 1413.

HISTORICAL AFTERWORD

After walking away from her heresy trials unscathed, Margery Kempe returned to Lynn and looked after her critically ill husband until his death. Some years later, she set off on another epic journey, this time to her son and daughter-in-law's home in Danzig (modern-day Gdansk, Poland) and she visited many revered pilgrimage sites on her way. And most significant for us, she preserved her story in *The Book of Margery Kempe* (c. 1436–38), the first autobiography in the English language. Kempe dictated her story to a priest, whose ecclesiastical authority gave gravitas to her narrative. After many years of battling the judgmental attitudes of her fellow townsfolk, Kempe finally achieved eminence in 1438 by becoming a member of the Guild of the Holy Trinity, Lynn's pre-eminent guild of the mercantile elite and the lynchpin of local government and religious life. The date of her death is unknown.

The Book of Margery Kempe is rambling and nonchronological, by turns pious and picaresque — a veritable treasure trove for medievalists that explodes our every stereotype of medieval women. We encounter Kempe's searing tales of postpartum depression, marital rape, and her thwarted attempts to establish herself as a businesswoman. Yet she triumphed in transforming herself from a desperate housewife into an intrepid world traveler and lifelong pilgrim — a mystic living in the full stream of worldly life. Suspected of heresy, she was tried by the Duke of Bedford, who did indeed go on to persecute Joan of Arc.

The major events in the novel are drawn from *The Book of Margery Kempe*. However, in the interests of narrative structure and cohesion, I conflated some of her trials while leaving out her trial in Leicester altogether. Some of her travel companions, such as Cecily, Rupert, and Derwa, are wholly fictional characters, but her compassionate and handsome Muslim guide in the Holy Land is mentioned in her autobiography, as is the young family in Rome who invited her to be godmother to their newborn, as is her absconding maid whom she later had to beg for charity. Richard the Irish humpback is also drawn directly from *The Book of Margery Kempe*.

Suor Lorenza at the Priory of Corpus Domini in Venice is based on the poet, playwright, translator, and Dominican nun Laurentia Strozzi of Bologna (1541–1591). Hawisia Moone was a real woman from Loddon, Norfolk, who was arrested and imprisoned in Norwich in 1430. You can read her confessions in *Women's Lives in Medieval Europe: A Sourcebook* edited by Emilie Amt. But it would have been highly unlikely for the young Margery Brunham to have encountered her in Lynn in 1392. I have taken further liberties with the historical timeline. William Sawtry, the vicar of Saint Margaret's Church in Bishop's Lynn, was indeed the first person to be burned as a Lollard in England, but his execution did not take place until 1401, when Kempe was twenty-seven. Kempe passed through Constance on her pilgrimage to Jerusalem, but her travel dates did not coincide with the Council of Constance or with Jan Hus's execution on July 6, 1415. Nonetheless, as a novelist, I felt it important to write the scene of Kempe witnessing Hus's burning so modern readers could get a visceral sense of just how dangerous it was to be perceived as a religious dissenter during this turbulent period of history.

The Book of Margery Kempe narrates how Kempe sought the counsel of Julian of Norwich before embarking on her pilgrimage to Jerusalem. This was an exceedingly vulnerable time in her life, for she had just left her husband and children behind and was filled with self-doubt and uncertainty. Julian's advice to trust God and not worry too much about what other people thought seemed to have a profound and empowering impact on Kempe.

My portrayal of Kempe secretly carrying Julian's manuscript, *Rev-*

elations of Divine Love, on her pilgrimage was inspired by Dr. Janina Ramirez's 2016 BBC Four documentary, *The Search for the Lost Manuscript: Julian of Norwich.* The first book written in English by a woman, *Revelations of Divine Love* reveals the radical theology of an unconditionally loving God so at odds with the official theology of the Church during Julian's time. She took the extraordinary step to write of her visions in English to make them accessible to ordinary people, and this at a time when one could be burned as a heretic for reading the Bible in English. *Revelations of Divine Love* was so highly controversial, it was possibly kept secret and passed from hand to hand. Dr. Ramirez speculates that Julian entrusted her precious manuscript to Kempe so she might share it with people sympathetic to Julian's ideas. Dr. Ramirez even suggests Julian inspired Kempe to write her own book.

As is too often the fate, both women and their books were cast into oblivion and forgotten. *Revelations of Divine Love* does not seem to have been widely circulated in late medieval England. The Short Text survives in only one manuscript copied from an original dated 1413. The Long Text survives in three manuscripts made after the Reformation by exiled English nuns in France and Flanders.

Not until 1901 did Julian's book reach a wide mainstream audience, thanks to Grace Warrack's modern English translation. Her publication of *Revelations of Divine Love* was popular and influential, an inspiration to the burgeoning women's suffrage movement as well as to poets such as T. S. Eliot, who quotes *Revelations of Divine Love* toward the end of his poem "Little Gidding."

And all shall be well and
All manner of thing shall be well

The Book of Margery Kempe was lost to the world for five centuries and only unearthed by accident at a country house party in Derbyshire in 1934. A group of young people were playing Ping-Pong at Southgate House, owned by the Butler-Bowdons, an old English Catholic family. When one of the players destroyed the Ping-Pong ball by treading on it, they rooted through the cupboards in search of another one. Instead, they discovered "an entirely undisciplined clutter of smallish leather bound books." One such tome was *The Book of Margery Kempe,* which medievalist Hope Emily Allen subsequently translated and published, attracting wide news coverage as Kempe was celebrated as one of the earliest known woman authors, a fascinating and contradictory figure, and a most unique personality.

So what was up with Kempe's uncontrollable fits of weeping that could empty entire churches according to her own account? Many twentieth-century pundits have used twentieth-century psychoanalysis to diagnose her as hysterical, psychotic, schizophrenic, or perhaps as a misunderstood epileptic. One male commentator even suggested her behavior was brought on by menopause — which as a menopausal woman, I find hilarious. (Personally, if I'd had fourteen children by the age of forty, I, too, would be throwing myself on the ground and weeping and roaring.) But in her own late medieval context, Kempe's weeping may perhaps be more correctly interpreted as affective piety rather than mental or physical illness. Affective piety is a highly emotional form of devotion to the humanity of Christ and the joys and sorrows of the Virgin Mary. This form of worship is still practiced in the Eastern Orthodox Church. I once witnessed a young man breaking down into loud, demonstrative weeping in Saint Sophia Church in Sofia, Bulgaria.

Not being proficient in Middle English, I relied on the following translations of the primary sources: *The Book of Margery Kempe,* translated by Anthony Bale (Oxford University Press, 2015); *Julian Norwich: Revelations of Divine Love,* translated by Elizabeth Spearing (Penguin Books, 1998); and *Julian of Norwich: The Showings: A Contemporary Translation,* by Mirabai Starr (Canterbury Press, Norwich, 2014). *A Companion to The Book of Margery Kempe,* edited by John H. Arnold and Katherine J. Lewis (D. S. Brewer, Cambridge, 2004), proved indispensable. I was especially inspired by Jacqueline Jenkins's essay, "Reading and *The Book of Margery Kempe,*" wherein Jenkins speculates that although Margery

Kempe claimed to be illiterate, it was highly probable that she could read English.

Other important secondary texts include Clarissa W. Atkinson's *Mystic and Pilgrim: The Book and World of Margery Kempe* (Cornell University Press, 1983); Anthony Goodman's *Margery Kempe and Her World* (Routledge, 2002) ; and *Mystics, Visionaries and Prophets: A Historical Anthology of Women's Spiritual Writings,* edited by Shawn Madigan, CSJ, (Augsburg Fortress Press, Minneapolis, 1998). To learn about the background of accused heretics and early women preachers, I was deeply inspired by Genelle Gertz's *Heresy Trials and English Women Writers, 1400–1670* (Cambridge University Press, 2012); and Margaret Aston's essay "Lollard Women Priests?" from the *Journal of Ecclesiastical History* 31, no. 4, October 1980.

For detailed accounts of medieval pilgrimage, I am indebted to Nicole Chareyron's *Pilgrims to Jerusalem in the Middle Ages,* translated by W. Donald Wilson (Columbia University Press, 2005), which contained the details of the alluring male belly dancers entertaining Christian pilgrims in Ramla.

I am indebted to the Julian Centre and the Friends of Julian in Norwich, England, for their warm hospitality and fantastic multimedia library. I spent a beautiful hour of contemplation in the reconstructed anchorage of Saint Julian's Church—Julian's original anchorage and church were destroyed in the Second World War. My research, of course, also brought me to Margery Kempe's haunts in Lynn, as well as Lincoln, York, and Rome. I walked part of the pilgrimage routes to Our Lady of Walsingham and Santiago de Compostela. I love my research, but this book was the first to wear out a pair of hiking boots! Alas, I have yet to make it to Jerusalem.

Deep gratitude to my agent, Jennifer Weltz, and my editor, Nicole Angeloro, who encouraged me to write about Margery Kempe and Julian of Norwich. My thanks go out to the entire team at Houghton Mifflin Harcourt and my indefatigable copy editor, David Hough. For friendship and feedback, warmest thanks go out to my writers group: Cath Staincliffe, Livi Michael, Sophie Claire, Sue Stern, and Anjum Malik.

For online support and fellowship, I am deeply grateful to the Fiction Writers Co-op community on Facebook and the Historical Novel Society and all my friends in the historical fiction community.

Endless love and gratitude to my husband, Jos Van Loo, for accompanying me on my research trips and book tours, and reading all my first drafts.